Charles R. Wilcox
December 21, 1997
"Merry Christmas"

P9-CNH-444

Objects of All Sorts

Objects of All Sorts

A Philosophical Grammar

Vincent Descombes

Translated by Lorna Scott-Fox
and Jeremy Harding

The Johns Hopkins University Press
Baltimore

Originally published as *Grammaire d'objets en tous genres*
© 1983 by Les Editions de Minuit, Paris
English translation © 1986 The Johns Hopkins University
Press and Basil Blackwell Ltd

All rights reserved

Printed in Great Britain

The Johns Hopkins University Press, 701 West 40th Street,
Baltimore, Maryland 21211

The paper in this book is acid-free.

Library of Congress Cataloging-in-Publication Data

Descombes, Vincent
Objects of All Sorts.

Translation of: Grammaire d'objets en tous
genres.
Bibliography: p.
Includes index.
1. Language—Philosophy. 2. Semiotics.
3. Object
(Philosophy) I. Title.
P106.D45713   1986   401'.41   86-164
ISBN 0-8018-2551-2 (alk. paper)

Contents

Introduction: Analytical versus Continental Philosophy?

The French edition of this book appeared in 1983. It has raised two
questions, which have been put to me both in France and in the United
States. They concern the familiar conflict said to exist between two
philosophical schools: the analytical and the Continental. In France there
are few analytical philosophers, and these resent the narrow options
open to them in teaching and publishing. In the United States, Continental philosophers, that is, American writers influenced by the Continental
tradition, complain in their turn of being marginalized by the analytical
establishment. We in France are perplexed as to the very meaning of the
expression Continental philosophy, in much the same way as we are
wary of the continental breakfast; unable to see quite what this means,
we fear that some misunderstanding will arise (cf. the deplorable case of
french dressing). Continental philosophy as understood by Anglo-Ameri-
cans seems to consist of two main strands of thought: *hermeneutics*,
which is of German inspiration, and *poststructuralism*, a loose label
attached to recent ideas circulating in France. A few years ago I wrote an
introduction to contemporary French philosophy—a decidedly Continental phenomenon—for a British publisher. It was therefore natural to
inquire whether I believed in the possibility of fruitful communication
between the two tendencies of modern philosophy. It was wisely suggested that I should preface the present volume with my answer to the
following questions:

1. What is the connection between this book and my *Modern French
   Philosophy*?
2. Is the purpose of this *Grammar* to offer an "analytical" critique of
   so-called Continental philosophy?

In answer to the first question, I would say that the *Grammar* is intended to complete my survey of modern French philosophy by means of an independent critique. But I cannot reply to the second question with a ready yes or no, for the perennial opposition between analytical and Continental does not strike me as very clear. I shall attempt to develop these two points.

I

My earlier work was written as an introduction to the past fifty years of French philosophy. The rule for this kind of survey is that it should strive to present each line of thought on its own terms, stressing whatever is most central according to the authors themselves. This does not preclude discussion—in fact, discussion is essential if we are to account for public reaction to the works concerned. However, I was barred from undertaking a critique of this or that thesis in terms of my own choosing; this would have been awkward and insensitive. I had thus to confine myself to what is called an *immanent critique*, the kind that questions a philosophical production on its own ground and measures it by its own standards alone. This procedure is familiar among philosophers. For example, an empiricist will be asked whether his concept of experience is derived from experience. Hegel will be examined for whether his notions of "the end of history" and "absolute knowledge" are suitably "phenomenological" and "dialectical." Nietzsche must be able to refute the suggestion that his "inversion of Platonism" remains Platonic. Heidegger will be asked whether his "overcoming of metaphysics" does not preserve a "metaphysics of presence."

In France, immanent critiques are most commonly practiced on the model of the *explication de texte*. In a French-style comprehension, one part of the text is played off against the rest. But this setting the text against itself requires that we identify hidden fractures, like dotted lines running through the text, the weak seams at which we can begin to dismantle what had appeared so homogeneous, so all of a piece. It is no doubt in the exposure of these secret fissures and latent tensions that the true professional can display his prowess. And like the old Sophist art of persuasion, the skill necessary for *explication de texte* can be made to serve opposing interests. The *conservative* would have a brilliant analysis shatter the text, pinpointing all manner of internal contradictions, only to demonstrate how these difficulties are ultimately overcome in the text itself. For him the great lesson of any text lies in that higher solution which shows the initial difficulties were merely apparent. The *skeptic*, on the other hand, uses the analysis to demonstrate that any synthesis must fail, that any thesis is its own antithesis, and that there is no higher solution.

In the eyes of many French (and other) philosophers, the immanent critique is much more than a method of exposition. To them it constitutes the only safeguard against dogmatism. Thus what began as a classroom technique now stands as the embodiment of philosophical rationality, eventually becoming the driving force of ideas throughout history. All intellectual advance is viewed as a process of immanent critique, the refutation of self by self. If the result of the immanent critique is deemed determinate, it will be called a *positive* dialectics. Otherwise it will be known as a *negative* dialectics.

Given that I myself resorted to this method of exposition in *Modern French Philosophy*, it might be assumed that I share the view so common in France: a good critique is an immanent critique, the only legitimate kind for philosophy. In fact I do not subscribe to this view and would suggest that there are grave disadvantages inherent in the exclusive use of such a method. In the first place, it always forces us to take the *broad view*. We are oriented toward the *text as a whole, the coherence of the system, the radicality of principles, the consonance of beginning and end*, and so forth. Unless the critique considers each object of study as a whole (a passage, a chapter, a work, a period), it will fail. The rule in this game is to block all the exits available to the object of the critique, except perhaps the one it cannot reach without crossing enemy terrain. But as we play out the dialectical game, we are in danger of forgetting that a general principle exists to be applied, or again that a general refutation must also be valid in detail. The immanent critique can tell us what holds good for the totality, in all cases, but we still do not grasp how it works in this case or that. We aspire to a more *applied* approach. Second, the prevalence of this method encourages illusions such as the "death of philosophy," the "end of history," or the "closure of metaphysics." When only one legitimate form of critique—the immanent critique—is to be recognized in philosophy, we begin to imagine that the course of human thought is irreversible. It becomes natural to start from our present position; the most recent doctrines appear to represent the critical gains of several generations. In this model of the history of philosophy, each writer of stature finds his place in the ancestral gallery. The work of one thinker is assumed to result from an immanent critique of his most illustrious predecessor, as in the traditional courses on "Aristotle, Critic of Plato."

We ourselves are necessarily at the end of the line, the last on the list, and hence our great problem is to know what remains to be said. What can we do or say after so many centuries of immanent critique? Everything, it seems, has been said already. All we can do is gild the lily: the practitioner of the immanent critique is immediately recognizable by his tendency to say that so and so *remains* a prisoner of the very fallacy he denounces. Kant, for example, "remains a dogmatist." Hegel "remains a thinker of the beyond." Nietzsche "remains both Cartesian and Platonic." There is something out of balance in this posture. The immanent critic is *too good an audience.* He surrenders too easily. He accepts everything about the text before him; his only wish is to reach the end of the road unimpeded. *In principle* he has no quarrel with this text; he insists only on consistency down to the final consequences. This attitude is all very well, provided it is balanced from the opposite side. The good audience must know how to be a bad audience. The critic must become a double reader: while one part of him, understanding every nuance, hastens in the direction of consequences, the other part must refuse to budge, obstinately unwilling to accept anything whatever without detailed circumstantial explanations.

In reality, a genuine immanent critique can only be marshaled fully from within a particular philosophical school, in which the reader uses the criteria established by the text itself. In any other case, we seek to address the text not with its own questions, but with ours. We are interested in the capacity of the text to suggest answers to questions *we* judge to be important. The elevation of the immanent critique to the status of absolute rational method indicates belief in a single philosophical school, beyond the apparent diversity of traditions and doctrines. But if there were only one philosophy, the reader of a philosophical text would invariably be a disciple, learning from the master (and none other) what may be objected to in the master. The disciple must search the master's teaching itself for reasons to part company with him. Such a relationship of disciple to master cannot be sustained for long without risking madness, violence, or suicide. The ordinary climate of thought then becomes *paradox* or *insistent repetition.*

For the past fifty years, French thought has been dominated by the immanent critique. Each new generation or school has announced a fresh victory over human illusion. According to this view, there have been three essential stages in French philosophy since the time of Bergson and Brunschvicg (if not since Taine):

1. The *phenomenological* victory over the "philosophy of representation," thanks to the concept of *intentionality.* "Philosophy of representation" is the dogma which holds that the human mind can know things only through the representation or idea it has of them. The emphasis on the intentionality of mental acts reminds us that it is the wolf we fear, not

our idea of the wolf, or that the Eiffel Tower itself, not an idea of it, is visible on the Champ-de-Mars.

2. The *hermeneutic* victory over "onto-theology," thanks to the concept of *interpretation*. "Onto-theology" is the supposition of an infinite mind at the origin of things, standard of their reality and guarantee of their intelligibility. Hermeneutics—the art of interpreting oracles in times of trouble—reminds us that we are not pure mind, dwelling in the land of eternal truths. Our reason cannot participate in the infinite understanding postulated by rationalist metaphysics. The concept of interpretation serves to suggest that, precisely because he is finite, man must inevitably advance interpretations, deciding at whatever cost that *this* means *that*. We must decide whether *this*—what appears to us, the phenomenon— means *that*—what our fate hangs upon—or whether it means something else.

3. The *semiological* victory over the "metaphysics of the referent," thanks to the revolutionary new concept of the *sign*. The "metaphysics of the referent" posits a *reality* that would be the unilateral measure of the validity of our assertions. The discovery of the true nature of the sign is the thesis whereby a sign derives its meaning not from its relation to an independent thing—the "referent"—but from its relation to other signs inside a closed system. We can conclude that signs refer us *indefinitely* to other signs.

If we accept the "immanentist" version of these three stages, we shall be quick to read into them the linear itinerary toward an ever-increasing critical lucidity. In each case a dogmatic residue carried over, either through carelessness or through naïveté, in yesterday's theories is unmasked by whatever school predominates today.

True, none of these dogmas deserves to be defended, and I have no intention of pleading the case of ideology against phenomenology, of rational metaphysics against hermeneutics, or of epistemological solipsism against semiology. However, I cannot feel unreservedly complacent about the progress of contemporary thought, because I do not know what to make of each principle invoked in turn: the phenomenological principle ("all consciousness is consciousness of something"), the hermeneutic principle ("all understanding is an interpretation"), the semiological principle ("there is only language—or text—nothing else"). These propositions present some difficulties. I do not level the charge that they are still trapped in ancestral illusion, or that they reproduce such and such a dogma. My problems begin much earlier. In brief, I cannot see what meaning is being ascribed to them, and I do not see, either, that anyone is concerned to give them a receivable meaning.

Thus I do not understand how I am supposed to interpret "something" in the maxim "all consciousness is consciousness of something." The phenomenological concept of object is not easily discerned. My problems are compounded when it is explained (in connection with the perception of an apple tree, for instance) that the phrase means *consciousness is consciousness of the apple tree.* We can understand the declaration, "I am conscious of *seeing* an apple tree," although of course there are not many opportunities to say such a thing; we might imagine a situation in which someone might say, "I have passed this apple tree a thousand times, yet only today, for the first time, *do I feel conscious of seeing an apple tree.*" But when the phenomenologist declares that consciousness is consciousness of the tree, he is expressing himself in these terms because he seeks at all costs to present the perceptual experience in the form of a relation between a self-conscious subject and a correlative object.

I am similarly disconcerted by the guiding principle of hermeneutics: "All understanding is an interpretation." For to interpret is to take the risk of saying that text A, initially enigmatic and opaque, has a meaning equivalent to text B, the text offered as the interpretation of A. Needless to say, text B must be comprehensible. If we take the hermeneutic maxim at its word, we shall not know how to proceed in order to interpret anything. This is how the hermeneuticist explains his principle to us: all understanding is itself an interpretation. In other words, the interpretive impulse never ends; indeed it cannot end. The reading of text A offered by text B must be interpreted in its turn, by providing the meaning of text B in a new text, C, and so on ad infinitum. But this explanation may be too charitable. The principle I have cited actually implies the opposite. It is not so much that interpretation is unending, that there are always more things to say and further readings to contend with, but rather that interpretation can never be begun. If all understanding is interpretation, then what passed for an *understanding* of text B offered by the reader of text A as an *interpretation* of that text A must in fact be an *interpretation* of text B. What we had taken for the understanding of text B (text B itself) was already an interpretation of text B—in other words, already text C. What we had taken for text B (*the understanding of the interpretation of text A*) was text C (*the interpretation of the interpretation of text A*). In other words, text B has never, according to the hermeneutic principle, been offered, nor can it ever be. Properly speaking, then, there has never been any interpretation of text A. For until the interpretation of text A is understood—until text B is understood—there is no interpretive reading of text A, but merely a gesture in that direction, an ambiguous and hopeless effort, an enigmatic failure. The hermeneutic maxim means that we have never read anything and never shall—that reading is impossible in principle.

In the strictly French version of hermeneutics, no one interpretation is nowadays championed against all others. In the knowledge that there will necessarily be several, and that it will ultimately be impossible to choose between them, we tend to read between the lines, coaxing out what interests, what forces, what parties confront one another at the moment of reading. The true interpretation of a text now becomes the discovery that it automatically offers multiple interpretations. Once this has been understood, there is no longer any need to be concerned with the "conflict of interpretations" (the title of a work by Ricoeur). There is no longer anything to defend, since we no longer believe in the validity of a single interpretation. It only remains to *play* with the possibility of these various readings. As Barthes comments:

> To interpret a text is not to give it a (more or less justified, more or less free) meaning, but on the contrary to appreciate what more or less *plural* constitutes it. Let us first posit the image of a triumphant plural, unimpoverished by any constraint of representation (of imitation). . . . The systems of meaning can take over this absolutely plural text, but their number is never closed, based as it is on the infinity of language. (*S/Z*, pp. 5–6)

But a text cannot simply be several; it has to be several *somethings*. For example, it might be several texts in one (as a pun is a "plural message," containing multiple messages in one). How many texts can a text be? Barthes asserts that their number is "never closed," but how can he be sure? Has anyone ever proved that there are, say, more than 18,593 texts in a text? Or more than three or four? In fact, the "infinity of language" is here posited on the basis of an a priori reasoning upon the nature of the sign: a text is made up of signs; each of these signs can carry an infinity of meanings by virtue of the infinity of contexts in which it can be placed; a text is therefore "plural." This argument is unfortunately sophistical. That a sign *can have* several meanings according to whether it is used in this way or that does not mean that it *has* several meanings in each use: the meaning it has when used in this way, but also the meanings it would have if it had been used otherwise. The doctrine of the plural text and of infinite language overlooks the fact that *potentially to say* is not yet *to say*, and that to play with the possibilities of play is not yet to make a move in the game. Does the hermeneuticist of the plural text play fair? Not if he pretends to have moved, to have started something, to have offered a textual reading, when he has done nothing of the kind. If the plural reading claims to be a reading in the usual sense of the word, it is a travesty. The reader of the plural text would be like a player who hankers

to play every possible move in one move, or like a child who receives two
dollars and tries to accumulate all the possibilities of pleasure it offers:
two dollars worth of candy, plus two dollars for the movies, plus two
dollars worth of comics, and so on.

But it is likely that the notion of interpretation is understood equivo-
cally here. The hermeneutics that takes the conflict of interpretations
seriously remains a discipline with a distinctly Germanic flavor. We shall
not understand its aims, or even its vocabulary, unless we bear in mind its
twofold origin: in the Protestant tradition of a direct reading of Scripture
by the faithful, and in the controversies over method in the "sciences of
the mind" (that is, those sciences that proceed from documentary interpretation and not from the observation of regular phenomena). In this
kind of hermeneutics, *to interpret a text* must be taken in the sense
Barthes seeks to reject. To read a text is indeed to endow it with meaning,
to find in it the answer to our questions. The French school of hermeneutics continues to speak of *interpretation,* but this now takes on the
sense of an artistic performance, as when an actor performs a part or a
pianist a piece.* Here the notions of text and interpretation have drifted
free of their original theological moorings. We have passed from the age
of the Wars of Religion to that of Symbolist poetry. As in late-nineteenth-
century art, we can see a retreat from the opus toward the sketch, from
the polished toward the vaguely suggestive. What we now call "meaning" is not a meaning proper, but the unfulfilled possibility of meaning.
What we refer to here as a "reading" is not a reading but a simulacrum
evoking what a reading might have been. Indeed, this is how it has been
accepted by the public, who have never demanded proof of the *infinity of
language,* even in a token handful of readings, in the ordinary sense of the
word. Our only objection to the plural reading can be that it persists in
masquerading as something it is ill equipped to be, namely a reading.

The misleading notion of the plural text has already led us to the
semiological principle that "there is only language." Now this principle
tells us very little so long as we do not know what else there *might have
been,* or what there *almost was,* aside from the language or the text. The
semiologist explains his principle as follows: "There is nothing outside
the text" simply means that the *referent* of the text cannot be considered
to be independent from it, since it cannot be identified independent of it.
But the explanation is deceptive. Had there been anything outside the
text, then, it would have been the *referent.* If such is indeed the meaning
of the principle, it is a hollow one. It is obvious enough that the referent
is, by definition, something found "in the text," in that the referent will

* In French, the usual word for "to perform" in this sense is *interpréter.* [TRANS.]

be *whatever the text refers to*. All we are saying, then, by stating this principle is that only by reading the text can we learn what the text purports to speak of. Consequently we learn about what there is "outside the text" by looking "in the text." In a frivolous sense, it is true that whatever is "outside the text" must nevertheless be included "within the text." But the problem is to know whether what is described as *the referent*, when found "within the text," still appears in the form of a referent posited by (and *only* by) the text when considered as it is "outside the text." If this were so, there would be no difference between fiction and nonfiction. The real would only be an *effect of language*, as the delightful phrase goes. But this remains to be proved, to say the least.

Clearly, the difficulties that should alert us to the dangers of adhering too quickly to these propositions are not of the kind we encounter after understanding overall, or following the broad lines; rather, they express an initial disquiet that manifests itself the moment we seek to grasp the matter in detail. This is enough to indicate that besides the immanent critique, invaluable in its proper place, there is scope for another kind of internal critique in philosophy (I take it for granted that philosophy cannot accommodate an *external* critique, or any kind of comparison between what philosophers tell us about the course of things and what we know from other sources). This alternative internal critique might be called *elementary*. The immanent critique demands that we understand a writer's theses better than he does himself. It requires the highest intelligence of us. But the elementary critique asks us not to understand any more than we are capable of explaining or applying in some way. The elementary critique does not address preoccupations such as: What can be said *after* all that has been said? It yields to the opposite pressure: What can be said *before* we can take up the philosophical challenge thrown down by the author? Not, What can be said after Plato, Hegel, and Nietzsche? But, What can be said before we are in a position to discuss what Plato, Hegel, and Nietzsche said?

II

I shall now tackle the second question posed earlier: Is it necessary to make a choice between an "analytic" and a "Continental" approach to philosophy? In our practice of philosophy, are we *scientists* or *essayists*?

It is indisputably true, I believe, that the divide between analytical and Continental is nowadays less pronounced. Once it was possible to equate Continental philosophy with Hegel or Dilthey and analytical philosophy with Russell or Moore. Fifty years later, Continental philosophy was phenomenology, and analytical philosophy was the analysis of ordinary language. Today the boundaries are more blurred, as we can see if we ask how our contemporaries might judge the following extract from *Philosophical Investigations* (90). Wittgenstein is trying to define what distinguishes a philosophical question. Once again, in the preceding paragraph, he has quoted Saint Augustine's famous question: Quid est ergo tempus? Si nemo ex me quaerat, scio—si quaerenti explicare velim, nescio. This is therefore for Wittgenstein, as indeed for most philosophers, the supreme question. He begins: "We feel as if we had to *penetrate* phenomena: our investigation, however, is directed not towards *phenomena*, but, as one might say, towards the '*possibilities* of phenomena.' " Thus far, many a committed Continental philosopher might endorse Wittgenstein wholeheartedly. Philosophy, they would say, must indeed be divorced from science. Philosophy is by no means a branch of scientific research. Science as a whole deals with *phenomena*, with facts, with what happens to be the case (although it might have been otherwise). Philosophy, on the other hand, is pitched toward the a priori, toward what can be established in advance or admitted in any hypothesis. However, while many Continentals would agree with the segregation of philosophy and science, the overwhelming majority of analytical philosophers would reject it out of hand. These conceive of philosophy as a theoretical activity, in the current sense of the word *theory*. Like their scientific colleagues, they see themselves as working toward hypotheses and overall explanations of the functioning of the human mind, or of language, or even of nature itself.

In traditional philosophical terminology, any study that bears on phenomena is known as empirical or *positivist*, whereas investigations whose results do not depend upon observation are known as *speculative*. Wittgenstein opts for the second. It is not that positivists ignore "speculation" altogether; they tend to view it rather as an area of preemptive thinking. Speculation consists for them in forging hypotheses about little-known domains with no facilities for proper experimental control. But there is nothing hypothetical about speculation in the eyes of speculative philosophers, and it has nothing to do with what is still hidden, pending eventual discovery. Philosophy as a speculative activity concerns what has always existed and always been known. Indeed, Wittgenstein goes on to explain the difference between "the study of phenomena" and "the study of the possibilities of phenomena." And at this juncture the Continentals will part company with him, while the analyticals will begin to recognize a fellow spirit.

We remind ourselves, that is to say, of the *kind of statement* that we make about phenomena. . . . Our investigation is therefore a grammatical one. Such an investigation sheds light on our problem by clearing misunderstandings away. Misunderstandings concerning the use of words, caused, among other things, by certain analogies between the forms of expression in different regions of language. Some of them can be removed by substituting one form of expression for another: this may be called an "analysis" of our forms of expression, for the process is sometimes like one of taking a thing apart.

Wittgenstein himself thus introduces the notion and functions of analysis in philosophy. The stated intention of all philosophers is to *clarify* or *sort out* our ideas, but there are few who would expect such a clarification from an examination of the *form* of our statements. This time Wittgenstein will have the analytical philosophers on his side, appreciating as they do the benefits that accrue from *logical* analysis of an expression (Russell's analysis of definite descriptions remains the best model of this). Continental philosophers, however, will find it regrettable that thought should be subjected here to a "logical formalism."

The antithesis of "analytical" and "Continental" is clearly inadequate. It must be completed by a further and more important antithesis, opposing the "speculative" and the "positive." If this is the case, the first question to ask of any philosophy will be: Are we dealing here with *phenomena* or their *possibilities*?

Philosophers of the positive school expect philosophy to have an object, and they expect this object to be "phenomenal" (not, according to what they term the "metaphysical" viewpoint, "suprasensible"). For classical positivism, philosophy has always been the attempt at a general theory, a universal science; the only difference between Thales and ourselves would lie in the greater complexity of the knowledge available to us today. Universal science; but science of what? A science of the most general *facts*; an inventory and a reasoned exposition of *constants* that are demonstrable from our experience in general. Another positivist school sees philosophy as the outbreak of a kind of speculative fever in a generation, coinciding with the birth of a new science. Philosophy is the speculative moment of theory, the theoretical inquiry into phenomena. Here again, *speculative* means *hypothetical* or *conjectural*. But now speculation has a bearing on a particular order of phenomena. There was a time, these philosophers tell us (for they are ever ready with a history of scientific concepts), when the great philosophical debates concerned the nature of motion and the principle of inertia. Later they centered upon the fundamental notions of psychology. Today, according to some of these philosophers, the intensity of the philosophical debate surrounding language in all its forms heralds an authentic science of language.

It is often said, on both sides of the Atlantic, that analytical philosophers operate in the realm of the sciences, whereas the Continentals, preoccupied as they are with questions of interpretation, operate in the realm of literature and the arts. This conventional wisdom is doubly misleading. Not only does it fail to identify the crucial question on which the so-called analytical camp is divided, but it is unaware of the richness and stature of Continental positivism. Anglo-Saxon philosophers and their followers are undeniably accustomed to encountering the *naturalist* version of positivism. But the positivism familiar to Europeans has more often been *historicist* or *culturalist*, addressing the "laws of history" or again the "elementary structures of culture." It arose now in the guise of Marxism, now in the guise of structuralism. In France classics such as *The Savage Mind* by Lévi-Strauss, *Reading Capital* by Althusser and his associates, *The Order of Things* by Foucault, and perhaps also *The Anti-Oedipus* by Deleuze and Guattari are all scions of this philosophical line.

For the naturalist school of contemporary positivism, this phenomenon may be studied according to the methods of natural science. For other schools, be they culturalist or historicist, a division of phenomena under the separate rubrics of *nature* and *culture* (or *history*) is indispensable. Here again, *phenomenon* does not simply mean *that which appears*; anything constituting a possible object of knowledge is phenomenal. But these schools concede that an independent science of cultural (or historical) phenomena is possible. This independence is seen by some as provisional and by others as definitive. What is the difference between the naturalist and the culturalist accounts of the same phenomenon? In the first, it is forbidden to ask what the behavior of agents under observation "means." In the description of their acts and deeds, no mention will be made of the agents' own views on the subject or of any commentary by the tribe as a whole. In the second, great emphasis is placed upon what these agents have to say—upon the *meaning* of what they say rather than the sounds they utter—in order to classify, identify, and compare their acts and deeds. This emphasis, however, serves not to explain the facts but to establish them. The culturalist positivist school does not hold that the true explanation of a person's behaviour is the one he himself is prepared to give us. Far from taking people at their word, this approach simply acknowledges that they speak.

In speculative philosophy, we are asked to shift our focus off the *phenomenon* and onto its *possibility*. These are Wittgenstein's terms, and it is hard to believe that the phrase "the possibilities of phenomena" occurs fortuitously at this point in the text, with no grounds for an evocation of Kant's "conditions of possibility." It seems that Wittgenstein wishes both to allude to the Kantian question and to register his own position: where Kantians seek sine qua non conditions and find them, by means of reflective analysis, in the subject of knowledge, Wittgenstein will turn his attention to possibilities and confine himself to a grammatical examination. The schools of *transcendental argument* (neo-Kantian epistemology, phenomenology) will ask of any object whatever: What are the conditions of possibility for experiencing such an object? In other words, Is it possible for what we are speaking about to be the object of a possible experience—an experience someone might have? Although the investigation, then, focuses upon the possibility of the phenomenon, this actually means the possibility of the object's being apparent to someone (the "phenomenality" of the phenomenon). Here, for example, is a condition frequently posited: in order to *appear* to *exist*, an object must be given to someone by means of a *sensible intuition*.

A "school" of *grammatical argument*, if there is such a thing, does not seek to set formal and general conditions for the phenomenality of phenomena in general. If *conditions* are at issue here, they are conditions for the understanding of what is said in a certain "type of statement." As Wittgenstein says: "That one empirical proposition is true and another false is no part of grammar. What belongs to grammar are all the conditions (the method) necessary for comparing the proposition with reality. That is, all the conditions necessary for the understanding (of the sense)" (*Philosophical Grammar*, 45). Here a typical question to ask would be: Is such and such a word used in such and such a proposition (for instance, "time *passes*," "being *is*," "a machine *can think*") taken in the ordinary sense or in another, unusual sense that can be explained? Or alternatively, have we simply omitted to give it a new sense even though it is not being used in its ordinary sense? The "possibility of the phenomenon" is thus no longer the possibility, for whatever we are dealing with, of appearing; it is the much broader possibility of this object's *being* in one way or another way. *The understanding of the meaning of the proposition is the understanding of the possibilities of phenomena.* To understand a description of phenomena is to understand that this description might have been false (in other circumstances). To understand that a proposition must be accepted without any obligation to compare it with reality is to understand that this proposition is "grammatical"—that it fixes what will be taken as *essential* in the phenomenon concerned.

All the current observations about the incompatibilities and convergences between analytical and Continental philosophies suppose that these are effectively two major definitions of philosophy. Yet nobody has managed to tell us what these definitions are. We are offered geography

find meaning in everything, for it would then become impossible to understand a meaning in this or in that. Here then is an alternative hypothesis: It is not the case that everything has meaning which claims it, otherwise nothing could claim to have meaning.

The problem of meaning would itself be meaningless were it not so banal and commonplace. However we take it—as the problem of the word *meaning* or as the problem of the meaning of words, that is, as the problem of the meaning of the word *meaning* or as the problem of the application of the word *meaning* to that which words, sentences, or discourses should offer—the problem must be posed in exactly the same way as the problem of the word *peplum* or of the word *dinner*. Philosophy begins at a point further along—not where we seek to elucidate a hitherto unknown meaning, but where we require that the meaning of something we ought to have understood be explained.

The meaning of something we have never expected to understand (a Chinese character, if we do not know Chinese) does not escape us; it is by definition inaccessible. Meaning can be said to escape us where we ought to have understood, where we think that we might understand by looking harder, where we were on the brink of understanding, or where we long to understand. Thus what gives rise to the philosophical problem of meaning is not the fact of there being texts that are Chinese or Hebrew to us. Others know these languages. Linguistics can help us learn them, and it even explains why this learning is possible. The problem is, there are texts in our own language that are Greek to us. The philosophical problem of meaning begins where the solution is not a corollary of learning. The philosopher cannot overlook the escape of meaning, for it opens to question the possibility of understanding in the most general sense. How can meaning fail us where others had found it, where we ourselves had a brief intimation of it? This is the experience Pascal described: "Thoughts come at random and go at random. No device for holding on to them or for having them. / A thought has escaped; I was trying to write it down. Instead I write that it has escaped me" (Br. 370). The point here is that we are dealing with the escape of my thought, of the meaning of what I was engaged in writing. Pascal does not say, "I no longer know what I wanted to write"; that would be a case of absent-mindedness. The thought that escaped is not the one he *wanted* to write and will therefore not be writing. The thought that escaped is the one he *would like* to write, in other words, the one he would like to write while he is writing it, but that he is nonetheless not writing because it has escaped him. "I write instead that it has escaped me." This "stead" is the place of an escape of meaning. It remains only to note the failure: "a thought has escaped, etc." This failure, like any experience of nonmeaning, generates thought. What Pascal wrote was not a thought of his, of which he would be master, since that thought escaped him. In its stead, we read a random thought bestowed by chance.

There is something universal about the experience Pascal describes so well. Not only can the writing of thought become the writing of a void in thought (without its being possible to tell whether some thought has fled or whether it was the mirage of a thought that evaporated at the moment of committing pen to paper), but equally it can be said that meanings come at random and go at random. There is no device in the reading of texts for holding on to them or for having them. A meaning has escaped: I was trying to gloss it. Instead my gloss records that it has escaped. *Random*: it is certainly the accidental fact of being born on this side of the water, where such formulations are charged with the highest meaning, and not on the other side, where they are merely an impenetrable historical document, that gives us the precarious sense of having understood.

Semantic questions are, in the first place, the questions about meaning we pose every day. *Please explain this sentence, this title, this poem.* These are semantic questions. We ask them because we know quite clearly that there are enlightening replies. We know what we are asking because we also know whether we have received the answer. That is the kind of meaning we are dealing with in the philosophical problem of meaning. It is the meaning that we know how to ask for, and not another kind that we had not envisaged until we began to philosophize. It is no more and no less than the meaning we know how to elicit in particular situations of everyday life. If this is so, why is there such uncompromising disagreement between the various contemporary philosophies of meaning? Why is there not even the glimmering of a consensus on what philosophy should clarify or explain?

At first one is inclined to believe that of all philosophical issues, the issue of meaning should be the most straightforward. Here, at least, we should have no difficulty in understanding. There seems to be no place for an obscure discourse on meaning. But this innocent trust in the skill of professionals also leads to the assumption that economists are good businessmen, that literature teachers write good English, and that psychologists always know what we are thinking. A confusion may also enter here concerning the philological explanation of the word meaning (or of the words *sens, Sinn, Bedeutung*, etc.) and its philosophical explanation. In reality, even if we were to maintain that "everything that can be said can be said clearly," it would not follow that we can say clearly what we mean by this.

Things would still be fairly simple if we could believe that the misunderstandings and deadlocks of the "philosophy of language" were the effect of a confusion of tongues. The various schools could always be distinguished by the idioms in which they operate. Phenomenologists could meet with other phenomenologists to discuss the meaning of experience; Hegelians with Hegelians to debate the meaning of history and culture; hermeneuticists to deliberate the meaning of texts, positivists to demolish nonmeaning, and analysts of everyday language to invent situations in which utterances would serve unforeseen purposes. We are told of the discomfiture suffered by students enrolling en masse in a first-year course entitled The Meaning of Life, only to discover at the outset that it would deal with the meaning of the word *life*.[1] No doubt they thought it would have been more honest to have clarified the special sense in which the word *meaning* was to be understood. However, this distinction would have resolved nothing. The confusion in the "philosophy of language" is not a confusion of tongues but one of philosophy. I suggest that the unhappy victims of this equivocation over the word *meaning* did indeed attend a course on the meaning of life, although perhaps not the one they had hoped for. For it is not immaterial, philosophically speaking, that a lecture on the meaning of life (the meaning to be given to one's life) can be delivered without a word about the word *life*. The curious thing is not that the meaning of the word *life* should have been left unexplained in the course of a lecture on the meaning of life. It is, rather, that a meaning—not simply the meaning of a phrase but the meaning of life—has not been addressed. Conversely, it would be interesting to know how long the zealous semantics professor for whom the meaning of life was nothing but the meaning of the word *life* could hold forth before coming up against the questions that arise in our lives.

I conclude from this that philosophers do indeed address the same meaning and for the same reasons. The same meaning: the one we seek when we do not understand. For the same reasons: because it is a matter of knowing why meaning sometimes escapes. Not to understand through ignorance of the language raises semantic questions only. But not to understand where one had expected to do so, when all the signs suggest that understanding should be possible—this is where the problem of meaning, as proper to philosophy, is actually posed. Now, it appears there are two irreconcilable ways of approaching the problem. One posits that meaning can never be lacking, while the other posits that meaning may very well be lacking. There is a *hermeneutic* and a *grammatical* way of positing the problem of meaning.

Sense or Nonsense?

To posit the philosophical problem of meaning in a grammatical fashion is to recognize that conditions of meaning exist. In order to say something, only certain constructions will do. Where meaning appears obscure or elusive, we must first establish whether there can be a meaning—an approach illustrated in Wittgenstein's formula. "My aim is: to teach you to pass from a piece of disguised nonsense to something that is patent nonsense" (*Philosophical Investigations* 464).

This doctrine clearly applies not to all signifying systems, nor indeed to all kinds of language, but only to a certain type of statement. The formula is designed for philosophical use. It implies, however, that certain uses of language do not signify at all. It is false to assume that the emergence of language confers meaning upon everything; nothing guarantees the signifying power of signs in combination. Such a reduction to nonmeaning could not be further from the phenomenological reduction to meaning. The phenomenologist reduces things to the meaning they offer us, *meaning* being understood here in a sense that remains to be explained. All that is not my (or perhaps our) lived experience is the meaning of our lived experience. Wittgenstein's stated aim may appear negative or destructive: where others speak of describing the meaning (of experience) and of bestowing meaning, Wittgenstein sets out to expand nonmeaning—a curious response to the demand for meaning. His semantics thus appears niggardly in comparison with the generous semantics of philosophies that take the risk of finding a meaning. This has indeed been the common interpretation, as if anything that did not clearly constitute a factual proposition should be jettisoned. The positivist retrenchment could tolerate only statements devoid of mystery; *it's a lovely day*, with its undertone of rejoicing, would be suspect.

We may sympathize with the heroism of the will to understanding. I belong to a generation raised in an intellectual climate bent on the decolonization of the mind. Our fathers had built an empire of science and power out of their refusal to understand a host of practices and customs, beliefs and daydreams, legends and sayings. It fell to the sons to resent the arbitrariness of this decision; it is their lot to hear the stifled voices, to decipher the faded palimpsests, to exhume the overlayered traces of another meaning. For them, the accusation of nonmeaning is a repressive gesture whereby some seek to protect the precarious ascendancy of certain axioms of modern reason—axioms that, on the contrary, cry out for ruthless genealogical scrutiny.

The will to understanding is not the same as understanding, however, and the only meaning we can offer is the one we have. If semantic generosity consists in attributing to the words we do not understand an equally mysterious meaning, then it is no longer an admirable display of magnanimity but becomes a deceptive conjuring trick. What matters, then, is not to assert that meaning has been attributed to this or to that, but to formulate this meaning we attribute, and to do so in the very language we speak. The bestowal of meaning will otherwise have a distinctly inflationary effect, analogous to the careless proliferation of monetary signs. Such galloping inflation is often celebrated in France as polysemic largesse, the cornucopia of signifieds—in short, the abundance of meaning. Meaning is multiple, meaning is the multiple. But if meaning is always multiple, let us at least state some of the meanings of one or two things. As Plato said, it is easy to jump straight from the *one* to the *many*; this avoids having to count in between.

On closer inspection, Wittgenstein's grammatical program is nearer than it might appear to the problem we have inherited. Here two points should be stressed. First, as I noted above, this program concerns only those words to which philosophers ordinarily attribute a meaning (although they cannot say which).[2] Thus it involves not the coercion of uncontrollable utterances into the realm of nonmeaning, but the grammatical scrutiny of certain philosophical utterances on which the classic conception of meaning rests. It is not our task to liberate the utterances of others—unfairly condemned by Western rationalism—from nonmeaning. Rather, we must establish whether we can rescue our own philosophical utterances from nonmeaning. Second, we can reassign meaning to those words we have deprived of it only at the price of a corresponding deficit in meaning elsewhere. If meaning has been unjustly withdrawn, for example, from traditional narratives or customs, it cannot be restored unless we are prepared to sustain a loss of meaning ourselves. In reality the meaning we stand to lose is rather like surplus fat, which it is beneficial to shed. The kind of reason that too readily condemns the time-honored practices of men and their life forms on grounds of irrationality and nonmeaning requires trimming down. In order to pass sentence, this reason has had to espouse principles and axioms that merit closer examination. We will understand afresh what has been dismissed as meaningless only if we abandon our claim to understand some of the things we had endowed with meaning. Thus the philosophical descent into problems of language need not be a symptom of decline after all: it is not for want of something better to do that we engage in splitting hairs. According to one widespread view, language was all that remained to philosophers once "real" scientists had taken everything else—but even language, of course, has been expropriated with the emergence of a definitive treatment from linguistics and anthropology. The philosophical decline (which invariably attends a philosophical flourishing) can be detected, rather, in the tendency to regard those issues that puzzle all genuine philosophy as minor.

The question of the conditions of meaning confronts us today not because we seek to outdo our predecessors in subtlety and finesse, but because we can no longer avoid it. As soon as we realize that meaning is escaping at every juncture, the urgent need to revise the immortal principles of the republic of philosophy no longer requires proof.

Interpreting the Sacred Sign

Hermeneutics, or the art of the hermeneuticist, belongs to anyone capable of interpreting divinatory signs:[3] oracles, auspices, omens, words that tell us what we are and what it is our lot to be. Essentially, the diviner's art is applied to messages. While they may sometimes be obscure, their character as messages is never in doubt. These signs that we may not understand are undoubtedly signs and undoubtedly destined for us. Meaning, then, is both given—the deity has spoken—and taken away, for it still remains to be understood, if we are prepared to run the risk of interpretation. All interpretation will involve an element of risk or danger. The possibility of misunderstanding the sign is one of the elements in the hermeneutic situation. There is tragedy when the sign is constituted in such a way that it dooms precisely as it claims to save. An error as to the meaning of an oracle is known as a tragic error: we trusted too soon in one or another possible interpretation of the given sign. We missed the warning it concealed, and our rash reading hastened the prophecy.

> *Often we encounter our destiny*
> *On the road we take to flee it.**

An authentically religious person will not be alarmed by disagreement among the diviners or by exegetical controversy. Such differences are inevitable. For all these reasons, hermeneutics is not an art of deciphering; it does not aim at an appropriate analysis that will pin down, once and for all, the code in which a cryptogram has been composed.

How do we shift from the hermeneutics of the diviner to the hermeneutics of the philosopher? The elementary hermeneutic situation—a person, a sign intended for this person, and a hermeneuticist—must be seen to

---

*From La Fontaine, *Fables*, 8: 16. [TRANS.]

embody the model of what takes place in the general understanding of
meaning. To understand is never to decipher by means of a code—
whether we possess it in advance or have to reconstitute it; to understand
is always to interpret signs that are singular on two counts: by the way
they signify in every instance, and by the person for whom they are
destined. What is properly hermeneutic here is the fact that we can
always construe a false meaning. It is possible for us to be deceived by
certain clues and to misinterpret. Thus the problem is to establish
whether we are not always more or less misconstruing. The anxiety that
attaches to this question might well be described as Cartesian, since it
arises from the acknowledged uncertainty of interpretations. Perhaps I
deceive myself in thinking this sign offers that meaning. Or perhaps I am
being deceived. Why prefer one meaning over another? In other words, is
there anything in my consciousness of having understood (when I clearly
have such a consciousness) to attest that my consciousness is not false
consciousness, that my consciousness of meaning is not a consciousness
blind to the false meaning that it is in the process of construing? To say
that this question is Cartesian in style is not to cast Descartes as a
hermeneuticist. It is rather to say that this doubt can be turned to
advantage, encouraging reflection upon the self. The situation in which
an understanding may be false is undoubtedly disturbing when we bear
in mind that the signs to be understood are destined for us. They are, in
the hermeneutic mode, messages we have incontestably received. The
sign that demands my interpretation is addressed to me. It carries a
meaning for me, intended for me. The entire problem is therefore to
know whether the meaning these signs have *for me* (the one according to
which I believe I understand them) is really the meaning they have *for me*
(the one they have to impart to me, the one I am destined to read in
them). The entire problem consists in crossing from the first meaning for
me to the second meaning for me. Herein lies the affinity between all
philosophical hermeneutics and phenomenology, in which every thing is
precisely that which it evidently is for me. It is true that the person for
whom a revelation is destined cannot easily be imagined in the guise of a
Cartesian or a Husserlian consciousness. However, he must be endowed
with what the phenomenologist would call "ipseity" or selfhood
(*Selbstheit*). He must be capable of suspecting that what he makes of
what he receives—the meaning he first apprehends when he understands
as anybody or everybody would—is not the meaning that has actually
been relayed to him; rather, it constitutes an obstacle that impedes his
understanding of the authentic meaning, the one he would be unable to
grasp without at the same time discovering who he is, himself, the person
for whom this sign was destined. The sign misleads the person it is

supposed to enlighten, because the receiver of the divine revelation has already gone astray and is lost to himself. False consciousness of meaning is false consciousness of self, a bizarre quid pro quo whereby we mistake ourselves for ourselves. Oedipus, the riddle solver, is nevertheless misled as soon as he takes the meaning of the oracle for him (in his hasty interpretation) to be the meaning of the oracle for him (which it has destined for him). But the conflict of the first self (what we are because we believe ourselves to be so) with the second self (what we are because we can be or are destined to be so) finds resolution in the following reflection: Whatever is addressed to me is necessarily addressed to me in a form I find intelligible, and there is thus a point at which, at my own risk, I have the right to take the meaning I grasp to be the meaning I should have grasped. According to a familiar phrase in modern transcendental philosophies, this "ought to be possible." The *for me* of subjectivity— lost, alienated, scattered, but also unnerved by its search for certainty— ought to be able to coincide with the *for me* of the sign that is delivered to me in order that I myself may be delivered. This ought to be possible, albeit at a high price: an infinite, laborious reading and exegesis of the revealed signs.

To say that a hermeneutic sign is addressed to a receiver split off and separated from himself is not to endorse those critics who locate the source of tragedy in the double meaning of oracles, itself made possible by what is called the equivocity of language. According to this view, the equivocal is what is tragic, whereas the search for meaning is a forgetting or even an active repression of tragedy. But the plurality of interpretations is not the plurality of significations. Here we ought rather to agree with Clément Rosset's point: "Sophoclean tragedy is tied not to double meaning but, on the contrary, to its gradual elimination. The misfortune of Oedipus is to be only himself, and not two selves."[4] Accustomed as we are to taking the plurality of readings for a plurality inherent in the text for which these readings are proposed, we find it quite natural to associate tragedy with the duplicity of the sign. It would take a narrow-minded positivist, we declare, to believe that a word could mean one thing without at the same time evoking another thing. Such eminently literary views are fairly widespread. I do not wish to discuss them in general, but I would point out that they are inappropriate to the oracle consulted by Oedipus. It may be that certain texts have several meanings, and it may be that *Oedipus Rex* is one such text, but it is certain that the oracular pronouncement of Oedipus's destiny has only one meaning. The oracle clearly stated that Oedipus will commit patricide and incest. To speak of ambiguity here is an error on two counts: first in terms of modalities, for it shifts from the possibility of misunderstanding to the obligation of understanding in several ways (that one word may be understood in several ways does not lead to the conclusion that it actually embodies all the senses in which it can be understood; a further step is required to establish that all the ways of understanding are equally in order); second, in terms of the nature of the meaning, equated here with what the receiver imagines he understands. For the initial conclusions drawn by Oedipus are no more what the oracle intends than a text that comments upon another text is in itself the meaning of the text being commented upon. The meaning Oedipus first reads into the oracle is his false interpretation of the revelation, not a secondary meaning to be appended to its real one.

The two great classic examples of hermeneutic reading are the Alexandrian reading of Homer and the interpretation of the Bible by Protestant theologians in the nineteenth century. Here the characteristic feature of the hermeneutic situation, as I have just described it, is clearly discernible. There is a text, ancient but not yet archaic, whose apparent meaning is deceptive. The reader can well understand the letter of this text; he knows its language, but he can find nothing there to arrest him or provide him with meaning (in the nonlinguistic, hermeneutic sense of the word *meaning*). The text says nothing to him. It is not hermetic; it is perfectly accessible to a positive philological reading buttressed by dictionaries and critical apparatus. But we who read it today do not find the decisive message it would yield if it were indeed the Text that an entire tradition has suggested (the Poem, the Bible). We could always leave it at that: *The Iliad* has aged, *The Odyssey* is a tissue of contradictions, and the Bible is a collection of obsolete books. These texts will then be stripped of their authority, remaining as nothing more than documents upon which to exercise our science. But we could also conclude that the meaning of the text for us today, with our innocently erudite reading, is not the one this text might have for us. Instead of proceeding from what we are or believe ourselves to be today to the ancient text, we might go the other way, from the ancient text that speaks to us about ourselves today, to ourselves: those to whom the text is speaking, not those to whom it says nothing. We shall learn from the ancient text about our place and about our time. In order to speak to us, and not in the manner of the first reading (literal, material, "objectifying"), the text demands a total transformation of our expectations and interests; we shall have to commit ourselves to a different reading (an allegorical or a symbolic one).

Hermeneutics as we have been approaching it is our solution to a particular situation. Philosophical hermeneutics is based on the postulate that this situation is much more common, and that it may define mankind's relationship with meaning. This generalization, however, is highly debatable.

The particular hermeneutic situation—that of the Alexandrine Greek confronting Homer or the modern Christian confronting the revealed text—is hermeneutic because of its particular characteristics. It is not a specific instance of a more general situation. Why must we think that an *interpretation* solves the problem posed by the dissipation of meaning? We must, because we know that this solution is the correct one. It is not justified simply by being a remedy for the deficiency of meaning. Nor is it merely designed to soothe, like some comforting illusion. We accept in advance that, from our position, the text requires interpretation. For we know—we take it for granted—that a message encapsulating an awaited truth has been entrusted to a chain of bearers in order to reach us. Each bearer is at once an intermediary (with a mission to pass on the relay) and an addressee. We know that any transmission across time entails losses and lapses. Such loss is inevitable, affecting any perpetuation through a family line; we are situated between our ancestors, who are dead, and our descendants yet to come. If a message is uniquely addressed to us—persons who exist in history—we are entitled to suppose that it was passed on in such a way as to survive the trials of the transmission process. Hermeneutic meaning, then, is not something we settle for in the absence of anything better or in order to avoid the problem of no meaning at all. The meaning to be disclosed through interpretation is the only meaning that can be transmitted down the ages. We are thus perfectly entitled to refuse all readings that offer no receivable meaning for us, but have a meaning only for the ancients, for the first receivers. So between ourselves and what is to be interpreted there is necessarily this very particular relation in which we know, before any interpretation, that we alone are being addressed.

Faith precipitates a manifestly hermeneutic situation, for faith is simply a matter of regarding certain signs as divine revelation—certain signs, but of course not every manner of sign, in every circumstance and on every occasion. The right to interpret is based on precisely this situation, in which I receive the sign of a power that reveals itself to me through the very sign it has sent. Interpretation is permissible wherever it is necessary, but such necessity is valid only for signs confined to the area of revelation, the *templum*: outside the temple, there are no hermeneutics. Beyond the temple lies the delirium of interpretation. The condition of interpreting signs given within the temple is that outside it, in profanity, there are different procedures for understanding. Here the word *interpretation* can be used only in the most banal sense, as in the interpretation of a diplomatic cable; or as in reading between the lines, or finishing another person's sentence, or suggesting the key to a difficult text. Such forms of interpretation draw upon procedures of inference, hypothesis, and calculation (*he wouldn't have said this if he hadn't meant that*). There is nothing hermeneutic about such intellectual exercises, for nowhere do they raise the question of a truth that could teach me what I should be—a truth I will not understand until I have *become* what I should be.

If philosophy wishes to use the concept of hermeneutic interpretation for sign spaces other than the temple, it must fulfill two conditions: (1) it must accept that interpretation is the exception, rather than the rule; and (2) it must justify this exception by a unique relation between sign and receiver.

Hermeneutic interpretation is legitimate where it is obligatory. It is never justified by the fact that it permits us to understand against all odds, but only because it may permit us to understand as we should. Hermeneutics is not a remedy for the deficiency in meaning, but only for the deficiency in the understanding of what presents the most definitive of meanings. All that is obligatory is permitted; all that is perhaps obligatory is perhaps permitted. If we cannot rule out that a text contains a revelation, then a hermeneutic interpretation may well prove justified. Needless to say, however, we are under no obligation to interpret a text that says nothing to us. The extension of hermeneutics to include any relationship of reader to sign is not legitimate. Although any sign whatever can (in the long run) be received by someone as the revelation of his fate, it does not follow that all signs may likewise be received by him. Thereby to approach the situation in which *templum* and *profanum* begin to merge is to fall prey to delirium (anything can be the revelation of anything).

Here again, as so often with the philosophical handling of the concept of meaning, we find that the alleged extension of a word results in the total loss of meaning. We will recall that Heidegger was the first to reject the "extended" currency of the word *hermeneutics*. The appearance of this word in *Being and Time*, he notes, is not as an extension of the original meaning (in this case, biblical theology); rather, it returns to a still more restricted, earlier sense, evoking Hermes' role as messenger of the gods.[5] *Hermeneuein*, then, means not to interpret (in the common sense, for example the philological), but to throw light on what informs us of our destiny.

The question now is to establish whether we can speak of hermeneutics outside the temple, on the grounds that a relation to signs may be found which is analogous to the relation within it. Can a relation be called hermeneutic when the term of the relation in which man stands is not a divine sign? This term must preserve the twofold singularity of the oracular sign. The hermeneutic space from which signs that cannot lack meaning emerge must be potentially separate; it can never be a common space. Account must also be taken of the interpretive debt, for signs that reach me from that space will tell me who I am and how to become what I am. Thus the hermeneutic space will not be literature so much as the book from which I learned to read, my reading primer, which I cannot therefore read as I would any other work. It will be not the world or the thing, but this landscape or that face (which have made me what I am). Aside from the gift of faith, then, the hermeneutic relationship appears necessary only in the name of a sense of homeland. Outside the temple the only place from which signs of this kind can issue is the homeland: not this nation (in the sense of a body animated by the national will) but the origin toward which we feel a debt, repayable through the cult of dead ancestors and the honor rendered to their memory. The sacred traces through which they continue to live among us (relics, mementos, icons, legends) can never cease to address us. Their remains speak to us still even when we cannot understand or are not interested, and they will do so until we become the self-made men of modern Utopia.

There is of course no conceivable hermeneutics of philosophical texts (or of "the philosophical text," in the words of those who behave as if there were only one). Philosophy knows nothing of the Book, and far from claiming to have any hold over us, philosophical works deliberately offer themselves up to the most meticulous scrutiny.

Understanding the Profane Sign

A situation is hermeneutic when it is necessarily meaningful. Certain sign spaces are conceivable where meaning cannot be lacking, although the interpreter may fail to understand it. But the conviction that meaning is present is actually the conviction that we are in the unique site—in the temple or homeland. Everywhere else, the presence of meaning ceases to be guaranteed, and it would be unreasonable to expect it. The difference can be put in the following way. Confronted with the sign offered for interpretation in the unique site, understanding is never enough, for a signification may always be challenged. Meaning is subject to arrest on grounds of suspicion, and in such circumstances no signification can remain indifferent to the conflict between the true meaning and the false.

An indifferent meaning is by no means neutral; beneath its casual appearance it conceals another meaning, which is the correct one. The necessary critique of the consciousness of meaning brings hermeneutics into a special dialogue with the great critiques of consciousness, in the tradition of cynics and moralists such as Nietzsche or Freud. Here, clearly, we may fail to grasp *the* meaning, but we never fail to come away with some form of meaning. Although meaning sometimes escapes us, or escapes us at first, it leaves an afterimage behind, a "screen" meaning—that indifferent meaning unlikely to contain any revelation. But if we now dispense with the hermeneutical assumption that we are in the site of interpretation, we find ourselves projected into the space of profanity, where signs may be meaningless. The escape of meaning is then no longer a Cartesian problem, but would be better described as Parmenidian. We should no longer say, I have understood, but have I understood correctly or am I mistaken/deceived? But rather, I have understood, but was it possible to understand? No longer, I thought I had understood correctly, only sometimes I misunderstand. But rather, I thought I understood, but sometimes there is nothing to understand. The escape of meaning that will concern us henceforth is no longer the dissimulation of authentic signification behind a deceptive meaning, or alleged nonmeaning. It involves the dissimulation of nonmeaning in the guise of meaning—a nonmeaning that must be exposed and made public in order to dispel the illusion of understanding.

"When a sentence is called senseless, it is not as it were its sense that is senseless [*sinnlos*]. But a combination of words is being excluded from the language, withdrawn from circulation" (*Philosophical Investigations*, 500). This remark by Wittgenstein highlights the absurdity of the following statement: *The meaning of this sentence is such that this sentence has no meaning.* Now this would not be absurd if it were applied within the temple to the readings debatable in hermeneutic terms. We should indeed say that the message, interpreted in such and such a way, affords a meaning, but if this is what it means, it is meaningless. For if the message were to be trite, or irrelevant to our fate, it would have no meaning for us. This entitles us to put aside any meaning that falls short of what we were promised. We have the right to reject any meaning that means nothing to us, because we have the right to find a meaning that means something. In a profane context, however, the statement criticized by Wittgenstein is absurd. At the same time, it emphasizes the absurdity inherent in interpreting signs within the profane space according to the laws of hermeneutics. In this profane space the combinations of signs that have meaning (whether banal or precious) have what meaning they have—that is, the meaning we attribute as we use them. Any meaningless combinations of signs are withdrawn from circulation; to say that they have no meaning is to say that their manner of construction automatically precludes any possibility of their use. This association of meaning with use should not be seen as a crucial thesis, as if a pragmatic or instrumental concept of language were now to be developed. More specifically, to refer to the meaning we attribute to a sign when we use it is not the same thing as to maintain that we should first attribute a meaning to signs and then use them. It is nevertheless worth repeating that a meaning is a usage. This will help us to identify the ascendancy of one example that prevails in much contemporary thinking about meaning:[6] the translation of an ancient language into a modern language. To understand Greek is to be able to translate from it. But I cannot say that I am really using Greek forms when I translate *into* Greek; it is an academic exercise, in which any corrections would be irrelevant to a conversation in Greek among Greeks. As such, it is purely a matter of my own progress in the language. Our relationship to texts in classical languages is not unlike our relationship, in hermeneutics, to the revealed sign. In both cases signs are received, but to understand them is not tantamount to being able to use them, as it is with the signs of common parlance. Perhaps classical antiquity slides into sanctity at this point. However this may be, exercises in the translation of ancient texts are never more than an example of the effort to understand, and certainly not an example that may be assimilated for the purposes of reproduction. Any theory of meaning that views this as the supreme example of understanding merely testifies to the preponderance of classical studies in the traditional training of philosophers.

It is the task of grammar to rule out meaningless combinations. But which grammar? Not the grammar of the French language (or that of any other language). Those combinations strictly excluded by the grammar of a language need not be withdrawn from circulation, because they can never seriously have entered it. Nor can its task be to codify correct usage, for this sets out not to exclude, but merely to rectify. It is what we shall call philosophical grammar, or speculative grammar (to adopt a medieval term that preoccupied Heidegger in his dissertation).[7]

The Idea of a Philosophical Grammar

How are we to define philosophical grammar? The difficulty is compounded by the fact that several disciplines or strands of research might in one way or another lay claim to this title.

It is certainly not the grammar of a single language, unless we maintain that thought has its own natural tongue. If this were the case, then the analysis of constructions native to this language would indeed be directly philosophical. Such was Rivarol's celebrated illusion:

Our language is distinguished from all others, both ancient and modern, by the order and construction of its sentences. This order must inevitably be straightforward and clear. French names first the *subject* of the discourse, then the *verb* that is the action, and finally the *object* of this action; this is the logic natural to all men; this is the nature of common sense. . . . Hence that admirable clarity, the eternal foundation of our language. WHAT IS NOT CLEAR IS NOT FRENCH; what is not clear is English, Italian, Greek, Latin, what you will.[8]

Rivarol's error does not derive, as we might at first expect, from the supposition that one idiom can be greater than others or one nationality superior to another. The magnanimity of such a criticism is a credit to its proponents but does little to dispel the illusion. Rivarol is mistaken not because he grants to French what he denies to English or Italian (without even mentioning German), but because he believes that the grammar of any language whatever can be the reflection of logic. In fact, no grammar of a language in spoken or written use is ever, as such, a logical grammar, for it incorporates a host of nuances and distinctions that may be important in all kinds of ways. Nor can any language by the same token be called illogical. As Wittgenstein makes clear, languages are no more designed for making known or for expressing thought than are clothes for emphasizing the form of the body (*Tractatus*, 4.002). Clothes have other functions. One might develop the analogy by saying that language no more fails to render thought than clothes fail to manifest the form of the body. The role of the habit is no more to conceal the monk than it is to reveal him.

Neither is philosophical grammar synonymous with general linguistics or the project for a general, reasoned grammar. At any rate, those who advocate the notion of a universal grammar of human languages with a view to discovering the "universals of language"—Denis Zaslawsky, for instance, in his *Analyse de l'être*—must understand that they are pursuing something other than what is being proposed here. A universal grammar, if it were feasible, would not be philosophical simply by virtue of its universality. As Zaslawsky observes, and rightly, there is little point in preordaining that the languages spoken on earth are far too various for us "to arrive through language analysis at structures that are abstract and general enough to provide an objective description of plausible a priori (transcendental) forms of human thought itself."[9] Perhaps, perhaps not; future research will tell. But if research is what will tell, then philosophy is not involved in this debate. True, the *transcendental*, in the Kantian sense, is not readily distinguishable from a "structure of human thought" capable of objective description. And yet Kantians insist on this difference, for transcendental philosophy would otherwise merge with general psychology. To liken Kant's a priori forms to "universals of thought" described by some "universal psychology" overriding the psychology of peoples would be to refute Kantian philosophy. If transcendental thought exists, then it cannot be another name for general psychology. Likewise, if a philosophical grammar exists, it cannot be another name for "the universal grammar" of linguists. This "universal grammar" is mere conjecture; future research will reveal whether it exists. Therefore I need only clarify the way we can speak here and now of philosophical grammar, in order to demonstrate the mutual independence of philosophical and universal grammar.

The simplest way to start would be with Wittgenstein's opposition between the "surface grammar" and the "depth grammar" of a word.[10] The depth grammar is the true one; in other words, it is the sum of rules for a meaningful use of the word—rules by which we do in fact abide. The surface grammar of the same word is the one we (we philosophers) are tempted to confer upon it, not when we use it as anybody might but when we are considering its meaning, in the course of a reflection along the lines of transcendental philosophy (where we ask about the concept F: *Such and such a thing is an F, but what is it to be F?*—as opposed to asking how we use the concept F: *In what case would something be the same F as this F?*). During this tête-à-tête with the word isolated from its uses, we run the risk of responding to suggestions that arise from the superficial resemblance between this word and others whose depth grammar is in fact different. As an example, Wittgenstein cites the word *meinen* (to signify, to mean). In French the example is more striking still. *Vouloir dire* (to mean; literally, to want to say) is superficially related to *dire* (to say). They appear to have the same grammar. The verb *dire* signifies a certain physical process, whether externalized (to speak aloud) or not (to say something to oneself). Such a process is linear and sequential and takes place in time. The surface grammar of *vouloir dire* thus encourages a search for an analogous, albeit less physical, process whereby we animate articulated words with a meaning. In the same way the surface grammar of *comprendre* (to understand) leads us to envisage comprehension in terms of *entendre* (to hear, to understand) or *lire* (to read).

A sound apprehension of these examples would demand that we enter into the Wittgensteinian critique of the "myth of interiority."[11] We will therefore choose a more direct example derived from the problem posed by Frege. Here is one possible version: If Rocinante is a horse, and if being a horse is a form of being (or a concept, in the Fregian sense of the reference, or *Bedeutung*, of a predicate), then why is Rocinante not a form of being (a concept)? The answer is that Rocinante is a name, that *being a horse* is not a name but a predicate whose reference is something that could also be signified in the following statement: "being what Rocinante (for instance) is." The reference of *being a horse* is thus not something with which Rocinante the horse need necessarily be identified or measured one way or the other. If this is the case, then the statement "being a horse is a form of being" adds nothing, but restates in another way what has already been said. If "being a horse" consists in being what Rocinante is, we can only conclude from this that Rocinante is what Rocinante, for instance, is—and welcome the facile truth of this conclusion because it means that the false problem has been dealt with. Such a solution is purely grammatical (even though it has nothing to do with a comparison of human languages). It necessitated the elimination of a certain phrase (*being a horse*)—that, taken superficially, appeared to designate one thing among others—and the substitution of an equivalent phrase, only without the appearance of a specific designation. What had been said in one way has been restated in another. With regard to the *res significata*, one *modus significandi* is equivalent to another.

In the same way, "Socrates is wise" allows us to speak of "the wisdom of Socrates" if what we say about the wisdom of Socrates can equally well be said according to the *modus significandi* in which the predicate clearly appears as such. To take an example from Dummett:[12] "Wisdom is not confined to the ancients." Our understanding of this sentence derives from the fact that we recognize it as another way of saying "The ancients are not alone in being wise." But the sentence "Wisdom is an ideal reality" could not be paraphrased in the same way (except by a highly reductive domestication, which produces: "There are those who wish to be wise, and strive to be so, in spite of the knowledge that they will never attain perfect wisdom").

The preliminary notion of a philosophical grammar emerging from these examples is that of an inquiry into statements from the point of view of their constructions (their *congruitas*, to use a medieval concept). Any proposition whose grammar is not readily discernible may constitute the object of this inquiry, which will involve the reduction of its *modus significandi* to an explicitly congruent manner of signifying.

It remains for us to establish the advantages of such an inquiry—no longer in academic examples contrived for the purposes of exposition, but at the heart of philosophical debate.

2

The Linguistic Turnout
of Contemporary Philosophy

The Critique of Language

According to Wittgenstein, all philosophy is a critique of language. This assertion is far from clear. It might mean that philosophy is the critique of philosophical language. Equally, it might mean that philosophy is the philosophical critique of language. The intention of this chapter is to justify the distinction. Expressions such as *critique of language* or *philosophy of language* encourage the confusion of the two enterprises, when nothing suggests that they are in fact compatible.

The greatest drawback of that worthy expression *philosophy of language* is that it raises false expectations. It seems to have been coined for a philosophical specialism oriented toward a certain field of study, as in *philosophy of law* and *philosophy of mathematics*. It is strange, moreover, that we say *philosophy of law* (and not *of justice*, as Plato does) or *philosophy of mathematics* (and not of *number*). These two examples are not taken at random, as though there were any amount to choose from. In philosophy as it is practiced today we will have trouble finding such well-delineated specialisms (in comparison with the less isolated specialisms of *aesthetics* or *epistemology* or with the would-be specialities of *ethics, political philosophy, psychology,* or *theology*). Philosophy of language is clearly constructed on this model. But in the instance of law—as with mathematics—we can see a marked remove between the philosophy and its theme. If we wish to discuss numbers, we must deal with mathematics. If we wish to discuss justice, we must deal with legislation. We can specify the nature of the detour that here appears mandatory for philosophy by suggesting—true to the spirit of the age—that human practices are the real business of philosophy. It could be said that in the course of a human practice (the practice of transactions or that of counting, measuring, displacing things) practical problems arise to which other practices are applied (law, mathematics); these in their turn encounter problems that are then called "philosophical" (problems of founding or of justification). I sketch the broad outlines of this conception of philosophy simply to throw light on the suggestions that are inevitably implicit in the expression "philosophy of language" and not at all for its own merits, which strike me as negligible. According to this model, a philosophical specialism grasps one thing by means of a detour via another. For example, it grasps number (or in the other version, the practice of classification and enumeration) via arithmetic. When it comes to philosophy of language, we should identify first a goal and then the detour toward this goal. What goal and what detour? There are two contending answers:

1. Philosophy of language reaches it goal (language) by means of the detour of linguistics (it is a philosophy of the sciences of language).
2. Philosophy of language reaches its goal (reality) by means of the detour of language.

According to the first answer, philosophy of language is interested in certain human practices—speaking, writing, expression, communication, the exchange of messages, wordplay, and so on. The study of these practices is linguistic science. As for philosophy, it will deal with the fundamental concepts in this field of study. *Language* as in *philosophy of language* will be strictly the same as in *linguistic science of language*. The second answer announces a very different program: here philosophy turns not to linguists or philologists but to the practice of language itself, in order thereby to grasp something else—the object of this practice. But the object of this practice may be anything and everything. It is "reality" or even the sum of real and imaginary reality. Philosophy of language, then, is nothing less than first philosophy, since it may have access, by means of its own special domain, to any other domain whatever (thereby reviving both the ancient oscillation of philosophy between the first and the universal and the mysterious solution: "first and therefore universal").

We could say a great deal about both answers, but it is already plain that they cannot be combined in a more complex formula that would run: Philosophy moves toward its goal (reality) by means of a detour (language), and it moves toward its detour (language) by means of a detour (linguistics). There is no detour toward the detour. There can only be a second detour within a first detour. Here we can easily verify that the detour via linguistics does not lead to this language-as-detour toward reality, for it is not at all the same language. First, the object studied by

linguistics (languages and their use) is part of reality. It is not therefore a
detour toward reality. Second, language as the detour we wish to take in
order to reach reality is not language in general, but a certain use
of language. Most uses of language are evidently inappropriate means of
leading us to any reality whatever, either because they have nothing to do
with a particular reality or because they are actually designed to inhibit
this access.

Several authors have maintained that the mission of philosophy of
language is to integrate with philosophy of action.[1] Thus its goal would
indeed be the practice of language, and philosophy of language would
have a privileged link to the study of linguistics. That in English we speak
of "linguistic philosophy" reinforces the impression that a parallel exists
between the philosophical inquiry into language and linguistic research
(not unlike the parallel Husserl detected between phenomenology and
psychology). But we will be utterly bewildered by any agenda for contemporary philosophy of language so long as we are looking for a
philosophy of linguistics. Searle, for example, states in his introduction to
an anthology actually entitled *The Philosophy of Language*: "The philosophy of language consists in the attempt to analyse certain general
features of language, such as meaning, reference, truth, verification,
speech acts and logical necessity."[2] For those who were not initiated in
the same way as Searle, this is a disturbing list. If we imagine that
language means the sum of language practices, we will first of all lament
that the aspects listed are all chosen from one language practice among
many others (that of speaking in order to inform), even though we might
think it more useful to begin with the language practice of writers or
attorneys rather than with that of journalists and professors. But this is
not an ultimate objection; the list can always be extended. More important, this list is unintelligible when it comes to the study of human
language, which is the object of linguistics. What are verification and
logical necessity doing here? Anybody who, like Searle, classifies them so
spontaneously within the study of general aspects of language can only
be heir to a whole tradition of thought accustomed to dealing with
verification at the heart of a theory about the meaning of statements
(Does an unverifiable statement have meaning?) and to considering
logical modalities as a fact of language (a necessary proposition is a true
proposition by virtue of the meaning of its constituent terms). This last
observation yields the key to "philosophy of language." It is the philosophy in which it is natural to say about a necessity that *it is only a fact of
language*. It is only a fact of language, for example, that leads us to
distinguish essences from accidents and necessities from possibilities. The
restriction of "only" evokes the opposition "and not————." And not

what? What should we oppose here, if not facts that concern things? Philosophy of language (construed in this way) arises from the opposition between language and the world (or reality) envisaged as two empires, each with its own laws, each open to comparison in the traveler's diary: "It is only on this side of the frontier that such-and-such a usage is compulsory; there is nothing like it on the other side." The whole program of a philosophy of language resides in this tracing of the boundary between the "linguistic" and the "extralinguistic." On one side are words, on the other "extralinguistic entities" that we assume correspond with them.

It is only a fact of language: a linguist would be unlikely to reach this conclusion even after years of research. Nor could it be the comment of a philosopher after studying linguistics. It is rather the decision to constitute as a topic of research something that constantly goes unnoticed, and that is no more the totality of languages than it is the sum of linguistic usages. The language philosophy takes as its genitive is the remainder of a subtraction calculation. From everything we take for reality, subtract reality itself and you are left with language. The world minus things in the world equals the language in which we speak about things. Taken in itself, Searle's list of the principal aspects of language that were important for philosophy-of-language* is a bemusing hodgepodge. But this oddity is explained, once we see it as the result of the operation that constitutes it as a philosophical theme. Language is like fishing minus the fish (the net) or like the sea at low tide (all kinds of driftwood, shells, and seaweed): not only words, but conventions, values, modalities, and negativity.

If this is the case, then the invasion of philosophy by questions of language—cause for complaint by many good souls—is nothing recent. It is at once older and more pervasive than we think. As MacIntyre has said, philosophy became a linguistic inquiry the moment it was considered worthwhile to state that definitions were nominal rather than real.[3] Once writers like Locke and Hobbes had reasoned that questions of essence were only questions of meaning, they inaugurated a new direction for philosophy; thereafter it would be preoccupied with what results (analytically) from the meaning we impart to the words we use when speaking about things.

That there are only nominal definitions means we can state what a dog is but not what Fido is, since we are certainly entitled to give any meaning we like to the word *dog*, but not to decide on what Fido is. Essential knowledge concerns a nominal essence, and nominal essence applies to

* See page 44 below. [TRANS.]

the species (what it is necessary to be in order to be a dog), not to the individual (what Fido must be in order to be himself). Once we are dealing with the individual, we must painstakingly learn its attributes by consorting with it in person: we cannot know in advance whether it will behave tomorrow as it does today. Now it is precisely this divergence of the *nominal* from the *real* that is challenged by the notion, in Frege and Wittgenstein, of a criterion of identity. How can I be familiar (acquainted) with the individual, Fido, except by meeting it—which would be impossible if in Fido I were dealing only with an initially indeterminate individual, whose characteristics I gradually learn. If the name Fido were for me only a kind of finger pointed toward an individual, I could never find Fido (for everyone is an individual). In reality, my first encounter with the individual Fido is already an encounter with what I will meet again as *the same dog* (I have deliberately chosen a common name for a dog). The use of the proper name is thus conditional upon access to a criterion of identity: in this case, what it is to be the same dog. It is therefore (nominally) essential for the said Fido to be a dog, since it is out of the question for a member of any noncanine species to evoke the response, "Why, it's Fido!"

The separation of real and nominal had given rise to a philosophy that, without yet describing itself as such, was already tracing the contours of linguistic philosophy by opposing language and the world. But what one philosophy of language believed it had established—in this case, that proper names have no meaning—another can overturn. The very notion of philosophy of language, for all these reasons, appears unserviceable. Nonetheless, the confusion we see here should not be regarded as a sign of weakness or decline. It might be that the term "philosophy of language," far from designating a set of learned investigations, is in fact the name of a very narrow contest being played out in contemporary philosophy, not only between schools or tendencies but even within a single school, or book, or concept. My objective will be to show that what is at stake in this contest is the concept of the object.

When Wittgenstein says that all philosophy is a critique of language, he is certainly not referring to philosophy as philosophers since the Greeks have generally understood it. Nor, apparently, is he referring to philosophy as it has been practiced. He therefore means to speak of philosophical activity as it ought to be. This definition might almost be the maxim of philosophy-of-language. Wittgenstein puts quotation marks around the expression *Sprachkritik* and cites several names, thereby emphasizing that he is not the first to define philosophy in this way: "All philosophy is a 'critique of language' (though not in Mauthner's sense). It was Russell who performed the service of showing that the apparent logical form of a proposition need not be its real one" (*Tractatus*, 4.0031).

The day philosophers were agreed on this, philosophy met what has been called its "linguistic turning point" or its "linguistic turn." In his anthology of the same title, Richard Rorty characterizes it as the change in method that produces "linguistic philosophy," governed by the verdict that "philosophical problems are problems which may be solved (or dissolved) either by reforming language, or by understanding more about the language we presently use."[4] We can see at once that this description leaves no room for the difference between scrutiny of the language *of* philosophy and scrutiny of language *by* philosophy.

Supposing it were to become a byword, Wittgenstein's formula would have at least two meanings, since *Sprachkritik* appears in quotation marks; the expression is borrowed from Mauthner, who receives no further mention in the *Tractatus* and is quoted only to be dispossessed; not of his thoughts—these on the contrary are returned to him with thanks—but of his language.[5] True philosophy can only be what Mauthner says it is; but not in the sense in which he said it and which Wittgenstein fails to specify. What follows introduces the new sense, credited to Russell, who had not stated it. This new sense of the critique of language is drawn from the theory of descriptions. Thus, for example, the true form of the propositions *God exists* and *God does not exist* is not the one ascribed to them by an analysis of surface grammar (subject, *God*, predicate, *exists* or *does not exist*), but the form that brings to light the logical paraphrase clarified by quantification theory (*there exists*—or not—*some such thing as the only divine being*).

If this is the case, we must add a third sense to the two mentioned in the text—that of Mauthner and that of Wittgenstein—namely the sense intended by Russell, in which he himself understands neither this critique of language nor the one ascribed to him by Wittgenstein. We know that in his introduction to *Tractatus*, Russell attributes to Wittgenstein the idea that the quality of services rendered by the languages we use should be measured against the idea of a perfectly logical language. This is not Wittgenstein's own view. For him everyday language, such as it is, is "in perfect logical order" (5.5563). What Wittgenstein meant according to Russell is not what Wittgenstein meant, nor is it what Wittgenstein meant according to Wittgenstein (when he alludes to the misunderstanding in *Philosophical Investigations*). From this it is difficult to see how we can avoid completing the three senses with a fourth: philosophy is the critique of language, in the sense of a scrutiny of discourses in the light of the fact that misunderstanding is the rule rather than the exception. Or even better, the fact that a misunderstanding is not a misunderstanding, since apparently one fragment of language (in this case, *Sprachkritik*) has been employed only to be instantly diverted from the use to which another writer had sought to put it.

It will be unnecessary to delve further into the expression *critique of language*, whose relevance here is to announce a transformation of philosophy. The critique of language is everything; to understand this would in fact be to understand the metamorphosis, or linguistic turn, undergone by philosophy. Is it possible to show how philosophy is transformed by having taken this turn? We can rule out the ill-disposed response: it becomes nonphilosophy, verbiage, vague talk. We rule it out not as a matter of conscience but because it prejudices the question of language. Such criticisms have already presupposed that the medium of language is only a stage, to be traversed as quickly as possible in order to arrive at things themselves. If it is necessary then it must be possible. The assumption here is that problems of "expression" (*modus significandi*) can be separated from problems of "content" (*res significata*). (In the preceding sentence, the quotation marks indicate a necessary reservation about the notion that a content is expressed, pending the critique below. The Latin words refer to the concepts of philosophical grammar that are to replace "expression" and "content".) The accusation of verbiage that threatens to engulf philosophy-of-language is nothing less than a critique of language invoking the founding divide, in philosophy of language, between language and the world. Philosophy-of-language was constituted in the ceaseless reiteration of this charge. We suspect that the most contrary exhortations may be addressed to us in the name of the critique of language: "Transcend language!" "Stop at language!" In this, as in every case, the critique concerns what has been omitted. Just as "literary criticism," in the sense of the critical review of new books, must point out omissions (lacunae, carelessness, lack of acquaintance with the rules), so too critical philosophy must turn toward human activity in order to rescue something fundamental from oblivion. In critical philosophy-of-language, the omission is language. We always overlook language. We forget that we are speaking. Imagining that we were doing something else, we had forgotten we were speaking. Critical thought curtails the omission of language (arguably a natural omission, if we accept that the nature of the linguistic sign is to efface itself by referring to something beyond itself). Critical reflection is based on the observation that language is first forgotten and always already unnoticed. It is only on reflection that language appears. Here, then, is the critical doctrine of language: we had not noticed at the outset that language was language, that it was no more than language. In this as in every case, critical philosophy delivers the human mind from its most natural errors.

In its "linguistic" form, an explanation or remedy is sought for illusions arising from language. The magical illusion, for instance, encourages us to believe we are acting on things when we manipulate symbols; thus the laws of magic are the laws of language (metaphor and metonymy). The religious illusion tells us that we are speaking to someone or being spoken to by someone because of certain irresistible suggestions involved in the use of the pronoun *you*. When I hear myself saying *you*, I am tempted to think there is someone I am addressing. And when I hear the word *you* but cannot identify the speaker, I take this to be addressed to me and ascribe it to an invisible source. In the case of political and social illusions, certain fictions in language are taken for bona fide realities: society, state, party, nation. To these misadventures of the understanding we can also add philosophical illusions: mistaking a fact of language (such as the necessity, in our language, that a verb should have a subject) for a general law (the so-called illusion of "substance"). To those who find this model of critical explanation dated, I would say that on the contrary it seems to me quite active in several works of contemporary anthropology, in a more refined form no doubt, but one in which the initial sophism persists: that illusion exists because illusion is truth itself. We believe in magic because there is a magic of words. We inhabited an enchanted world because we were under the spell of language.

If philosophy-of-language is the philosophy that says language is not the world, then the critique of language to which it gives rise will be essentially paradoxical. All the illusions it exposes derive from the fact that we had not realized that language was language and nothing more. We had not realized that in speaking, we were merely speaking—nothing more. We did not know how to transcend language. But this was because we had overlooked language from the start. Thus we did not know how to stop at language, to lodge there, to reconnoitre it (as one reconnoitres unknown territory). We thought that we were already beyond language, in the world, precisely because we had not paid sufficient attention to words. We passed too quickly over the question of language. We transcended it too fast; now we have to admit that we did not know how to transcend language, because we did not know we had transcended it. In transcending it we became locked inside it. We remained at the level of words because we were thinking only of things (forgetting about language), and we were thinking only of things because we did not wish to remain among words. And yet at the same time we were thinking only of words; we forgot that they were only words and took them, instead, for things. And the preceding formula must be reversed, for it is the world we had forgotten. Trusting naïvely in language, we remained trapped among words, believing all along that we were consecrating ourselves to things themselves. We forgot that the world was beyond language, that words needed to be transcended in order to arrive at things. It is by transcending language that we failed to transcend it; by remaining with it that we left it behind. It is by forgetting language that we failed to find the world and by forgetting the world that we also forgot language.

Once again it becomes apparent that the principle of philosophy-of-language is the line of the forgotten frontier between the realm of words and the realm of things. The remedy for those illusions it criticizes will be this very distinction, as paradoxical as the oversight itself: it is by remaining with language that we will resist its seduction; it is by no longer transcending it that we will finally transcend it. There is surely something paradoxical in the imperative to trace this frontier. And by virtue of the paradox we shall always find ourselves in the wrong place (already on that side, when we wished to remain on this side).

For all these reasons, the project of a critique of language cannot nowadays lay claim to a clear or stable meaning. In such an uncertain state of affairs, the distinction drawn at the beginning of this chapter may perhaps prove useful. It is contradictory, in my view, to demand that a philosophical examination of language should also be an examination of philosophy of language.

Scrutiny of philosophical propositions is practiced, in France and in the so-called Continental tradition, in the form of a rereading of philosophical texts that have already been written. We reread in the acknowledgement that there will be no new works of philosophy to be read. Heidegger's disciples believe that this rereading should be meditative; others call it hermeneutic. In Derridean circles it is generally referred to as deconstruction. The remarks that follow by no means offend against the significant, and in the view of interested parties, insurmountable, difference between these readings. Those who see the examination of philosophical propositions as the philosophical activity par excellence would be unable to counter the charge that they have confused philosophy and history, had they not admitted first of all that philosophy is a reflection upon philosophical matters as such. Philosophy exists only as the philosophy of philosophy. This is why the form of the philosophical proposition must be studied. In this instance it makes no difference whether we call it *the form of the proposition* or *the form of propositions*, since we are no longer examining theses (with a view to pitting them against others), but rather are considering what is *philosophical* about those theses. All philosophical propositions say "the same" (Heidegger). And yet this statement is no longer exactly a philosophical proposition (otherwise it would have the frivolous sense that all philosophers are basically in agreement). All philosophers say the same, and this is what allows us to speak of "Western metaphysics," even though all philosophers do not say the same if we confine ourselves to the philosophical concept of identity (which would require philosophers to propound the same theses in unison). Measured against the philosophical concept of identity—and against the principle of identity as it is variously expressed by philosophers—philosophies vary. It is therefore quite true in one sense that they are diverse. But something—"the same"—is always implied in all philosophy; something that comes closest to declaring itself in the principle of identity but that it is no longer up to philosophy to conceive. Or again, if we were to grant that philosophers do not in fact say the same thing (in the ordinary sense of identity), we could maintain that philosophers have the same way of saying different things. The philosophical proposition can then be described in its sameness in terms of the way it is signified—its language, which is "the language of metaphysics." Or again, if philosophers have different ways of saying different things, they have the same way of reading these differences, and they hold that their various ways of saying something differ in the same way one from another; in which case the sameness to be sought in the diversity of philosophical texts will be this philosophical determination of the same, as it is applied to diversity.

In certain "therapeutic" tendencies of so-called analytical philosophy, the procedure for scrutinizing the philosophical proposition has been inverted. Philosophers are unanimous in maintaining that the philosophical proposition begins where the proposition of fact ends. In the light of this an attempt has been made to establish a priori that no meaning whatever can be assigned to it.

As a result, philosophy takes a linguistic turn, becoming a critique of the language in which the propositions of philosophers are stated. It shows that this language is not innocent, since it exposes thinking to the seduction of a thought that remains concealed within the very form of the philosophical proposition, or again to the illusion that a philosophical proposition has only a single meaning, or finally to the illusion that the philosophical proposition has a meaning of some kind, whatever this may be.

The other approach to the critique of language is to undertake a philosophical (as opposed to philological) examination of language. This second type of critique supposes a philosophically relevant description of the proposition (or perhaps of propositions). We could also call this a *logical critique*, but taking *logic* in its fullest etymological sense (as an examination of *logoi*, propositions, or discourses) and not in the narrower, traditional sense (the study of valid inferences). How can the description of the form of propositions (or types of propositions) be relevant to philosophy? This will be the focus of the chapters that follow. For the time being, it is enough to state the mutual exclusion of the two kinds of critique. If I embark upon a critique of the language of metaphysics, it will already be too late for a philosophical critique of the proposition; I have already conceded that there is only one philosophical doctrine of the proposition. This doctrine is "Western metaphysics," the philosophy of the "identity principle." All I can do thereafter is to take up a certain distance from this doctrine, in other words, from the entire logic (sometimes known as "logic of identity") that is supposed to govern philosophy. Since this is a distance in relation to philosophy, any reservations we have are no longer philosophical and can no longer be stated philosophically. Heidegger took this path, believing he could show that the same doctrine of the proposition (as attributive discourse) dominated philosophy from start to finish.

If I begin now with the philosophical critique of propositions, it is clearly too soon for a special critique of philosophical propositions in particular. And it is subsequently too late. Too late not because I will already have introduced certain ontological prejudices into the analysis, nor because the first kind of critique would seem subversive and inadmissible from the viewpoint of the second, but because in trying our hand at a philosophical critique of propositions we soon realize that there is no uniform, traditional doctrine of the proposition. If such a doctrine were to exist—stating the "logic of identity" and the reduction of all utterance to an attributive discourse—then we should be able to express it somehow, though not necessarily in the "language of metaphysics." This doctrine should at least have a relative coherence in terms of elementary philosophical requirements. But until such time as we have articulated what the metaphysical doctrine of the proposition consists of, any comment upon "Western metaphysics" as a whole will be premature.

The attraction of studying the way thoughts are signified should now have become more obvious: it stems from the interest that contemporary philosophers may find in the conflict between critiques of language. Assuming we conclude from the above that philosophy of language is as old as modern philosophy, I consider it more appropriate to speak of the *linguistic turnout* of contemporary philosophy than of its linguistic turn. For in the latter, nothing turns very far: philosophy confronts only that inaugural division of language and the world which declared itself most clearly at the outset of modern philosophy with the empiricists.[6] Rorty mentions this in his work on linguistic philosophy: the "linguistic turn" is the most conspicuous (but not the most important) development in recent philosophy. The most important is undoubtedly the challenge to traditional epistemology.[7]

Until now I have spoken of *philosophy-of-language* (indicating by this graphic device the disparity between the philosophy, so called, of language and a possible philosophy of the object in linguistics). Henceforth I shall speak of two philosophies of language (without hyphens): in the narrow sense, contemporary linguistic philosophy (with all the ambiguity, already noted, of its relationship to linguistic science); in the broad sense, the philosophy of experience, or even epistemology. The remainder of this chapter sets out to ground these definitions not in a history of the philosophy of language but in certain connections I shall make between a number of well-known facts relative to this history.

Language in the Philosophy of Experience

The expression *philosophy of language* first occurs, apparently, in Mill's *System of Logic* (1843).[8] Here the philosopher who corresponded with Auguste Comte comments upon the nature of scientific inference from a standpoint that is now justly held to be dated and indefensible. But where does logic come in? Since the *Logic* of Port-Royal, it has become commonplace to associate the exposition of logic proper with that of method in the search for scientific truth, by means of a compromise between traditional teaching and Cartesian inspiration. The *Critique of Pure Reason* was itself organized along these lines.[9] Nonetheless, Mill begins with an exposition of formal logic before dealing with what was then regarded as the consummate refinement, the theory of method. The novelty lies in prefacing the exposition of logic with a section on words— a new initiative for his readers but not, needless to say, entirely unprecedented. In the Port-Royal *Logic*, whose conception of logic was to be "widely accepted and continue to dominate the treatment of logic by philosophers for the next 200 years" (i.e., from 1662 through Frege)[10]— the opening chapter is entitled "Of Ideas According to Their Nature and Origin." First place is given to ideas because they are introduced as the necessary intermediary between ourselves and things.[11] Words are indeed discussed, but not until chapter 11 of part 1: "We have already said that the necessity we are under of making use of exterior signs in order to express our thoughts, causes us to affix our ideas to words in such a manner, that we often consider rather the words than the things."[12] In other words, logic has no need to go through language in order to analyze thoughts, but only in order to identify it as one source among others of the faults we commit against the "art of thinking." This is why it was necessary to deal first with ideas, so as to see more clearly when it came to communicating through signs. In Mill's logic, the first chapter is called "On the Necessity of Beginning with an Analysis of Language." Here we suddenly find ourselves on the terrain of a prodigious, or at least prolific, posterity: analytical philosophy. A philosophy is analytical if it recognizes that necessity; it remains to be seen, of course, how such an analysis of language is to be carried out.

Mill's chapter heading itself suggests a concern to justify this way of beginning. The epigraph he chooses for his book 1 ("Of Names and Propositions") points quite clearly to the kind of objections that might have been raised against his analytical starting point. It is a passage from Condorcet, quoted in French: "Scholastics, which in logic, as in ethics and areas of metaphysics, produced a subtlety and a precision of ideas unknown to the ancients, contributed more than we are apt to believe to the progress of true philosophy" (Condorcet, *Vie de Turgot*). This quotation does not merely prime the reader to accept the revival of certain "barbaric concepts" that Mill was to undertake with regard to notions such as the *abstract term* and the *concrete term*, the *categorematic* and the *syncategorematic term*, the *denotation* of the term and its *connotation* (and here the disparity between Mill's usage and that of his medieval sources scarcely matters). There is a lot more at stake here than the simple rehabilitation of certain distinctions. The concepts I have just referred to belong—in the *logica moderna* treatises of the thirteenth to the sixteenth century—to what was then called the study of the properties of terms, and in particular to the study of the various functions that can be justified by one and the same term in the context of different propositions. *One and the same term* means that the same term can be recognized in two contexts, including cases where it does not stand for the same thing. What a term preserves in every context (and what may therefore be considered as independent of any particular context) is the *significatio*. What varies according to context is the *suppositio*. Let us now look at an example of the *suppositio* under analysis—an analysis that appears to be superior to commonplace semantic doctrine.[13] Let us take the difference between

       1. Aristotle is a philosopher.

and

       2. "Aristotle" is a Greek name.

According to the most prevalent theory nowadays, quotation marks around a word produce a new sign which may be treated as the name (in the ordinary sense) of that word. In (2) we would therefore regard the subject of the sentence as the name of Aristotle's name. But what is

Aristotle's name? There is no reply to the question: What is this name that is a Greek name? We cannot reply Aristotle, for we are talking about Aristotle the philosopher as soon as we use his name. Nor can we reply "Aristotle." Between the quotation marks there is Aristotle's name (which is a Greek name). The sign constituted by the combination of what is in quotation marks (and which is the object of the question, What name did you say?) and the quotation marks themselves is the name of Aristotle's name. Aristotle's name is a Greek name, but the name of Aristotle's name is not a Greek name (if only because there are no quotation marks in ancient Greek). The name that I name by writing, as above, "Aristotle" (using the sign " 'Aristotle' ") is a Greek name. But Aristotle is not a Greek name, nor is it the name of Aristotle's name (i.e., " 'Aristotle' "). It is impossible, then, to say what Aristotle's name is. Medieval analysis, of course, did not have to deal with quotation marks, an artifice unknown at the time. Instead, quotation consisted in a particular use of the same term—with the kind of use being indicated by the context. In the example above, we would find the same sign, *Aristotle*, that is, a word with the same *significatio* in both contexts. What changes is the *suppositio* (today we would call it the reference). In (1), the name *Aristotle* stands for (*supponit pro*) a certain individual, that is, Aristotle the Greek (*suppositio personalis*). In (2) this same name acts on behalf not of itself, but of all words similarly constituted (*consimilia*) and having the same meaning: there is a *suppositio materialis*.

For the medieval distinction *significatio/suppositio* (whose subtlety is a result of the theological approach to the mystery of the Trinity), Mill was to substitute his distinction between connotation and denotation, which survives today in the work of certain semiologists and is sometimes confused with the distinction Frege was to introduce, between sense (*Sinn*) and its reference (*Bedeutung*).

Mill embarks on his treatise by saying that it is necessary to begin not with the study of ideas (like all philosophers since Descartes) but with the study of words (as in "terminist" logic). His initial reason for this, however, is not the right one. Since reasoning is constructed by means of words, Mill argues, it is important not to mistake their meaning. But this explanation is incorrect. It tells us only that we must look to language, without explaining why this should be our starting point. The correct reason is that logic is concerned with inferences. What can we conclude from what we know or believe? Inference takes us from one proposition to another. Knowledge and belief are stated in propositions. For example, says Mill, we can say (= proffer): "the sun." What we have said has a meaning; it can be understood. However, nothing has yet been said (= stated). We cannot ask, "Do you believe it?" ("Do you believe the sun?")

"Is it true?" ("Is it true that the sun?") It is in order to analyze a proposition, then, that logic must begin with an analysis of the language in which that proposition is stated. And this is why Mill can be regarded as the precursor of philosophy of language, as the expression is currently understood (or of what I referred to earlier as philosophy-of-language). Even if Mill were not the inventor of the phrase *philosophy of language*, we would still have to regard him as the Abraham of the immense family tree that was to practice this kind of philosophy. More noteworthy still, his *System of Logic* was to act as a foil to the two tutelary figures of twentieth-century philosophy—Husserl (for Continental philosophy) and Frege (for analytical philosophy). After Mill, philosophy of language abandons the old eighteenth-century concerns: hypotheses on the origin of language, discussions of the priority of poetry over prose or gesture over speech, or polemics regarding the superiority of this or that national tongue. Instead, in an unexpected resurgence of interest in *proprietas terminorum*, we find chapters on naming, on the reference of the name and eventually of the predicate, on the construction of propositions, and so forth. If this "philosophy of language" were merely a study of language, it would indeed deserve all the criticisms it so often incurs for its narrowness and formalism and for restricting itself to declarative or descriptive language alone. But in fact it has always been a logical investigation—an investigation conducted in the interests of logic.

In Mill's logic, the entire range of scholastic concepts—lifted more or less faithfully from medieval logic—is marshaled to resolve a problem of empiricism. Mill remains loyal not only to empiricism (any general truth is the generalization of a particular observation) but also to the nominalism he finds in Hobbes (all categorematic words are names). However, he is not satisfied with Hobbes's analysis of the proposition. For Hobbes, the true proposition is one in which the predicate names the same thing as is named by the subject. Subject and predicate are names, and all propositions are statements of identity. Mill certainly intends to maintain that any proposition is a linking of two names. To remove the unacceptable aspect of classical nominalist analysis, he introduces his distinction between proper names (names that denote but do not connote) and common names (names that simultaneously denote individuals and connote properties). In a proposition, we attribute properties connoted by the predicate-name to the denoted of the subject-name; the proposition is true if the denoted of the subject is equally denoted by the predicate.

The nominalist doctrine of the proposition is unsatisfactory in that it fails to distinguish between a statement of identity (*Murat is the king of Rome* = is the person whom we also call *king of Rome*)[14] and a general proposition (*All the marshals of the empire have boulevards in Paris named after them*). In the first case, reference is made to someone (and we can always inquire to whom). In the second, reference is made to nobody (the proof being that to understand what is said, we do not need to ask whether Murat was a marshal of the empire).

Mill is the founder of analytical philosophy not because of any one of his theses (all have since been fiercely contested), but because he realized that logic was not primarily a methodology, an art of thinking and forming an exactness of judgment. Logic is in the first place the study of the consequences of having said this rather than that. But Mill's position is remarkably ambiguous. He corrects the nominalist interpretation of the proposition (what would most readily occur to an empiricist) because he can see its shortcomings but believes it can be salvaged. We must indeed cease to view the proposition as a linking of two proper names. But according to Mill, we can analyze it as the linking of two common names (for general propositions). The obscurities in Mill's theory of the name would later force philosophy of language, from Russell to Kripke, to make, more or less willingly, increasingly radical revisions of the initial doctrine.

The problem confronting all philosophy of experience is that of the language of this experience. The notion of experience may well seem very immediate, and yet it is the anticipated result of a labor of purification and reduction described, in an unconscious antiphrasis, as a "return to the original," as the rediscovery of "the immediate data of consciousness," as a genealogical return to our sources. Experience is anything reduced to what is really given. It is anything at all purged of interpretation and assumption, hypothesis, reckoning and assimilation, belief and personal association. What we are left with after this filtration is the impression, the perceptible data, to which we must now adhere. How can we give an account of experience? In other words, what language is capable of expressing what is really given without in the least deforming it, adding to it or subtracting from it? And this is the only intelligible use of the verb *to express* as applied to a declaration. The declarative proposition is one that restricts itself to expressing the content of experience, without adding the judgments or emotional associations that the "experiencing subject" inevitably blends into it. Once it looked as if the nominalist theory of the proposition could explain as follows how a language purely descriptive of experience ought to be constituted: each sign we use corresponds to an idea of something; we assemble in a proposition those ideas we have that represent the same thing to us all. Since this theory is flawed, we must revise the analysis of descriptive language, unless we are prepared to conclude that experience is ineffable and that there can be no language without deformation.

The philosophy of experience gives rise to a philosophy of language in the course of a debate between empiricism and itself. The question is to isolate a language of experience, a language confined to the unadorned account of our experience. Henceforth the word *language* ceases to have its ordinary meaning (*Je vis de bonne soupe et non de beau langage*).* Language now means the account of experience; in other words, a faithful version, a dependable testimony, an authentic narrative, and also the inauguration of a relation between two things (between our representations and the facts, or between the subject and the object of experience). Thereafter the critique of language may herald a reform of ordinary language as well as a revision of the concept of experience: a reform of language if ordinary language seems to betray the genuinely given content of experience, and a revision of epistemology (or the concept of experience) if it is the commonplace notion of experience that does not match the account offered by language.

The "Meaning" of Phenomenology

In France the work of Edmund Husserl was first encountered in the *Cartesian Meditations*. Thus the French are accustomed to viewing phenomenology as a fresh attempt at the radical founding of science upon a *cogito*. For them Husserl is the descendant of a philosophical lineage characterized by Kant, Fichte, and Hegelian phenomenology. And in phenomenology's concern to describe, together with its constant proximity to psychology, they like to detect a trait that belongs to their own tradition of thought, from Maine de Biran to Bergson. All of this may have obscured the fact that, in Husserl's own estimation, the decisive readings for the formation of phenomenology were not the *Metaphysical Meditations*, the *Critique of Pure Reason*, the *Doctrine of Science*, or the *Phenomenology of Mind*, but rather the works of Locke, Hume, and Mill.[15] We will of course recall that Mill was criticized in the *Logical Investigations*. But we are inclined to forget that he provided the material for the first of these *Investigations*. In the immensity of Husserl's published work, the problems of philosophy of language (in Mill's sense and in the sense of analytical philosophy) are not really tackled except in the *Logical Investigations*—and even then, with the exception of the fifth and sixth (which, much to the surprise of the reader, introduce a study of acts of consciousness into what had been presented as a quest for a nonpsychologistic philosophy of logic). Phenomenology is not a "philosophy of language," but it is undoubtedly a philosophy of experience.

* From Molière. [TRANS.]

Yet this philosophy of experience is constantly inquiring into the meaning of experiences. And the concept of *meaning* is of course linguistic.

Phenomenology has popularized a very particular use of the word *meaning*, by virtue of which it may be applied without regard to any of the conditions of language. Phenomenology is happy to speak of the meaning of experience, the meaning of the world, the meaning of a perception, or the meaning of the object, and of the object as a "unit of meaning" for consciousness. A philosopher's phenomenological background is always betrayed by his lack of qualms in the face of such usage. It does not astonish him, and he uses it when it suits him. Note too that this meaning is not even equivalent to a "relevance for my own projects" or an interest for me (as in *the meaning of life* or the *meaning of art*). For to the phenomenologist, the "meaning of the world" is not, after all, the value we attach to worldly things. Husserl himself is still aware of the novelty of this usage (although his awareness was not to outlive him). Thus, in a passage from *Ideas* that argues in favor of idealism, he adds a note to indicate what is unusual about his concept of meaning. Having explained that the "natural attitude" (which the phenomenological reduction will "suspend") is not a philosophy and so no more realist than idealist, he continues: "Absurdity first arises when one philosophises and, in probing for ultimate information as to the meaning of the world [*der Sinn der Welt*], fails to notice that the whole being of the world consists in a certain 'meaning' [*ein gewisser "Sinn"*] which presupposes absolute consciousness as the field from which the meaning is derived [*Feld der Sinngebung*]." And now we are referred to a footnote as follows: "I allow myself here in passing, and for the purpose of an impressive contrast, the use of an unusual and yet in its own way trustworthy extension of the concept of 'meaning' [*Sinn*]."[16] This extended use of the concept of meaning, unusual in ordinary language, is commonplace in the language of the phenomenologist, as obstinately employed as it is ill explained. Husserl intends no more than a mild audacity of usage, a manner of speaking that is easily comprehensible in itself. But an unprepared reader will consider this usage not only unusual (or *inusité* as indeed Paul Ricoeur translates it in French) but extraordinary (*ausserordentliche Erweiterung*, says Husserl, meaning of course, "unusual" or "*inusité*" rather than "outside ordinary rules"). In phenomenology, the ordinary is out of the ordinary. Phenomenological language is not comprehensible in itself; to be understood, it needs to be presented in more ordinary terms. This is precisely the explanation Husserl omits to give. But it is also this sort of explanation that phenomenology should never have to give. The language of phenomenology ought to be that of experience. It should be the language of all presentation (since phenomenology seeks to be a description prior to any construction). If phenomenological concepts had also to be introduced or presented, the qualification "phenomenological" would have to be withdrawn and conferred instead upon the concepts by means of which they were presented. But assuming that the extraordinary concept of meaning is necessary for phenomenology as practiced by Husserl, then an infinite regression would be inevitable: the presenter would be presented, in his capacity as presenter, by another presenter who had himself expected to be presented by the first.

The extension moves from the linguistic sphere to affect all mental acts. It is ordinary to say that a sentence has a meaning. But it is extraordinary to say the same of a perception. Take the case of how to describe the act of seeing an apple tree in bloom in the garden (a familiar example to Husserl). Such a description is complicated by an ambiguity attaching to what we understand by the perceived object. Am I really seeing an apple tree in bloom? The question can be taken to bear upon the reality of my perception (Am I seeing or imagining?) but also upon the reality of the perceived object (Is there an apple tree?). In order to set about a description of the act of perceiving, it must be freed from the hold exercised over it by the reality of things as this is "naturally" understood (in the "natural" attitude). To obtain the description of what is really given ("to consciousness," as the phenomenologist says) in a perception, we must address ourselves to the reality of the perception, not to the perception of the reality. The "phenomenological reduction" is a response to this shift of interest on our part, from the perception of reality to the reality of the perception. What makes the orthodox formulation of this reduction unintelligible is the inseparable character of the two functions it is meant to fulfill, in the description and in the "constitution" of things. The reduction is classically presented as a sovereign decision that has to be taken, although its real motives cannot really be explained to someone who persists in the "natural attitude." We are told that the reduction makes sense only with hindsight, for it is the free return of the subject to himself. Like the slave who has lost all memory of freedom, the subject has forgotten from the first that he was the absolute; instead he holds the naive conviction that objects can exist without him. In a word, the phenomenological reduction is presented as an initiatory process. We will understand why it was necessary once we have been through it. But the descriptive function of the reduction is in fact quite independent of its constitutive function. The descriptive reduction reduces nothing at all; it merely answers the ambiguity contained in the statement of perception from a logical standpoint, that is, from the standpoint of the consequences that may be inferred from it. Ordinarily

we believe that the statement *I can see an apple tree* (spoken straightfor-
wardly, by a normal observer in favorable conditions) allows us to infer
that *there is an apple tree*. But the description of mental acts necessitates
the suspension of this right to inference. Indeed, we can describe mental
acts only by applying to them the language that, in its direct, elementary
use, serves to describe the objects of such acts. In order to describe
perception, we must therefore speak about the apple tree—not that we
have any interest in the apple tree as such, in the apple tree as tended by
the gardener. Psychological description necessitates a retreat away from
the thing toward its perceptible appearance. We can, if we insist, compare this retreat to that of the skeptic and characterize it as an epoche,
provided that this makes no difference and that the suspension has
nothing to do with the apple tree itself. Clearly, perception is not the best
example of an intentional act that we can invoke in favor of this measure
of suspension (for perception involves a presumption of reality, except in
special environmental circumstances altered by simulacrum or trompe
l'oeil). The reason for the suspension, and its perfect innocuousness,
becomes clearer if we change our example and replace the act of seeing
with the act of drawing. If someone draws an apple tree, the object
drawn—in other words the object he draws—is an apple tree; not that a
particular apple tree must necessarily be drawn by him. This apple tree
study is not necessarily the study of *an* apple tree in the sense of a certain
apple tree (of the kind that yields apples) drawn by someone. The
description of this activity known as drawing requires that I be able to
describe the objects drawn without raising the question of existence, or
as a result the question of identity (Of what apple tree is this drawing of
an apple tree the drawing?). Unfortunately, Husserlian phenomenology
links these observations, correct in themselves, with an epistemological
thesis expounding the dependence of "objects" upon the "subject." It
introduces reduction and constitution as two aspects of the same operation, as we can see in the passage from *Ideas* quoted earlier: it is in
reducing objects which transcend their "meaning" for consciousness that
we discover its transcendental function. But the "reduction" in itself is
limited to distinguishing the intentional object from what could be
referred to as the material object. We will call an *intentional object* one
that corresponds to a statement such as "I remember that there was an
apple tree in that garden" as opposed to the *material object*, which
corresponds to the logically distinct statement "There is an apple tree I
remember being in that garden." The reduction may have to seek its
justification in the exigencies of description, but it does not go beyond
this simple distinction. As for the famous "constitution," it is the epistemological thesis that the statement bearing on the material object must

be susceptible of a reduction to the appropriate coordination of statements bearing on the intentional object. This thesis, which lacks any
founding description, thus produces a reductive reduction, namely, the
reduction of things to the various objects of our intentional acts—in
other words, to what Husserl was thenceforth to consider the "meaning"
of these acts. Now the distinction between the intentional object and the
material object can be made only by clarifying the logical difference
between two statements. An inept hunter can say both "I shot at a
rabbit" (intentional object) and "There is a dog that I shot" (material
object). We will note that "material" is not the same as "physical" but
stands in opposition, here, to "formal." The inept hunter shot a dog, not
inasmuch as it was a dog (formal object) but inasmuch as he mistook it
for a rabbit.[17] What he shot turns out, irrespective of his intention, to
have been a dog. The same holds for the perception of the apple tree,
which we can understand as the perception of the real tree or of the
intentional tree.

Husserl argues that the intentional apple tree is the meaning of
the perception of the apple tree. For him, the meaning of a mental act is
the object of that act. The perceived as such (i.e., the formal object)
is the meaning of the perception.

The *tree plain and simple*, the thing in nature, is as different as it can be from this
perceived tree as such, which as perceptual meaning [*Wahrhnehmungssinn*]
belongs to the perception, and that inseparably. The tree plain and simple can
burn away, resolve itself into its chemical elements, and so forth. But the meaning
[*Sinn*]—the meaning of *this* perception, something that belongs necessarily to its
essence—cannot burn away; it has no chemical elements, no real properties
[*realen*].[18]

The apple tree in blossom that has been planted and tended, and that
yields apples, is a thing of nature, exterior to the act by which it is
perceived. The apple tree perceived as such is the meaning of the perception. How does Husserl come to treat the intentional object as a meaning? To answer this, we must look at the meaning given by Husserl
himself to the word *Sinn*. It is the restricted notion of meaning that leads
us to the broader notion. The blossoming apple tree in the garden,
viewed as the object of a perception, becomes a meaning precisely on
account of the way Husserl explains that the expression *the blossoming
apple tree in the garden* has a meaning. And this confirms that phenomenology, if not actually a linguistic philosophy, is not so very far removed
from it. Husserl deals with signification in the *First Logical Investigation*,
where he is concerned to challenge psychological conceptions of meaning. To avoid a confusion between meaning and the representations

suggested to a listener when certain signs are used, we must, according to Husserl, distinguish several components in the "content" "expressed" by an expression. In any expression, he says in paragraph 14, something is intimated, something is signified, and something is designated. But all this becomes confused if we talk of expressed content. The *intimated* is a state lived by the speaker, the *designated* is a corresponding state of things. For instance, someone who expresses a wish intimates a lived experience (his desire) and designates an objective situation (one that would satisfy it). For Husserl, meaning is the intermediary between the intimated and the designated. His analysis is constructed on the model of the name (which is, for no clear reason, given priority over other kinds of sign). The function of a name is to designate something. But the bearer of the name may be either present or absent when it is uttered. In both cases it has the same meaning (it is, in both cases, understood). However, Husserl subordinates the use of the name in the absence of the named object to the use of the name in its presence. In paragraph 9, he observes that the use of the name in the absence of the object (or strictly we should say, in the absence of its visibility, since for phenomenology the absence of an object is its absence from perception) is a sign that derives its meaning from a "meaning intention." But this intention remains void (much as "good intentions" remain void when no act substantiates them in practice). The object is "intended" in a void, and the reference of sign to object is not fulfilled. If the object appears, if it is plainly given, then the meaning intention is fulfilled, the relation of the name to its bearer is realized for consciousness. A *Bedeutungsintention* thus calls for a *Bedeutungserfüllung*. In Frege's view, the reference of a name is void if this name names nothing, if nothing bears this name—if it is, in other words, a fictional name. For Husserl the meaning intention remains void as long as the object is not present in person, as long as it remains at a remove. This is a strange doctrine of the name, inevitably suggesting an affinity between nomination and invocation. The absence of the named object becomes something regrettable or untoward. The act of signifying remains incomplete and unfinished, awaiting an epiphany. It is as though Husserl believed that the circumstances in which a name is conferred on a thing must also be the conditions of its most common use: when the thing named and the person naming it are present to one another. It is impossible, then, not to read any use of a name as a kind of summons. But in reality it matters less that the referent is present than that it is identifiable (as we can see in the case of homonyms). Certainly the name is introduced in the presence of the thing named, but only so that it may still be possible to speak of that very thing in its absence (not so much, as the phenomenologist says, when the object "absents itself" as when it is no longer in *our presence* or when we are no longer in *its* presence and cannot designate it with a demonstrative pronoun).

The same approach is applied to propositions, where we also find a meaning intention and a meaning fulfillment.

"Anne, sister Anne, what can you see?"

And each time sister Anne answers,

"I see nothing but the sun gleaming and the grass greening."*

Each time Bluebeard's wife asks her question, she hears the same answer given. The meaning is the same, since sister Anne sees the same thing. But what Anne sees is not seen by her sister, even though she understands it. Bluebeard's wife hears what her sister tells her. She is understanding not only signs that she herself could reproduce, but a language that says something. For Husserl, the language of sister Anne says something because it is expressive. Sister Anne is in a position to see what presents itself (which is nothing—the absence of brothers). To say as much is to express it: her perception of the sun gleaming and the grass greening is the content signified by her expression of it. And so it comes to the same thing whether we treat *the sun gleaming* as the meaning of this statement of perception—what this statement says is seen—or as the meaning of the actual perception. The wife herself can see nothing at all; she has the "meaning intention" (since she can speak English) without its fulfillment (since she is not at the top of the tower). What does she understand? She knows, having heard and understood her sister's words, what she would see if she were in her place. She understands, in other words, that she would have this perception.

It is no doubt by a transition of this kind that Husserl comes inevitably to broaden the concept of meaning, treating intentional objects as "sense units." Phenomenology thus presents itself as an inquiry into the meaning of experience. Barring its transformation into *hermeneutics* and *semiology* (tendencies to which phenomenology, in its orthodox form, was to give way, as we shall see, and which we will be dealing with later), phenomenology is not yet a philosophy dedicated solely to the question of language. It is not a linguistic philosophy. But neither is it anything else. For it does not simply aspire, in the classical manner, to be a philosophy of experience or of the givens of consciousness, but seeks to be an inquiry into the meaning of experience. And this is why nothing in principle distinguishes its intentions from those of linguistic philosophy. The difference is entirely a question of descriptive procedure. In certain circumstances, Husserl's reasoning will follow the course of the most

*From Perrault, "La Barbe Bleue." [TRANS.]

orthodox semantic philosophy, which is in search of what we are bound
to accept if the beliefs we share are true. Since these beliefs are expressed
in sentences, we must establish the "ontological" suppositions that are
necessary for "common talk" to be meaningful.[19] Must we accept that
there are bodies, and also events, and again, persons, numbers, facts, and
so forth? This is how Husserl argues in an effort to counter classical
empiricism by establishing his theory of ideal objects: it is impossible
to claim that such objects are not given, because it is a fact that
we understand the locutions we use to designate them and the statements
we use to describe them. We speak, he says, of *"the* number two, *the*
quality of redness, *the* principle of contradiction"; we say that "four is an
even number."[20] Husserl proceeds from a fact of language to what must
be postulated in order to account for it. The fact, in this case, is the
presence of certain locutions in what we say. (If we understand the
sentence, "Four is an even number," then we understand what object we
are dealing with—*the* number four; and this object "must have being"
because the statement is true.) The difference between phenomenology
and semantic philosophy thus resides entirely in their respective use of
the fact of language. Semantics will proceed to analyze this language in
order to quarry out the "ontological suppositions" entailed in its use.
Husserl eschews any such analysis of language, summoning it instead as
witness to a "phenomenological fact," the existence of a mental act (the
eidetic gaze) by which we all have access to what is designated. Husserl
invokes language; he does not analyze it. (This assessment would have
seemed unfair to phenomenologists of the classical period. What, after
all, they would retort, are the *Logical Investigations,* or at least the early
ones? They are, precisely, an invocation of language in order to elaborate
a description of consciousness. For an analysis of language must extract
the logical form of this language, in other words, its scope for inference.)
Husserl finds that we speak of *the* number four or *the* color red as we
speak of *the* city of Paris or *the* apple tree in my garden, from which he
concludes at once that we have an intentional perspective on all these
objects, a signifying intention, pending a fulfilling intention. Husserl does
not question the *modus significandi* of these terms, and this is why to
every utterance with an ostensible designatory function he assigns a *res
significata* cut from the same pattern—that of the named object. To say
that we refer to *the* principle of contradiction in the same way as we
would to *the* apple tree in my garden is to maintain that we speak of it as
we might speak of an individual. But there is no individual without the
principle of individuation (*no entity,* as Quine says, *without identity*). In
effect we are speaking about an individual as soon as we can identify the
thing we are speaking about. The analysis Husserl overlooks would show

the principle of individuation that allows us to deal with "the principle of contradiction" as we would with an individual. Husserl is not concerned with this because he reckons that the individual in question is sufficiently identified by my intentional perspective, by the fact that I am thinking of that individual—as though we could explain precisely who "N" is by saying that he is the person known as N. For Husserl, the named object is the given object, not the identified object. Husserl is plainly the victim, here, of the traditional concept of identity that is thought to be applicable without the least criterion of identification. And so in the difficult paragraph 131 of *Ideas*, we witness the disaster, no less, of Husserlian phenomenology. In it Husserl explains that the reduction of objects to the "intentional meaning" they have for consciousness is not the last word of phenomenological description. The apple tree planted in the garden is reduced to the intentional apple tree, but this "meaning" is not sufficient to itself. It is the "meaning" offered by something—something about which I say that it offers itself to me with the appearance, or the meaning, of being an apple tree in the garden. Thus we can distinguish the object (that which presents itself from different angles) and the meaning (the totality of these appearances). And so Husserl says, *the same object* offers itself now from one angle or perspective and now from another.

We say that in the continuous or synthetic process of consciousness we are persistently aware of the intentional object, but that in this experience the object is ever "presenting itself differently"; it may be "*the same*," only given with other predicates, with another determining content; "it" may display itself only in different aspects whereby the predicates left indeterminate have become more closely determined; or "*the*" object may have remained unchanged throughout this stretch of givenness; but now "it," the selfsame, changes, and through this change becomes more beautiful or forfeits some of its utility-value, and so on.[21]

Quotation marks and italics abound in this text, but they do nothing to conceal the failure of the description. The process that needs to be described is not particularly enigmatic: we see a thing now from in front, now from behind, either because we have moved or because the object of our gaze has itself revolved. Thus it is a case of distinguishing the object viewed in certain circumstances (for example, a house seen from the backyard or before renovation) and the object of reference viewed independently of any one circumstance, in such a way that we can say we have enriched our description (having seen the house both from the backyard and from the front) or completed our narrative (before and after the renovation). The distinction sought here by Husserl between the "noematic meanings" (predicates, descriptions, what we say about the house) and the "determinable object" (the house itself) must explain the process of identification: the view is not the same, but it is assuredly the same house. It appears that identification can take place, to judge from Husserl's text, by means of mysterious allusions to something unsayable: "[It detaches itself as] the '*object*' [*der Gegenstand*] the 'objective unity' [*das Objekt*], the 'determinable subject of its possible predicates'—*the pure X in abstraction from all predicates*—and it disconnects itself *from* these predicates, or more accurately from predicate-noemata."[22]

Quotation marks abound precisely because meaning has drained away. "It," "the object," is a pure X, while at the same time it is the subject of predicates: how can it be a pure X (an unknown quantity) when it is also what the predicates say it is? "It," "the selfsame," has just begun to change. How can it be "it," "the selfsame," if it is in the process of changing? Husserl seems to think that it is enough to say *it, the same object*, to have designated an object and to have identified it as the same object "in abstraction from all predicates." This is sheer assumption, easily shattered by a question about the individuation of this "selfsame object." The same object presents itself to consciousness now from one angle, now from another: descriptions of it can vary. But the various descriptions of the same object are not descriptions of "it, the selfsame." Moreover, *it* authorizes the question *What?*—a question that demands an identification. The descriptions are the descriptions of "the same object" because they are descriptions of the same house, in other words, something that is neither an indeterminate subject of determinations nor an identical subject of changes. If we now wish to deal with the predicate of being a house, as a description that can be exchanged for others, we will have to say—for example—that these bricks and tiles did constitute a house, but that they have ceased to do so. They are the same bricks, but the configuration is no longer the same, leaving no trace of an "it, the selfsame."

It is now possible to answer the question raised in this section: What is *meaning* to a phenomenologist? Or more clearly: What relationship is there between the phenomenological project of describing that which is authentically given and the descriptive endeavors grouped under the heading "philosophy of language"? Furthermore: How has phenomenology, which is not an overtly linguistic philosophy, spawned the hermeneutic and semiological schools (both engendered by a question concerning the impossibility in principle of any phenomenological description)?

Like all philosophy of experience since the seventeenth century, phenomenology asks: What is incontestably given? True, it adds the inconvenient rider, given in a lived experience. But it refers to the given that it seeks to circumscribe in this way as the *meaning* of the experience in which it is given. This meaning should not be construed as an adjunct to the crude data, to facts initially bereft of meaning. *Sinngebung* in no way seeks to lend meaning to what lacks it, nor does it pretend to find order in what was, in its primitive state, nothing but an absurd chaos. It is here that the extraordinary aspect of phenomenological usage emerges. *To give a meaning* is normally applied to the appropriation of a hitherto available sign for a certain use, or to the decision to complete a fragment of language with a provisional context in order to understand it. The phenomenologist does not say that we confer meaning in either of these ways (giving a meaning to a sign or interpreting a fragment of discourse). He describes *meaning* as that which distinguishes one lived experience from another. How is the difference between one experience (seeing Venice, for instance) and another (imagining it) synonymous with the difference between the meaning of the first and that of the second if not because it is the difference between the meaning of the statement relating the first and that of the statement relating the second? But then the real given is not a totality of lived states. It is a totality of ways of speaking. To describe what is given to a perceived subject (sister Anne) is to listen to what she says. The difference between intentional acts is manifest in the difference between ways of saying that we are performing them. As a result, the description of a mental act is a description of the language of this act. The description of perception is the analysis of the language of perception, and this holds good for all acts. And where are all these acts to be found? In ways of speaking. From every difference that comes to light in the logical form of various kinds of statement, we deduce a difference in psychological acts, states, or dispositions. Each time, the description consists in analyzing the possible place of a statement in a chain of inference. For example, knowledge is not belief, because the inference from *he knows that p* to *p* is valid, while the inference from *he believes that p* to *p* is not. This extension is perfectly natural; the description of mental acts implies an analysis of the meaning of those statements that "express" them. Only in this way can we elucidate psychological concepts.

But Husserl seeks to practice something other than descriptive psychology (though he does not actually diverge from this course). By means of the reduction, the description of a lived experience is at the same time the description of its corresponding intentional object. Phenomenological extension consists, then, in the decision to maintain that with each manner of signifying something a certain type of object is given. We signify in this way, and we understand; thus objects of this type can be given to us intuitively. We say we perceive the apple tree in the garden; therefore objects of perceptual intuition exist. We say that four is an even number; therefore we have access to ideal objects. We say that farmers rejoice at the advent of spring; therefore we have access to certain states of affairs—"objects" that correspond to the propositions we use to describe them.

The question is why this extension struck Husserl and the bulk of his readers as so natural. The explanation lies in the fact that the confusion of philosophical psychology and primary philosophy is not confined to phenomenology. This confusion also characterizes epistemology, or theory of knowledge. Psychology is there to answer questions such as What is it to feel? What is it to perceive? What is it to undergo an experience? In elucidating all these concepts psychology deals, as it were, with data. For example, it will ask whether the act of remembering consists in interpreting immediate data as traces or vestiges of a past, or alternatively whether it operates independent of any immediate data. Now philosophy becomes an epistemology when one philosophical question governs all others: How were we able to learn all the truths we claim to possess? And epistemology becomes more particularly a philosophy of experience when it puts the question of principle as follows: In what experience have we felt that such and such was so? *Epistemology* is the theory of knowledge, *Erkenntnistheorie.* Note that here I depart from the current use of the term in French (as recommended by the French Society of Philosophy's *Vocabulaire de philosophie* by Lalande) in order to recover the use that has been preserved in Anglo-Saxon literature, where it translates *Erkenntnistheorie.* This term was coined during the neo-Kantian era in order to guarantee philosophy, as it was understood after the "collapse of German idealism," its place in the universities and hence a proper status alongside the other activities of the mind.[23] I consider the French use to be the source of many false problems. Lalande maintains, for example, that we must separate theory of knowledge (which, erroneously in his view, the English call *epistemology*) from "philosophy of science." Which science? As it happens, the French do not describe all knowledge susceptible to orderly exposition (and therefore to being taught) as science: the word is reserved for certain disciplines only. But if epistemology were the philosophy of sciences (plural) and not the philosophy of knowledge (in the sense of *Wissenschaft*) how could it tell whether a given theory (psychoanalysis, say, or historical materialism) was or was not scientific? Yet we expect this of epistemology because its very function consists in asking whether inquiries conducted in a particular way contribute to knowledge. If epistemology were the philosophy of sciences, however, it could only confirm a particular line of research in its own right (having already included it in an initial inventory of acceptable sciences) or else condemn it as a deviation (in terms of the model provided by those acceptable sciences already inventoried). But what we really wanted to know was not whether a particular line of research could be subject to the same tests and sanctions as astronomy or chemistry, but whether it had anything to teach us.

Epistemology, or theory of knowledge, is the study of the psychological concepts required to explain the fact that we learn, that we understand, that we know, and so forth. It may well be that the best way to study the concepts of sensation, observation, recognition, judgment, and concept itself is by studying "scientific method." Such was Comte's view: we should study the mind (or what is sometimes misleadingly known as "the workings of the mind," as though we were literally to dismantle a machine) through what is observable about it; in other words, through the procedures followed by men of science. And we should study these methods through their history, since retracing the history of a method is, according to Comte, the best way of describing it. Psychological concepts, then, for a positivist faithful to Comte, are to be explained through a study of the history of science. It does not follow, however, that this history is of itself an epistemology.

The Deconstruction of Descriptive Phenomenology

Speaking as they do of the *meaning* of experience, phenomenologists provide a fair indication that for them the real given is not lived experience, but in fact the lived experience of which it is possible to speak. In phenomenology, the question of language (in the sense of the one and only philosophical question) is impending: we need only consider that everything is given us in a language we can use. The implications of this emendation now remain to be assessed. But at the same time, as we have seen, phenomenology never performed an analysis of language, unlike the classical empiricist school, which aimed with its analysis to elaborate a language that was purely descriptive of the given; this analysis was finally to destroy the belief in a purely given given (in an "it, the selfsame, the same object in abstraction from all predicates"). The study of the properties of terms underwent a kind of suspension, an unconscious bracketing out. The consequences of this omission can still be seen today in the work of Husserl's successors.

The epistemological assumption urges those who subscribe to it to confine themselves to the object as it is given. Psychological descriptions are thereby elevated to a new preeminence. The material object must be equated with the intentional object, and from this point on, paradox abounds. Let us return to the apple tree in bloom in the garden. How many blossoms does it have? It has, of course, as many blossoms as there are blossoms attributable to it. In other words, the number of its blossoms is thoroughly determined. But if we are only looking at the apple tree through the window of Husserl's study, we are unlikely to be able to answer the question. The intentional apple tree already has a few blossoms or many blossoms, but not necessarily a particular number. The phenomenologist will therefore find himself obliged to maintain heroically that the apple tree bearing an exact number of blossoms is a result obtained by certain operations based upon the authentic apple tree encountered in perception, which it is essential to approach in less rigid a fashion. Thus Merleau-Ponty has no compunction about saying that optical perspective is a property of the thing itself[24] and that the cube never has six sides at once but only these or those sides in turn, since the real cube is the cube-for-me, the intentional cube.[25]

If we accept the epistemological assumption—what exists is conceivable only in the presence of an observer—we are then forced to concede the paradoxes that follow. To become aware of these paradoxes is to radicalize phenomenology and to begin to "deconstruct" it; that is, to undermine its descriptive ambitions. I think we can go further: *deconstruction*, in what I take to be Jacques Derrida's sense of the word, is nothing other than the dissolution of phenomenology as an effect of that epistemological injunction which has always governed it. Deconstruction is a way of bringing to light the "play" in the language of phenomenology which is also that of Western metaphysics ("play" in the sense that there may be play in the articulation of mechanical parts). This "play" means that metaphysics can never fulfill its brief to declare the presence of things. On the contrary, though unwilling to admit as much, it does what it most condemns: it prattles on, unable to decide between the chicken and the egg, rebounding endlessly from one marker to another and destroying any possibility of settling on some fixed point from which to aspire to the good and search for the true. "Contrary to what phenomenology—which is always phenomenology of perception—has tried to make us believe, contrary to what our desire cannot fail to be tempted into believing, the thing itself always escapes."[26] It can be shown that deconstruction operates, not as it claims, upon "Western metaphysics" (with phenomenology as one variant, not to say a faithful reproduction), but upon Husserlian descriptions. Deconstruction subverts the descriptive facade of phenomenology. It does not attempt to rescue the description from epistemological requirements but seeks instead to honor them meticulously, so much so that "the thing itself" will escape us forever.

Indeed, in his commentary on the *First Logical Investigation*, Derrida notes that the Husserlian requirement for the signified object to be present in order to fulfill the signifying intention is unjustifiable, simply with regard to an analysis of signification.[27] We certainly have no need to see the show in order to understand the comments of someone who has. (If anything, the reverse is true. To see something and emerge from an imbecile stupor like Proust's narrator seeing Berma in the role of Phèdre, it is not enough to look harder; and even if we are not quite expected to have read all the reviews, including those as yet unwritten, we nonetheless tend to preempt possible commentary, which involves mastering a particular language appropriate to the game, say, of "describing one's response to a great actress.") More surprising is that while Derrida points out the arbitrariness of Husserl's requirement, he simultaneously declares it to be classic and inevitable. All philosophy, he says, thinks in this way, subordinating language to presence and the sign to truth. The notion of the sign, as it has always been conceived, demands that the signifier be secondary to the thing signified, existing only in order to lead back to that thing. The metaphysics of presence is so called because it claims to derive the sign, giving it the status of a witness that announces or recalls the presence of the thing itself.

But such observations about the concept of the sign or about language are so general as to remain indeterminate; as soon as the analysis of language begins, it will compel us to replace this notion of the sign by others: simple and complex signs, signs that are propositional or constitutive of the proposition, designative or descriptive signs, and so on. Let us therefore turn to an example raised by Derrida: "Let us consider the extreme case of a 'statement about perception.' Let us suppose that it is produced at the very moment of the perceptual intuition. I say: 'I can see a particular person through the window' while I really do see him" (p. 92). If we call the *meaning* of this statement that which will have been understood in hearing or reading it, provided only that we understand English, we shall have to admit that the apprehension of meaning is dependent neither upon a perception nor upon a perceptual anticipation or representation. Derrida correctly continues: "Whoever hears this proposition, whether he is next to me or infinitely removed in space and time, should, by right, understand what I mean to say" (p. 93). We must now inquire how what is said by the perceiving subject at the very moment of a perception allows another person to understand, even though this person perceives nothing at all of what the statement refers to. This is possible, says Derrida, only if we admit that the statement of perception already states not only presence, but absence.

> My non-perception, my non-intuition, my absence *hic et nunc* are expressed by that very thing that I say, by *that* which I say and *because* I say it. . . . The absence of intuition—and therefore of the subject of the intuition—is not only *tolerated* by speech, it is *required* by the general structure of signification, when considered *in itself*. It is radically required: the total absence of the subject and object of a statement—the death of the writer and/or the disappearance of the objects he was able to describe—does not prevent a text from "meaning" something.[28]

The statement of perception in the example would say all that. It would say that subject and object can disappear. It would even say that subject and object, inasmuch as they are only stated, have already disappeared (or perhaps have never appeared). Later on, Derrida explicitly asserts that the use of "*I*", even in "*I am alive*" must include the possibility that I am dead, since this statement will be understood irrespective of whether I am dead or alive. Consequently, the *I* of *I am alive* already has the meaning it will have when I am dead. "The statement 'I am alive' is accompanied by my being dead; its possibility requires the possibility that I be dead, and conversely."[29]

From the first, this example of a statement of perception presents some difficulty. Nobody says such things while looking out of the window. Instead, we say: I can see someone (if we do not name the object of perception). Or again: I can see N ("N" standing for some proper name the reader can supply at will). And so we do not know if the example is itself the example of an example ("I can see so and so—we shall call him Paul") or if it is to be taken literally. There are four possibilities:

1. "I can see *I know who* (but I'm not telling you who it is)."
2. "I can see *I know who*, namely N (whom you don't know)."
3. "I can see *you know who*" (and here the statement assumes one meaning for the destined interlocutor, even though it says no more than the two preceding statements for anyone who happens to overhear).
4. "I can see *you know who*, namely General de Gaulle."

Now let us consider what will be understood by a hearer in the infinite. Let us assume that this sentence has been written on a scrap of paper, which comes to light later on. A reader would thus have occasion to see it out of all context (having found it in the drawer of a desk of unknown origin purchased at a flea market). A certain meaning survives even if it is unclear whether this is a fragment of narrative, an excerpt of translation, or a grammatical example. According to Derrida's analysis, the sentence could not conserve a meaning throughout every imaginable vicissitude unless it also always said: I, who am already dead, can now see—and always at the instant already previous to this (never precisely now)—such and such a person, who is already absent from my view, through a window that has already ceased to exist.

A curious analysis, since in any circumstances the sentence ought rather to mean that someone at a given moment saw someone else through a window. The sentence does not say who saw whom, where, or when. How could it mean that a walking corpse had seen another, similar creature through a phantom window? The Husserlian requirement for the intuitive presence of named objects was arbitrary, but the complementary demand for the absence of these same objects seems equally unjustified. In fact, the phenomenological concept of presence produces these paradoxes because it necessarily confuses phenomenal presence and real presence, or visibility in the presence of a viewer and the fact of being here or there.

Let us first suppose the possible absence of the object of perception. It goes without saying that the sentence loses none of its meaning in the intuitive absence of the object of perception, since it did not derive its meaning from the object's presence. Let us suppose now that the sentence contains a name, the name (known or unknown) of a stranger to the hearer (a stranger in the sense that the hearer would be unable to describe this person's outward appearance). Let us suppose that the hearer is the speaker's neighbor and that he rushes to the window to experience the intuitive presence he lacked. But if he discovers from the window a crowd of passersby, he will be none the wiser. The phenomenal absence of the perceived object is thus tolerated because it is a wholly indifferent absence. The same is true for the real absence of the same object at the moment the sentence is encountered by a reader: its disappearance between the moment the sentence was produced and the moment it is read is incidental. The sentence says nothing about the perceptual possibilities available to this reader. What matters is not the absence of the nearby hearer or the distant readers at the point when the presence of the object has been announced, but rather whether the object of this sentence is or is not in the presence of the speaker. The sentence says that this object was visibly present to the author. Phenomenal presence is thus more than real presence (since the person could have been there without being seen or recognized). This phenomenal presence is required by the meaning of the sentence, if the sentence is true. But the meaning of the sentence does not, of course, require it to be true (it might, perhaps, be a quotation, a translation, or the opening of a novel). That is why the reader's understanding of the sentence does not demand that he enter into relation (through intentional perspectives or by any other means) with someone who happens to be the person seen from the window. If such a relationship were to exist between the reader and that person, it would have to do so independent of the sentence. For example, the sentence could say that someone had seen de Gaulle from a window; and the reader, recognizing this name from elsewhere or taking it, correctly let us say, in its household sense, might add this incident to the general's biography ("was seen from a window").

All that the example establishes is the gap between the meaning of a statement and its truth. The sentence can retain the precise meaning it has—that someone saw someone at some time from some window—even if the reader has no means of verifying it or of knowing whether it makes any claim to truth. The reader need not have been present at the moment the sentence was written; he need not have been in the presence of its author, or of the object it indicates, or of the window. Nor is it necessary for the sentence to inform the reader that he need not be in the presence of all these things. For if he understands quite simply that someone saw someone else from some window, what absences should he be advised of? "My non-perception, my non-intuition, my absence *hic et nunc* are expressed by the very thing that I say." A strange analysis, since, even if the sentence stated as much, the reader would not read it and the listener would not hear it. Absence of whom? Nonperception of what? Derrida's deconstructive analysis can be explained by the following epistemological reasoning: Since the sentence, contrary to Husserl's assertion, puts the reader into relation with no presence (neither the presence of the subject of a statement nor that of the object), it must put him into relation with the absence of a subject and the absence of an object. If a thing is not given in the presence of someone, it must necessarily be given as absent from all that is given to him. However, our sentence can no more put the reader into relation with the absence of the subject or object of the statement than it can with their presence. First, if the simple meaning of the sentence does not require that the sentence be true, neither does it demand that it be false. But to maintain that things which might be absent are, in fact, absent already is to admit (incorrectly) that only the necessarily present is actually present, and only what is nowhere absent is truly present, and only those things whose phenomenal absence is inconceivable are truly given. Second, the sentence retains the meaning it has even if it was not written with this meaning in mind, by someone, say, scribbling at random to try out a new pen. The author might have written with no thought of any particular person, or window—or indeed, perception. In such a case we cannot say that the absence of anything has been indicated, for whom could we possibly identify as the person who had not been seen?

But what of the subject of the statement, the author of the sentence? If his identity is not discernible in this statement, should we not say that he is indeed signified as absent, anonymous, a walking corpse of a subject? Somebody has written this sentence, but it tells us that he is unknown. "When the word *I* appears, [it is] just as if *I* were written by someone unknown."[30] But this is not so, unless we commit an inadmissible elision. If I receive an anonymous letter, I conclude that it has been written not by an anonymous subject, but simply by someone who has not signed his name. That I do not know who wrote the letter does not mean I know it was written by an unknown figure (if anything, it is more likely to have been written by someone I know). Likewise, that the sentence could have been written by anyone (if I know nothing whatever of the context) does not mean that it has been written by someone who could be anyone. Understanding that someone has written the sentence, the reader will say:

There is no one about whom I know that he was the person who wrote that sentence.

It will be impossible for him to say:

I know that there is no one about whom it would be true to say that he was the person who wrote that sentence.

Let alone:

The letter was written by someone who is no one.

It is only the phenomenological habit of assimilating what is the case to what is the case for me that could cause the author of an unsigned letter to be taken for an anonymous subject, distinct from all subjects endowed with names.

The Hermeneutic Radicalization of Phenomenology

Within "Continental" philosophy, those schools that succeeded orthodox phenomenology established themselves with what they have called "the question of language." In France, Michel Foucault's *The Order of Things* disclosed for many readers a new orientation in thinking, a new state of mind that was already manifest in the anthropological disciplines but had not yet made inroads into philosophy. In this book, we read that "our entire curiosity as thinkers now resides in the question: What is language, how can it be circumvented in such a way as to make it appear in itself and in its plenitude?"[31] Thus Foucault too registers a preoccupation with language in philosophy, and here he speaks not only for himself but also in the name of the public he is addressing ("us").

The content of "the question of language" as it has been approached (if not formulated) in the hermeneutic and semiological schools remains to be determined. I believe it can be adequately epitomized as follows: Would we have the same experience if another language were available to us? (I assume in posing such a question that we can distinguish whether two forms of lived experience constitute a single experience or two; whether two ways of saying something constitute one or two languages.)

The stress upon language Foucault observed in France in 1966 is comparable to the *linguistic turn* in some (not all) trends in Anglo-Saxon analytical thought apparent since the thirties. In both cases we remain at the hub of a theory of experience. The matter is clear as regards logical positivism. It remains to be established for the postphenomenological schools. I shall show that they too are critiques of phenomenological language and not phenomenological analyses of language. I shall begin with the question of hermeneutic philosophy.

Merleau-Ponty has on several occasions quoted a phrase from Husserl that struck him as peculiarly apt to encapsulate the philosophical intention of phenomenology: "It is that as yet dumb experience . . . . which we are concerned to lead to the pure expression of its own meaning."[32] Here we have the blueprint for an investigation into the meaning of experience—a meaning it is credited with, even before the language of its expression or its being told has been conceived. Phenomenology thus sets out to find a language capable of describing what is given prior to all language, and *as* it is given prior to language. In so doing, it repeats the impulse of all philosophies of experience. Those philosophies challenge the (philosophical) illusion that arises each time we do not begin by establishing the division between what is given, independent of all language, and the human language we use in order to speak about it. In ordinary language, we are told, evaluations masquerade as descriptions (*this man is just, this landscape is beautiful*), knowledge of words as knowledge of things (*no bachelors are married*), modalities of the proposition (*necessarily, nine is greater than seven*) as real essences (*nine is necessarily greater than seven*). The philosophy of experience is thus a critique of the language to be used for philosophy: it seeks to conquer—perhaps at the end of an infinite labor of purification—a descriptive language that would add nothing to the pure account of the given.

It is curious to note the slight change Merleau-Ponty makes in the quotation from Husserl. After some deliberation, Husserl determined to begin not with a theory of association of sense impressions but with a "descriptive theory of consciousness." He continued: "Its beginning is the pure—and, so to speak, still dumb—psychological experience, which now must be made to utter its own sense with no adulteration. The truly first utterance, however, is the Cartesian utterance of the *ego cogito*—for example: 'I perceive—this house' or 'I remember—a certain commotion in the street.' "[33] The discrepancy between the two texts is significant. According to the text quoted by Merleau-Ponty, we shall express any experience whatever as though we were ready to take anything at all to be the meaning of experience, as though nothing were yet decided. According to Husserl's actual text, we already know very well what the primary expression of experience is. It has already been discovered; it is the Cartesian language of *cogitatio*. Here is how this language is constructed: to every designation of an object (*this house, this street gathering*) is prefixed an appropriate intentional verb in the first person of the present tense (*I perceive— this house*). Such an alignment enables the "proper meaning" of each lived experience to be expressed; in every proposition so constructed, this meaning is the grammatical object of the intentional verb prefixed in the first person of the present tense.

Cartesian bias

The point of this construction is to oppose the given—what is really given—to the alleged. I perceive this house. The phenomenologist's task is to describe this given, as against all those who would hasten to interpret it in the light of instructions issued elsewhere. Some expect us to adjust the description of what we have seen according to divine command, others would have it tally with the strictures of speculative thought, or perhaps of the exact sciences. But none of their terms—whether *creature* or *image* of a higher reality, or *force field*—is necessary to express the fact that I perceive a house. To use them, we would need to introduce each in turn as constituents of a language suited to the expression of a particular lived experience.

Since phenomenology aspires to doing precisely that, we will find the critiques converging on the same point. There is no language to describe what is given independent of all language. A language of pure telling does not exist, and the language used by phenomenologists is not utopian in that sense. The critique must then focus upon the philosophical project of a purely descriptive language. It will not address the concept of experience or of the given, and this is why it may be viewed as a radicalization of phenomenology. There is no language to say what is given independent of language; therefore all language describes a given relative to the language used, and therefore what we are given is always the gift of language. To describe the constitution of our experience we must turn to our language, not to the intentional operations of consciousness.

A phenomenology that grounds the question of language (the language responsible for the constitution of what is given to us) in history or origin may be characterized as *hermeneutic*. As Heidegger puts it, primitive vocabulary is historical.[34] Here the word *hermeneutic* should be taken to indicate a particular kind of textual reading consecrated in (and by) tradition. What this reading may consist of becomes clear in its own explicit opposition to the reading it regards as "narrowly philological" or "positivist"; the reading that prides itself on keeping to given data or facts (thereby reproducing in textual terms the program devised by phenomenology in terms of objects of perception).

Now the positivist philologist claims to read texts from the past in order to know more about that past, whereas the hermeneuticist is well aware that for him the texts of the past are informative about the present. Thus the past is not some distant, poignant, primitive time, but an origin, just as we speak of *original sin* (which is original not with regard to the primal misdemeanor, but with regard to the definition of our present status). But what connection is there between the reading of texts and the question of a language of experience? It will be helpful here if we consider what differentiates hermeneutics from plain historical relativism, for it is not at all a matter of explaining the present through the influence of the past. Historical relativism easily dispenses with any question of a language of experience. Hermeneutics, for its part, is not concerned to reconstitute causal links between past and present. If we are conditioned, as the hermeneuticist sees it, by Platonism and metaphysics, this is irrespective of our reading of Plato or of Descartes. Metaphysics holds equal sway over the thinking of those who have never troubled with it—except perhaps as an example of outmoded quaintness. So what is our relationship to Plato or Parmenides? In a lecture delivered in 1951, Husserl's former assistant, Eugen Fink, offered an interesting expression of the hermeneutic motif. Fink took up the objections to classical phenomenology that arise from the position of a Heideggerean convert.[35] The phenomenologist watchword had been: *the return to things themselves*. This return was designed to avoid purely speculative constructions. But what are these things themselves that demand description? The prototype of "the thing itself" is the thing in nature, inasmuch as we are aware of its being in front of us. Yet phenomenology did not *see* that this was the prototype of the thing itself; it *thought* it, by means of an unconscious speculative operation, prior to any description. This ignorance of the speculative moment was possible only because phenomenology had overlooked the question of language. Hermeneutics shows how it is the language we use that for us has constituted the thing perceived as the prototype of the thing itself. The thing itself was not always the thing perceived, however, precisely because this language has a history. To every epoch in language there is a corresponding epoch of the thing itself.

The phenomenologist imagines that he can apprehend the thing itself by divesting the given of all the predicates attributed to it through habit, hypothesis, or interpretation. But while it is possible to move back from the thing, as described by science, for instance, to the same thing as described by someone ignorant of science, the hermeneuticist contends that we cannot move from the thing as described by metaphysics back to the thing described as naively as if metaphysics had never existed. For outside metaphysics no project of a pure description of the thing itself survives—no description in which only those features belonging to it by virtue of what it is will be attributed to the thing itself (taken as *hypokeimenon*, the subject of predication). Fink expresses this idea as follows:

The ontological labor of the entire history of Western philosophy remains present in the structure of the thing. The smallest pebble in a field, the fleeting cloud that crosses the sky, or the cricket hiding in the grass—everything is pervaded by the thoughts of Plato and Aristotle, Leibniz and Hegel. Everywhere the ontological structure or pattern, whereby each *ens* is what it is, prevails.[36]

I have reproduced this rather lengthy extract of Fink's demonstration because it is important for us to grasp what he considered its strengths. In the present state of French philosophy, his reasoning will appear obvious to some—even elementary—and unintelligible to others. If only the first could articulate their understanding and the second their bewilderment! This gulf highlights the point at which our work of elucidation should begin. How does Fink find it helpful to conceive of the "smallest pebble in the field" as the habitat of philosophical thought? Needless to say, Plato's thought is not situated in the pebble in the same way as the pebble is situated in the field. The speculative phenomenology mooted here by Fink is therefore concerned not with the pebble as it lies in the field or the stream, but with the pebble inasmuch as it is talked about in various ways, now on a metaphysical plane, now otherwise. Plato's thought resides not in the stone, but in the phenomenologist's description of the stone, and so Fink reiterates Husserl's epistemological postulate, whereby whatever necessarily belongs to the description of a thing must be attributed to that thing. Just as the phenomenology of perception maintained that cubes never have six sides at once (since we can never see all six sides together), so hermeneutic phenomenology arrives at the contention that pebbles have "categorical structure"[37] since they can be described only in the propositions known as "categorical": those that say something (the predicate) about something (the subject). Fink tells us that this propositional pattern is the effect of the ontological work of Western philosophy as a whole. Thus it is only because we are the receivers of a language in which the labor of metaphysicians has inscribed this pattern that we take for granted our dealings with things as they are.

Fink's reasoning, then, runs as follows: that our language is a product of the ontological mode of metaphysics affects not the presence of the pebble in the field, but rather the way we shall describe that presence. Our language obliges us to do so in accordance with an ontological or categorical pattern in which each being or *ens* is what it is. Consequently, an orthodox phenomenologist seeking to apply Husserl's instructions might well divest the pebble of all the predicates assigned to it by myth, science, or common sense—but he would necessarily conform to the predicative pattern itself. Each *ens* is what it is. "The thing submits to being divested . . . without ceasing to be an *ens*. Whatever we think about a thing is unimportant; but what we think *as* thing is its ontological status, its 'nature.'"[38] These conclusions would be clearer if we could find some clue in the argument as to the concepts of *ens* ("each *ens*") and *esse* ("is what it is").* The reasoning we are offered rests entirely upon the notion that a certain analysis of the proposition, characterized by a practice of the concept of *esse* ("each *ens* is what it is"), belongs to a particular historical tradition (if we were not from the Western Hemisphere we would not speak like this) while at the same time it is inevitably present in all metaphysics. If this premise were justified, it should be possible to indicate which "categorical" analysis, imposed by metaphysics, applies to each of the examples Fink provides. But his examples are really only images. If we embark upon a statemental discourse about them, we apparently have the choice between several possibilities:

1. A stone is what it is, namely, a stone. A cloud is what it is, namely a cloud. A cricket is what it is, namely, a cricket.
2. A stone is what it is, namely an *ens* (or a thing). And so on.
3. A stone is what it is, namely, in a field and of all stones in that field the smallest. And so on.
4. Something is what it is, namely, the smallest stone in a field. And so on.

* For the purposes of this passage we have, on the author's advice, translated *étant* as the Latin *ens* and *être* as *esse*. *Étant* and *être* are themselves renderings of the Heideggerean *Seiende* and *Sein*. [TRANS].

5. If there is a small stone in a certain field, then there is a small stone in that field. Likewise, the fleeting passage of a cloud through the sky is the fleeting passage of a cloud through the sky. And so on.

Fink's argument does not enable us to decide between all these possible analyses. Since the thoughts of philosophers reside inside the stone or the cloud, we may at first imagine that the *ens* is, in each case, the individual(s) referred to in a singular (or collective) proposition. The *ens* would be now the stone, now the cloud, now the cricket. In this case, the fact of mentioning them in the language of Western metaphysics would be straightaway to attribute a particular structure to them. But does metaphysics decide that the stone is endowed with a physical constitution that makes it a stone, or that the cloud has a physical constitution that makes it a meteoric mass of vapor? No, for metaphysics is not concerned with such merely "ontic" differences, but attributes in advance to each *ens* the composition by virtue of which it is what it is. Short of returning to the earlier thesis (the stone is something, namely a stone), we must assume that this metaphysical constitution is not the same as the ontic or physical constitution: whatever the thing may happen to be (stone, cloud, or cricket), its ontological status as *ens* is already predetermined. This status, Fink tells us, consists in "categorical structure." But *categorical* is simply the Greek word for *predicative* or *attributive*. The only thing to which we may give the same structure as the attributive proposition is the state of thing, the fact signified by a statement. The *ens* would then be rather the passage of the cloud, the invisible presence of the cricket in the grass, and so on. We can speak of *the fleeting passage of a cloud across the sky*. The thing so signified (*res significata*) incontestably displays a "categorical structure," since this phrase (*the fleeting passage of a cloud across the sky*) is the apparent singular designation of an event, a designation that is erased by any paraphrase of a propositional kind: *there is a fleeting cloud passing across the sky*. Do we need to posit something which is precisely that: an *ens* that is the fleeting passage of a cloud across the sky? No; it is sufficient that something should be this cloud (for there will be the fleeting passage of a cloud across the sky not if something is precisely that—the fleeting passage of a cloud across the sky—but if there is a cloud about which the truth is that it passes fleetingly across the sky). And so the *ens*, in all this, is the cloud; and what is endowed with a categorical structure is its passage across the sky.

An objection may, however, be raised: the *ens*, in this example, is the cloud crossing the sky, and what it is, is precisely a particular cloud crossing the sky. In that case the categorical structure of the thing (for metaphysics) would be the use of the verb *to be* in first distinguishing the two and then identifying them. A particular cloud is the same thing as a particular passage across the sky. Here, undoubtedly, is the only way of guaranteeing a "categorical structure" to the *ens* taken in the sense of a *tode ti*, an individual. But this way leads to the highly paradoxical theory of nominalism—which effectively holds sway in certain areas of modern philosophy, without in the least claiming to embody the invariable doctrine of all Western philosophy.

In short, while Fink successfully demonstrates that descriptive phenomenology is not devoid of speculative presuppositions, he fails to establish that these presuppositions are inherent in the language of philosophy and moreover that philosophical assumptions regarding *esse* and identity affect not perhaps the constitution of things, but their constitution as they are given to us.

The reasons for the passage of classical phenomenology into hermeneutics are set down better still in Jean Beaufret's *Dialogue avec Heidegger*, which includes a subtle critique of the *Phenomenology of Perception*. We know that Merleau-Ponty had advocated the primacy of perception in philosophy. Phenomenology, being the quest for an original encounter with things, must indicate the site of this encounter. It was located by Merleau-Ponty in the act of perceiving, that is to say in a prescientific relationship with our surroundings. Science is secondary to the perceptual experience, like "geography in relation to the countryside in which we have learned beforehand what a forest, a prairie, or a river is."[39] Had we not seen landscapes, we could not have practiced geography. Beaufret sees this as a naive idea; he calls it the "phenomenological schedule of a city dweller on holiday."[40] Merleau-Ponty is confusing the return to things with a "return to the land." The hermeneuticist's true return is to the Greeks. We should therefore recognize that it is from the Greeks, not from our country rambles, that we have learned " 'what a forest, a prairie, or a river' is to us."[41] (Note the deliberate emendation of the wording *what a forest is*, to the more phenomenological formulation *what a forest is to us*). We gain access to landscape via the Greeks. But what does this mean? It was not from the Greeks that we learned to cut wood or to swim. The Greeks are our tutors in philosophy, not forest management. Returning to the Greeks is thus justified in the language we use; the wording *what a forest is* issues from Greek metaphysics. This observation, though quite correct, does not in itself justify a hermeneutic reading of the Greek philosophers. It demands that we read them (so as to understand the wording above) but does not prescribe them as utterances addressed to us, in which our fate is sealed (in which, for instance, "what forests, prairies, and rivers must be to us" is enshrined). If the forest is what it is by being what it is to us, and if it is what we say it is because we have learned from the Greeks to render up to each thing the "what it is" that is proper to it, then the Greeks are much more to us (much more for us) than masters of philosophy. They are our masters of truth. "The holy word is truly the Greek word, provided that we receive it at its source."[42] Thus this philosophy of language, hermeneutics, is indeed a philosophy of experience. It deals with language, like any philosophy of experience, in order to describe the constitution of things as they are "to us." Things are given to us in the way they are because we are the *intended receivers* of an utterance constantly infused with our *fate* as we hear it, the *utterance of being*.[43] Philosophy, in the course of its history, is attentiveness to these words. Beaufret concludes that philosophy is the "dictation of being." This is not to say that philosophers are like students to whom a master, "being," dictates an accomplished text that they transcribe with varying degrees of accuracy. (To substitute the auditory model—attentiveness to the utterance of being—for the optical model of eidetic vision immediately confronts us with the problems surrounding the inspiration of the sacred text.) "The dictation of being is rather the transformation of the text itself into another text, and another, but in such a way that the sole theme of this dictation is the ever other sameness of being itself."[44] All philosophical hermeneutics, then, clearly postulates no more than a single text. All texts are the permutations of a single text, which is not itself to be confused with the writings of philosophers. For the dictation of being is not confined to thinkers seeking the meaning of the verb *to be*. It transpires each time the verb *to be* is used in some way. The hermeneuticist asserts (1) that our use of the verb to be (in the languages of the metaphysical continent) decrees the kind of language we speak (the "era of being" to which we belong) and (2) that this usage is not only inevitable for us (it is our fate, our destiny) but also entirely contingent or historical. Being has not always "dictated" itself in the same manner; furthermore, the "dictation" began when the verb *to be* imposed itself, as evidenced in Parmenides, as the "paramount verb." Thus the metaphysical text (or the dictation of being) embraces all uses of the verb, including those that appear to lack any affinity with metaphysical speculation. Being is dictated, writes Beaufret, in our most modest judgments: "Ultimately, it dictates itself in the copula of judgment, when I say for instance that the earth *is* round, that a door must *be* either open or closed, or to echo Don Juan that '2 + 2 *are* 4 and 4 + 4 *are* 8.' "[45] I think we can now see why hermeneutics insists that all theses concerning being and all languages featuring the verb *to be*, not necessarily explicitly, form part of a single text: that of metaphysics. The copula itself affords proof of the unbroken continuity of one "utterance of being" from the pre-Socratics down to ourselves. Here is what I take to be the hermeneutic argument: All Western tradition falls within the scope of the verb *to be*, for it is always used, if only in the humble guise of a copula. True, there is a considerable disparity between the copulative sign in predicative propositions and a genuine verb, but it was precisely in the course of a singular history, the history (of the text) of being, that the verb gradually diminished in this way from its original meaning of presence (in the temporal sense) to the lowly rank of copula. The history of philosophy reveals the increasing subordination of the question of being to the question of the meaning of the copula in a proposition. For the Greeks, on the other hand, the verb *to be* is not limited to the copula, and this observation may be understood in two possible ways. It could simply mean that a thinker such as Aristotle acknowledges diverse uses for the verb *to be* (its equivocal character). Alternatively, and quite differently, it could mean that *being* is invested with several meanings. If it has *more than one meaning*, and thus more uses than the copulative function alone, it is merely equivocal. But this is not yet to say that it has in its copulative use *more meanings* than the copula alone possesses for us. This latter thesis is the one advocated by hermeneutics, which may thereby invoke the "ever other sameness of being." For example, Beaufret maintains that in Aristotle's work, "*being something* is finally understood on the basis of *being, pure and simple.*"[46] If that were true, there would be some single meaning subsisting throughout all attested uses of the verb *to be*, so that an echo of being, in the sense of presence ("simply being"), would linger in the copulative function of *to be* ("to be something"). There would be "the ever other sameness of being itself" throughout the history of metaphysics, thanks to the semantic sameness of *to be* in all its uses. Yes, but to substantiate this idiosyncratic reading of Aristotle, Beaufret invokes a passage from the *Treatise on Interpretation* (21–25) that tells us no such thing. It is impossible, says Aristotle, to infer from *Homer is a poet* that *Homer is*. The chapter discusses the meaning of propositions containing a composite predicate. If a person is *good* and is also a *cobbler*, this does not suffice to make him a *good cobbler*. Conversely, if he is a *good cobbler*, he can be defined as a *cobbler*, but not as *good*. In the same way, it is legitimate, while rejecting *Homer is*, to allow that *Homer is a poet*. This example gives very little credence to any notion that copulative being is reasoned out of verbal being; on the contrary, it confirms the insignificance in Aristotle's view of what we call the copula (he did not even have a term for this use of *to be*). Any retroactive application of the concept of copula (which first occurs, it seems, in Abelard) to the philosophy of Aristotle must reckon with the following declaration from the same work: " 'Being' alone . . . . is nothing; it signifies a composition which cannot be conceived apart from the things composing it."[47] Beaufret does not, of course, overlook this text; his reference merely obscures it to the point of standing it on its head: "This nothing is doubtless not nothing at all. It conceals secret riches within itself, yet from it, we can derive only such statements as we might make about anything whatever."[48] Might not the copula be credited with secret riches simply in order to sidestep a failure, that of the theory according to which the question of the meaning of the word *being* (as *ens*) in Aristotle bears upon the entire range of uses for this word, including the use we refer to as copulative? In any event, the failure cannot be avoided, for the meaning attributed to the copula is reduced to "what we can say about anything." Now, we can say about anything that it is one thing or another. Thus the copula has no meaning proper to it (such as "existential" or "parousiac") that would in predication add something to the meaning of the predicate. It is possible to claim a meaning for *to be* by reasoning as follows: If a predicate is true of a thing, then that thing *is* (and may thus figure in any question about the meaning of *to be*). However, this being, which apparently has been attributed, remains purely logical: this spurious property of being says nothing about the thing except that one or another predicate can be applied to it. In reality, then, we have added nothing to the initial predication.

The textual doctrines of Western metaphysics ultimately assume, then, that there is only one metaphysically acceptable analysis of the proposition. In other words, there is no real history of logic, but only a series of secondary incidents. As the "destiny of being" unfolds, so too the verb *to be* is increasingly interpreted on the basis of its recognized function in attributive propositions. For Kant this function is positional, whereas for Hegel it serves to identify the subject with the predicate over and above their difference, by positing the predicate as the subject's other, which the subject must become in order to be, in the final instance, what it is— namely itself. But this is only a variation on a very specific theory of the proposition—proclaimed by Hegel's distinction between *judgment* (*Urteil*, with a play upon *Ur-teil*, or the "original division" of the concept *die ursprungliche Teilung*) and the *proposition* (or *sentence*, *Satz*). "Propositions" are statements of ordinary language, devoid of internal dialectic (*Caesar crossed the Rubicon; I had a good night's sleep*). Dialectical "judgments" are those propositions susceptible of being cast in the so-called logical form upheld by textbooks of the period, in which a *subject* is joined by a *copula* to the *predicate* period.[49] As the logicians of Port-Royal put it, "But though every proposition does necessarily include these three things, yet . . . it may consist but of two words, nay but of one."[50] The logical formulation will thus consist in manifesting the duplicity of that which presents itself as *one* (*Urteil*, or again, *one divides into two*) and the triplicity of that which presents itself as *two*, divided and separated (by the mediation of a *third*, *the two are fused into one*). The old logic invested the copula *is* with the function of linking what had earlier been distinguished. If we take these reckless theories literally, out of irony, we shall have to agree with Hegel that the copula identifies what we are speaking about (the subject) and what we say of it (the predicate). In a judgement, *the subject is the predicate*. But in a judgment of knowledge, the subject is singular—*this thing*—and the predicate is general—a concept. By positing their identity as a result of the copula, we are saying that each thing is a concept. So then, all things are concepts. Conversely, each concept must also be a thing, but it can achieve this only through self-division (*Ur-teil*) prior to reunification with itself by means of the copula.

Like Pascal, we may protest: I have no use for dialecticians; they would mistake me for a proposition (or rather a "judgment"). The dialectic of judgment is plainly the paradoxical expression of the contradictions inherent in traditional logic. But it is equally clear that the analysis of *logos* we find in the Greeks is oblivious to such judgments, dealing only in honest propositions: those composed of a noun and a verb (but in the examples given by Plato and Aristotle, not necessarily the verb *to be*, nor an abbreviation of a formula made up of the copula plus an adjective).

And we may venture to question the hermeneuticist about the doctrine of the proposition hidden in Western metaphysics in these terms: Is it the one that requires a copula or the one that dispenses with it? Whatever his answer, the effect will be salutary, for the text of the dictation of being will be fragmented.

On Semiology and the Experience of Literature

The study of sign systems is referred to as a *semiology*. For example, a semiology of cooking would develop if someone were to analyze the way food is selected, prepared, presented, and consumed, just as we can analyze the production and circulation of signals between transmitters and receivers. Such a semiology should not be confused, of course, with the systematic study of the language of cooking. Meaning is conferred upon things insofar as they are part of a communication system.

At the height of its prestige, semiological thought was not referred to as such in France. Instead it was invoked under the mysterious and somewhat intimidating name of *theory*. This theory represents the effort to develop all the philosophical consequences arising from the central fact—highlighted by certain linguists and their followers in anthropology—that a sign can be conceived only within a system. Semiological philosophy did not arise from any precise work. It should be seen instead as a discernible tendency in recent French philosophy, not confined to any one writer or indeed to professional philosophers. Semiology is obviously a philosophy of language; let us therefore look at its treatment of the "question of language."

No linguistic sign (or anything akin to it) can signify outside a system. In any study of meaning the first step should be to reconstitute the system to which the sign-figure (*the signifier*) belongs. Oblivious to the necessity of this operation, phenomenology crucially neglected to perform it. Had it been otherwise—so the semiological thesis asserts—phenomenology would have been obliged to abandon its ambition for a pure description of what is given prior to all language.

In the anthropological disciplines to which semiological philosophy makes frequent reference, the difference between nature and culture has displaced the old dualisms of the nature of the body versus its freedom or its soul (not to mention the dualism of nature and grace). The distinction between natural and instituted, conventional signs will be made as follows:

1. No sign is present in the realm of the undifferentiated.
2. An instituted sign is present only when differentiation itself (between the sign and other elements in the system) is significant.

There are, in fact, conditions of meaning, conditions governing whether something acts as a signal. Where natural signs are concerned, the condition is the difference between the presence of something and its absence. (Although here, as in the case of phenomenology, we ask, "What presence? Phenomenal or real presence?" Since we are now dealing with semiology, the presence in question must signify; it must be more than real, then, it must be phenomenal without, on the other hand, being merely phenomenal.) A sign is natural if its presence indicates something and its absence indicates nothing at all. Natural signs are therefore not semiological, for they are not elements in a system. The natural sign is precisely the Stoic *sēmeion*. Smoke is a sign of fire because the presence of smoke indicates a fire; its absence indicates neither that there is no fire nor that there is a fire with no smoke. The presence of smoke is the presence of a sign of fire, the absence of smoke is the absence of any sign. The Stoics theorized natural signs: anything that can constitute the antecedent of a conditional is a sign. *If there is smoke, there is a fire* gives us *if there is no fire, there is no smoke*, but not *if there is no smoke, there is no fire* or *if there is a fire, there is smoke*. I quote this basic example in full so as to make it quite clear that what we call a natural sign is described by a proposition. The formula is sometimes abbreviated to read: *if this, then that*. Here the demonstrative pronouns *this* and *that* stand for propositional signs, not singular designations. *If smoke, then fire* makes no sense. The natural sign is not the smoke, but its presence: *there is smoke.*

Instituted signs, when used, are vehicles for intention. But intentional is not the same as deliberate. The intention need not be conscious, for it is unnecessary to know why we signal, or even that we have made a particular signal. In phenomenology, the intention associated with using the sign is a "meaning intention," a perspective of which the ultimate model is the mental act of thinking of a certain thing, bringing one's attention to bear upon it, conjuring it into presence by means of a perception or a memory, and so forth. The system to which the sign, in its usage, belongs is thus of no interest to a phenomenologist. And yet the difference between natural and conventional signs is precisely that the absence of a natural sign does not signify, whereas the absence of a conventional sign signifies. If, for example, a party of treasure hunters divides into two groups, each agreeing to communicate discovery of the treasure by a prearranged set of smoke signals, then the absence of any such signals means that nothing has been found. We have seemingly passed from conditional to biconditional. In reality, however, we have entered the realm of deceit (so long as the smoke signals are not emitted, no treasure has been found; but it is always possible that one group has discovered the treasure and decided not to divulge this to the other).

Workable examples of gestures that are significant as part of a system are easily found in the domain of social custom and ritual: codes of propriety and manners (table manners, modes of dress), rules governing the image we project of ourselves (conspicuous consumption, lavish spending, observance of rank), polite formulas, ceremonial behavior at key life events, symbols of kinship within the tribe. Here the stability of the analytical principle in play is best illustrated by the model of applause at the end of a concert. Applause—produced at the appointed time—is scarcely the impulsive expression of a lived state of gratitude or admiration, for the absence of praise would likewise be a sign (and not, perhaps, the effect of a greater restraint in expressing it or the symptom of exceptional rapture). There are, as Mauss has suggested, social circumstances in which the expression of feeling is mandatory. The individual's only margin of freedom is to select the degree of intensity, each measuring for himself how much pain he is prepared to inflict on the palms of his hands. Once applause is no longer an unpredictable exuberance of the body but a signifier, to withhold it becomes by the same token an abstention loaded with significance. Should we share the Rousseauist dream of an idyllic state of nature, we would say that the signifier wrenches us from a condition of innocence; henceforth our expressions are not sincere, they are summoned forth by the expectations of other people, since they occur within the system we use to communicate with others.

The transition from "nature" to "culture" operates at the point where sign becomes signifier, where smoke is no longer simply the sign that there is fire, but the sign, for instance, that something has been found. This transition coincides with the emergence of language, in the sense that signs are selected in order to undergo a further restriction: *if p, then q, but if non-p, then non-q*, in other words *p iff q*. If a man wears his old school tie, this is because he wishes to be known as a certain kind of gentleman, and if he does not wear it, this is because he would rather not be identified as such. Here again, the sign does not stand for Eton (say), but for the fact of espousing or rejecting it—the fact of sporting the old school colors or keeping them buried at the back of a drawer.

I have just defined a "language," in the semiological sense of the term, by the transition from signs, which may be invoked to support an induction, to signifiers, in which there is a discernible intention (conscious or unconscious) to signal something. If this is indeed the semiological view of language, it has absolutely nothing in common with language as we have discussed it up till now. Any philosophy of language asks how propositions mean what they mean. Semiology does not, so far, appear equipped to analyze propositions. When I suggest that cooking is a language, this language has nothing to do with the "language of cooking," that is, the language we use to speak about cooking. True, some semiological research has attempted to play it both ways; but this need not concern us since we are possessed of a formal argument with which to establish the confusion here. In the language we use to say something, it is always possible to form the negation of a proposition. The semiological system as described above, however, includes the "vacant slot" of structuralism, but not the negative. This does not emerge clearly so long as we confine ourselves to rudimentary examples of one-signal systems (i.e., to two signifiers: the emission of the signal or the absence of emission). In a two-signal system, we find three signifiers, assuming that the two signals cannot be used simultaneously (as if we had simply coupled two systems of communication). The instructions for using a communications setup of this kind correspond to the following outline: *p iff q, r iff s, neither p nor r iff neither q nor s* (in other terms something like this: *You make the first signal in such and such a case, you make the second in such and such another case, otherwise you do nothing*). Three signals would make four signifiers, and *n* signals *n* + 1 signifiers (the "extra" signifier occupies the system's "vacant slot"). In codes having more than one signal, the presence of a sign is no longer in opposition to its absence, but is in opposition to the presence of another sign. By the same token, the absence of any sign is in opposition to all signs; it is the negation of their disjunction. Such a code allows us to indicate the presence of an extra situation beyond all those specified by a certain signal. What we cannot do, however, is to signal the absence of one of the latter situations. Let us imagine a village where the supporters of a particular cause advertise their views by wearing black ties, while others do the same by wearing white scarves. Those villagers wearing neither would be declaring themselves to side with neither Black nor White, which would be tantamount to forming a third faction, the Grays. This political code would mean that no villager could state simply that he was against Black (without specifying whether he supported White or Gray).

Once we have set aside the misunderstanding that informs the semiological study of discourse proper (that is, the language in which anything once said can be negated), what, if anything, remains of the dispute between semiologists and phenomenologists? There can be no dispute without common ground. It will help matters, I think, to recall the weighty and rather arrogant tone adopted in the sixties to talk about *theory* (always in the singular). This curious celebration of "theory" can be explained by the failure of the phenomenologists' polemic against what they called "objective thought." "Theory" is precisely the rehabilitation of "objective thought" through semiology. In his *Phenomenology of Perception*, Merleau-Ponty examines the difference between geometric space and lived space. Objective thought, he says, takes account of only the first, rejecting such experiences of space as the "oneiric," the "mythic," and the "schizophrenic." But it is forbidden in any philosophy of experience to reject an experience. By what authority does objective thought presume to dictate to the dreamer or the madman what he is really living or feeling? For objective thought itself speaks in the name of an experience—the experience of evidence. Why, if dreamers or madmen are not the arbiters of what they experience, should scientists be the judges of what they experience as evident? Conversely, if the scientist is justified in speaking in the name of the evidence he experiences, the dreamer must equally be the judge of his oneiric experience and the madman must be the judge of his schizophrenic experience. Merleau-Ponty writes: "If the person who experiences something knows at the same time what he is experiencing, [then] the madman, the dreamer and the subject of perception must be taken at their word and we need only to confirm that their language in fact expresses what they are experiencing."[51]

The struggle between "theory" and "lived experience" is a classic conflict of authority. Who can tell me what I feel? No one, because others are *themselves* and only I am *myself*. We may object that theory is not the consciousness of the subject: it is an impersonal science, and besides, "I am myself" is debatable. However this may be, Merleau-Ponty has clearly defined the task of phenomenology: simply to confirm that a language expresses an experience. The snag is that there are several languages. Since mythical, oneiric, and schizophrenic experiences of the world exist alongside perceptual and scientific experiences, how do we know that these are all experiences of the same world? Merleau-Ponty's solution is to invoke philosophical experience: the oneiric meaning of the world for the dreamer is founded upon the philosophical meaning of the oneiric experience of the world for the philosopher. To show that experiences converge upon a single world, a phenomenology of mind is required, as Merleau-Ponty suggests.[52] But he does not say how this is to be achieved. Other phenomenologists, unconvinced, were drawn to the conclusion that experiences are irreducible, languages incommunicable, and worlds innumerable.

While the means of achieving a phenomenology of mind may elude us, the project itself remains clear. A phenomenology of mind is a philosophy of language, and it is a philosophy of language because it is a philosophy of experience, albeit in a wider sense than usual. Philosophers put a narrower interpretation on the concept "experience" than we find in ordinary language. Outside the academy, the perception of an apple tree in bloom, and the registration of a sense impression do not qualify as experiences, compared, in an ordinary person's life, with finding true love or being wounded in battle. Such is experience in life. But the ambition of Hegel's *Phenomenology of Mind* is the same, deep down, as that of the philosophy of ordinary language. Or again, *ordinary-language philosophy* is a phenomenology of mind respectably turned out by an Oxford tailor, minus the trimmings. It rests on the principle that ordinary language holds good against simplistic philosophies of language, and experience holds good against theories of experience. If the statement of the experience of having a sensory impression is indeed *this, here and now*—if we have established that this is indeed the language of that experience—then the statement holds good against the philosophy of sensation (which claims that the felt is singular and concrete). If the statement of a perceptual experience is the judgment of perception *there was a spell of sunshine and then the stone was warm*, that statement holds good against the "philosophy of common sense." Likewise in the practical domain: if the master's command to his slave is *recognize me, you whom I do not recognize*, this statement holds good against the philosophy of the victor's sovereignty (when it denies the master's dependence upon his servant). It remains to be shown—and this is more problematic—that all these truths concatenate to form a single "experience of consciousness."

The phenomenology of mind (as opposed to the phenomenology of intentional mental acts) resorts to a concept of language that matches its amplified concept of experience. Like all modern philosophy, it is prepared to recognize only the language of experience, but whereas theories of a strictly empiricist order recognize no more than one language of experience (that which is reducible to sense impressions), phenomenology of mind entertains several, thereby transposing the word *experience* into the plural. All language—now understood as an identifiable form of expression—must be taken seriously. And by virtue of the coincidence in any authentically lived experience of meaning and what is felt, the seriousness of an utterance derives only from the original experience it puts into language. The only way not to construe poetic language, for example, as misguided or inept is to make it the expression of a poetic experience in which a relative truth can be recognized.

This principle might serve as a procedural guideline in anthropology: Ask your informant to speak freely and take him at his word, once you have made sure that his language is a faithful expression of his lived experience. But how can such a thing be confirmed? Since I acceded to the experience through the language, it is now too late to measure the language against the experience. (Here is the vicious circle found in certain versions of the so-called transcendental argument: *he would not speak as he does if he had not undergone a certain experience, therefore he has undergone a certain experience; now let us see if his language expresses that experience.*) Reasonably enough, we have to ensure that the subject speaks as he does in order to express himself, not to please or manipulate us and not by rote. Unfortunately, most of the uses of language encountered by the anthropologist will consist precisely in the effort to influence others or to repeat traditional utterances, proverbs or sayings, legends or tales. Merleau-Ponty's reasoning, outlined earlier, betrays this vulnerable spot common to all anthropology of a phenomenological inspiration. The phenomenologist speaks happily of an "oneiric" or "mythic" consciousness of the world. But to dream is not to be conscious of dreaming, nor is it to be conscious of the world in one's dream. To recount a myth is quite the opposite of having a "mythic" consciousness of things. According to Merleau-Ponty, objective thought seeks to reduce mythic consciousness, while phenomenology intends only to describe it. But whose mythic consciousness? The mythical narrative is not a form of language in which a specific "mythical" experience of the world can find expression, with the narrator as subject—except after reconstruction by the anthropologist (the victim of psychology). For the myth, taken at its word, does not tell of ourselves at all but tells of our remote ancestors, of the founders of the family line or of the nation. It tells us that they lived in conditions wholly unlike our own, so extraordinary that they belong to another time altogether (the time of the awesome foundation of the world preceding the profane time of its habitation). The hunt for the lived states that might be expressed in a narrative of primitive time therefore requires the extrapolation from each utterance of what the subject has himself experienced. Such a retranscription of the language under study thus plunges us back into objective thought: while intending to speak of what took place before all merely human history, the narrators are unconsciously evoking certain outstanding moments of their own experience.

What if we stopped here, concluding that language is not generally supposed to express an experience? This would explain the failure of the anthropological application of phenomenology. Two languages would now demand separate definition: language in the common, anthropological sense and language in the specialized, philosophical sense. A kind of friendly settlement would adjudicate to each party the language of its choice. But this solves nothing. The anthropologist's subjects of inquiry may also want to talk about their lives, publicize their exploits, and communicate what they feel. How do they express their lived experience? By ringing their own changes on a communal tune. The statement reporting an experience can never be taken as a sure expression of that experience. It is fashioned according to a set of rules which the anthropological subject has assimilated—since he follows them—but does not control, since it is we who theorize them. And so the demonstration is complete: the statement does not hold good against the theory.

The philosophy of experience wishes to relate what is given, as it is given, and in the proper language. But anyone attempting to implement this is also bound by the rules. He cannot determine these rules—on the contrary, they will determine what he can express. If one were really to record the most immediate given, faithfully and meticulously on a sheet of paper, truth would dictate as follows: *I am writing on this sheet of paper*. The phenomenology of experience amalgamates here with the practice of literature, one that, for writers such as Maurice Blanchot, consists in *this insane game of writing*.[53] Just when it seems that the concept of experience is about to dissolve, *literary experience* propitiously intervenes to restore the credibility of phenomenological description.

Narrating, teaching, even describing, these lead . . . Where do they lead?

Suppose an observer has been posted in a certain spot to report what takes place there. For instance, a newspaper sends a correspondent to a remote city. The correspondent, instructed to describe what happens, is the epitome of anyone using language for the purpose of reporting (*of the universal reporting that enlists every kind of contemporary writing, with the exception of literature*). The newspaper is awaiting his dispatches. But a dispatch can hardly be improvised. The correspondent will stick to his instructions, mentioning only those events he is expected to mention. The news desk already knows what is likely to happen; the reporter has learned from his editors what the parameters of his experience are likely to be. Our reporter's relationship to his employers is thus perfectly consonant with what semiology teaches about the relationship of the speaker (in this case, the scribe) to the signifier. The news desk will learn from the reporter what is happening (whether q or s or neither), but before taking up his post the reporter has already mastered the formulas he is to use (*p iff q, r iff s, nothing iff neither q nor s*). Whatever the scope of his jurisdiction, he will on due occasion report that there is nothing to report. This too has been foreseen. The ultimately banal message "nothing to report" is the semiological vacant slot. But is "nothing to report" the description of the absence of something, or is it the absence of a description of something? It is the description that is offered when other formulas are ruled out. It is thus not the description of a mere absence, but that of an absence permitted at the limits of the correspondent's mission; these limits are included in the "signifier" with which he has been equipped in order to write his reports. "Nothing to report" does not mean that there is nothing left, that the town where he is posted has been suddenly obliterated (this would have been a major story). The message indicates that no occurrences fall into the category of events the reporter has been charged to monitor. Supposing that instructions from the news desk are treated as definitive and absolute, etched forevermore into the order of things, then "nothing to report" will coincide with *something—namely nothing—to report*. The more we treat the code that governs the formulation of messages as intangible, the more we tend to regard the vacant slot in a communications system as providing for the eventuality of a vacuum in things or events. The dispatches reporting this vacuum relate to nothing. They describe a state of nonoccurrence, describing without describing, narrating without narrating anything at all. Interpreted in this way, such dispatches propel us into an empty area that is the *literary space*.* If the code is absolute, the dispatches that report nothing are pure literature, in the absolute sense. For the concept of

* Cf. Maurice Blanchot, *L'espace littéraire*. [TRANS.]

literature has two uses. Accompanied by an adjective or a determinative complement, the word *literature* refers to genres of writing rather than to writings in general. *Literature* then stands for writings in every genre: the literature of a topic, pulp literature, escapist literature, children's literature, avant-garde literature, and so on. When the word is used without qualification, it applies to all writing: if it is written, then it is literature.

There are times when our reporter has nothing to report. But as soon as his editor expands the scope of his brief he quickly finds a wealth of things to communicate: life has suddenly become richer, more stimulating. The reporter's experience of this means that things happen or do not happen as a direct result of the instructions received and of the system in use. What is happening at any given moment is not affected by the directives issued at the office. But whether what is happening rates as something or as nothing is a function of the language within which the correspondent is committed to operate. This seems to substantiate the semiological thesis: the correspondent's experience would not be what it is, or have the same meaning, if a different language were available to him. This is how semiology becomes a theory of experience. When we undergo a certain experience, its content is prescribed in advance by the character of our own language. If we endeavor to break free of this restriction, we discover that we are powerless to do so. The inadequacy of language when measured against what actually happens cannot be remedied by a process of completion, for language can only be complete (a closed system) by being incomplete (by including a vacant slot). All languages require an ancillary slot in order to achieve closure. But this ancillary adds nothing, being necessarily empty. It is occupied by the experience of language itself—literary experience. A person who is merely writing does not experience anything (since by virtue of the limitations of the language used, nothing has occurred for him to report). Yet something is indeed happening to him, for he is writing, combining the twenty-six letters of the alphabet on his sheet of paper. What is happening is that nothing is happening. Semiology thus affirms that the theory of the signifier overlaps perfectly with the theory of experience. The occupied slots of the code correspond to particular experiences, in an order decided by the organization of the code. The empty slot is devoted to experiences of the indeterminate or the indefinite. Since here we are persevering in the phenomenological assimilation of the intentional object to the thing itself, there are indefinite objects and indeterminate events, things that are something without being one thing or the other, agents that are never more than *it* or *they*, events that happen although they are uneventful in themselves.

How can it happen that nothing happens? We are all familiar with the

hidebound provincial town, the sleepy village where nothing, according
to the local youth, ever happens, where events themselves incur disap-
proval. All that happens is a kind of nothing. In these sleepy purlieus,
that something should have happened at all is even more startling than
the event itself. Balzac is a master of the device whereby the event is
elevated to the status of a superior force at a stroke of the pen. In the
provinces, the news is not that a book of poems has been published, but
that there is a second literary lady in Berry (Dinah, the county muse), or
another sublime child in Angoulême (Lucien de Rubempré). Thus the
event is not that a person writes poetry, but that there should once more
be someone to do such a thing. It is as if the event were so highly
improbable that it must be registered twice—once for its own sake as a
literary event (the *Echo du Morvan* publishes *Paquita La Sévillane*) and
again as an event that affects the earlier event (George Sand is not the
only author from Berry, Victor Hugo is not the only *sublime child*). It is
as if, besides the event, there were an event of the event. But this
description is misleading. If something happens, the reporter does not
telex *something has happened and what happened was . . .* and so on. His
sending the dispatch shows that something—that is, the content of the
dispatch—has happened. But it may happen that nothing happens, and in
that case something has indeed happened, namely that nothing has
happened. In spite of appearances, then, there is no such thing as an event
of the event, since the reporter will send a telex in any circumstances to
confirm that he is at his post. The event of the event (or indefinite event)
is not an event and is not included among the material to report. The
event of the event is the sending of the dispatch, and the event itself or the
absence of any event worth mentioning is the content of the dispatch.

   In our semiological model, literature begins beyond the *elementary use*
of the system. The reporter tires of cabling "nothing to report." Out of
idleness, he begins to introduce variations: *still* nothing to report,
nothing *further* to report, nothing to report *to date.* He attempts to relate
the event of this nonoccurrence. *Nulla dies sine linea.* Having been
posted in a place where nothing happens, he must convey this fact and
run up simultaneously against the impossibility of conveying it—experiencing the lack of language in the very attempt to convey this lack. Such a
concept of literature did indeed take shape outside the domain of semiology (although not outside phenomenology of mind). It has strong links
with notions of the end of history. In the past, things happened, and there
were literary genres that celebrated events: epic, drama, ballad, and so
forth. What happened thereafter was that nothing happened, whence
literature, in its purity as written text.

"No thinking! Let us copy! The page must be covered, the monument completed—in the equivalence of everything, good and evil, fair and foul, insignificant and characteristic. Only phenomena are real."

End on view of the two little men bent over their desks, copying.[54]

Only phenomena are real: such is phenomenology of mind *for them*, Bouvard and Pécuchet, as they experience it. As for the final frame of the two little men copying, that is *for us* who witness the experience, understanding that everything which can be said has already been written. After the end of history, experience becomes pure literature. *The page must be covered, the monument completed.*

But we can endorse neither the semiologist when he speaks of the totality of the signifier nor Blanchot when he invokes the deficiency of language. As Jacques Bouveresse noted in this context, to draw attention to a lack within language is misleading.[55] A book may be a *spiritual instrument*,* but language cannot be. A book may contain lacunae, for a more complete book can always be imagined; but a language can be said to manifest a lack only if it is measurable against another, faultless language. This comparison is meaningless. Any meaning it appears to have is the result of replacing language by something akin to the semiological system of communication. All semiological systems have a deficiency: they do not allow for the possibility of negation (except perhaps in the case of canceling a message or withdrawing a signal; to deny a piece of information is not, however, the same thing as to erase a message). A semiological system does possess a vacant slot, and this is the token of its limitations as well as the condition for its use (for the system has to cover every possible eventuality, the entire "field of experience"). For any and every given system, therefore, one can conceive of a richer and more satisfying one, by means of which whatever unforeseen events occur might be stated. But in order for this improved system to be closed, it must also have its vacant slot. Whatever system we envisage, it will never be language. Semiological speculation, then, seems to be grounded in a misapprehension.

A Question of Grammar

Nowadays every philosophical school claims to operate a critique of language. But the contrast generally drawn between the analytic (traceable back to *Principia Mathematica*) and the phenomenological—later the hermeneutic—critique (that which more readily invokes the *Logical Investigations*) is insufficient to enlighten us. This contrast exists. It

---

* "Le livre, instrument spirituel," from Mallarmé, *Variations sur un sujet*. [TRANS.]

˙might be said of the second school that it represents an extreme critique of language, since it involves confronting language with its Other (in the sense of *alterum*, not *aliud*). Sometimes the Other of language is posited as given (in lived experience, in the phenomenal presence of things), sometimes as essentially elusive (in the experience of the equivocity of language). This kind of critique is legitimately counterposed to the analytic, insofar as it remains removed from research, by an analysis (that is, a paraphrase) of the logical form of propositions.

But we cannot let matters rest there. The analysis of a proposition is not an end in itself. It is no more than a laborious means of confirming the validity of a particular reading. That a school does not normally practice the formal analysis of propositions is thus of far less consequence than its inability to do so; and even this is an overstatement, for there are many propositions we can understand although their logical grammar remains controversial (for example, certain modal propositions, or again narrative propositions). The crucial point is rather this: depending on the school an author belongs to, he may consider either that the critique of a language is an accomplished fact or that it has yet to be undertaken. The first view is surely wrong. As for the second, the fact is that any analysis, once contrived, will simply succeed or fail in confirming an initial reading of the proposition in question. It may well succeed. In principle, any philosophical doctrine can attempt to enlist in the analytical ranks.[56] It would be more useful, then, to examine a different contrast, lying at the heart of analytical philosophy.

The analytical philosophy of language was born at a time when theory of knowledge or epistemology was taken to be synonymous with first philosophy. As a result, many of the relevant writings reveal an inextricable confusion between questions of experience and questions of the logic of language. The epistemological question is, How is it possible that we should know a thing? The logical question is, What results from what has been said? The psychology of knowledge has always presented itself as a postulative discipline. It reasons as follows: *We would not be able to . . . if we were not able to . . .* ; or again, *For us to be able to . . . , we would have to be able to. . . .* For example, we would not be able to identify objects (*it's him*) if we were not able to form concepts (*it's the same man*). Ever since *Phaedo* and *De Anima*, philosophy has sought in this way to establish the requisite abilities for performing certain operations. Which operations? Ours, those that come naturally to us (*ab esse ad posse valet consequentia*). Postulative reasoning cannot therefore begin without prior description of a behavior; the epistemological question is secondary. First say what you know, then ask how it is possible that you know it. The postulative approach in philosophy loses all relevance if it is limitless, and this is what occurs when epistemology becomes the dominant philosophy. The postulative approach then becomes what is sometimes called the *transcendental argument*. Certain versions of this argument generate a perpetual vicious circle. Does the subject (of the verb *to know*) know anything for certain? Yes, if he is capable. Is he capable? Yes, if he can distinguish between the subjective order of his representations and the objective order of events. Can he do so? Yes, if he is capable of subsuming all received intuitions within a pure concept of understanding. Can he do this? Yes, if he knows something (for if he has done so, then he must have been in a position to do so). But does he know anything? We are back at the beginning. On the other hand, a noncircular version of this argument starts out from the fact that certain truths are well known. They can therefore be stated so as to provide a sample model of knowledge. Thus the question of a language of knowledge precedes the epistemological inquiry.

There are a number of domains in analytical philosophy where the confusion of logic and epistemology is particularly obvious. The term *logical positivism* is one symptom among others of this confusion. I think such a confusion may account for the relative failure of language analysis to take root in Continental Europe—a failure that may well be followed by a belated and no less confused triumph. So long as analytical philosophy is presented as an epistemology, it will appear as a competitor, a rival doctrine, one that is in some sense naive and in another sense open to recuperation. This is why the method of analysis applied to a proposition in argument and function has been cited more than once by various neo-Kantians in support of the alleged opposition between the "logic of terms" and the "logic of relations." Theoreticians of knowledge were quick to align this with their pet duality of *function* against *substance*—and of *mind*, ever flexible and active, against the *thing*, in its crudity and inertia. More generally, the advance of logical questions has been veiled by the retreat of philosophy to unhelpful or obsolete strongholds. The reader of Hegel or Husserl (let alone Nietzsche or Heidegger) must be dismayed at the prospect of discussing such futile topics as the mind/body problem, the causal theory of perception, scientific philosophy, or again *the* language of morals (as if there had never been more than one).[57]

Nonetheless, in the wake of Frege the analytical tendency has shelved questions about the foundations of certainty in scientific propositions in favor of very different issues that belong in one sense to a more ancient way of thinking. As Elizabeth Anscombe remarked, Frege and Wittgenstein owe more in some respects to Plato's *Theaetetus* than to Descartes's *Regulae* or Kant's *Critique of Pure Reason*.[58] Indeed, the reform of philosophy of logic recaptures an era when logic had not yet become *the art of thinking*, the study of *scientific method*, in other words, an unappetizing hodgepodge of arbitrary psychology and presumptuous pedagogy with a moralistic aftertaste. Before its decline in the Renaissance, logic was concerned not to investigate mental activity (with the idea of regulating it, as if an art of acquiring and preserving thoughts were possible), but to examine thoughts, the reasons offered by propositions or *logoi*.

One principle subtends the entire project of an epistemological foundation of certainty where propositions of knowledge are concerned. It is that the proposition which provides an account of a phenomenologically guaranteed given is, logically at any rate, anterior to the proposition providing an account of the thing itself. This is to say, in Kantian terms, that the judgment of perception precedes the judgment of experience. The former confines itself to the subject and the subject's representations. The latter supplements these representations with the "relations to an object," which allows us to treat them as the respresentations or phenomena of an object. (What object? We have no idea, since the transcendental object is still something = *x*.) This anteriority is also invoked by Descartes in his twelfth *Regula*:

Here it must be noted that no direct experience can ever deceive the understanding if it restrict its attention accurately to the object presented to it [*rem sibi objectam*], just as it is given to it either first-hand or by means of an image; and if it moreover refrain from judging that the imagination faithfully reports [*referre*] the objects of the senses, or that the senses take on the true form of things, or finally that external things always are as they appear to be.[59]

According to the now classic example, a man with jaundice is not wrong to say that everything looks yellow (that everything is yellow to him), but he would be wrong to add that things actually are yellow. The error is induced by what Descartes calls *compositio* (composition, the precursor of the phenomenological "constitution" and the "logical construction" invoked by some analytical writers). Any judgment that finds things to be such and such invokes the "composition" (or combination) of what is represented to the subject (that they are yellow) on the one hand and, on the other, the act of asserting (here, with no supporting evidence) that the *res externa* is indeed what it appears to be.

The epistemological argument—and I mean the argument which elevates epistemology to the rank of *prima philosophia*—states that logically, if not historically, the description of appearances precedes the description of things. This argument is logical sooner than epistemological. Before maintaining anything about the domain of knowing, it adopts a position on the grammar of phenomenological propositions of the *something is such and such to me* variety. This is why Wittgenstein was able to shatter the epistemological argument, which had prevailed in philosophy since the beginning of the modern age, by means of a purely grammatical argument, without recourse to any epistemological (i.e., psychological) given. The grammar of the language play involved in the description of appearances is more complex, he says, than it is in the description of things. In reality, then, physical descriptions are logically anterior to phenomenological descriptions.

"It looks red to me." "And what is red like?" "Like *this*." Here the right paradigm must be pointed to.[60]

This looks red to me. But what is the appearance that has been so described? The appearance of a red surface. But what is it like when it is red? Exactly like what has just been indicated! What looks red seems to be whatever is like what looks red is. What looks red is like red, exactly as it would be if it were red. The epistemological argument assumes that *this may be red* is understandable before *this is red* can be understood. It assumes that the second statement is more informative or complex than the first, because a judgment of perception (my representation, presenting me with something red) has been combined (*composed*) with a judgment about the thing, endorsing the represented of the presentation with the "relation to an object" or "objectivity." A conjunction has therefore occurred: *It looks red to me and it is indeed as it looks.* Put like this, the phenomenological proposition is logically anterior, since it figures as an element in the conjunction. Epistemological philosophy does not, of course, suggest that the logical order is historical as well. In fact, dogmatism precedes criticism, in philosophical history as in the history of mind. But the initial impulse is to trust appearances, to deal in phenomena. Only subsequently does disappointment intervene, followed by distrust and suspicion. The mature mind becomes more reticent; it qualifies its discourse with *perhaps, it seems to me, as far as I'm concerned.* Reflexive philosophy accounts for the belated discovery of subjectivity through an inevitable rashness in the youthful mind. To advance in terms of thinking would then be a retreat on the heels of a sudden leap forward. Phenomena were always what was initially given, but they were quickly overshot by our earliest judgments. By returning to the real given, we are only effecting (through epoche) the provisional suspension of this inevitable dogmatism, in order to set the limits within which our assertions can be maintained. Thus the skeptic epoche can be described as a retreat toward appearances inasmuch as we assume a prior movement forward, however impulsive, from phenomenological propositions to propositions bearing upon objects. Molière provides a perfect illustration of this in scene 5 of *Le mariage forcé*. Sganarelle, the future cuckold, approaches the skeptic philosopher, saying that he has come to consult him. *Master Sganarelle, pray alter this manner of speaking*. But is he to alter it to a more complex and subtle language or to a more originary one, closer to what is actually given? *You should not say, I have come, but rather: it seems to me that I have come*. Sganarelle cannot make head or tail of this. *Of course it seems so to me, for so it is*. His objection is the skeptic's cue to embark on the epistemological argument. *That does not follow: it may seem so to you, and yet be false*. The skeptic pounces on this invalid inference to condemn it: the appearance of a thing is not necessarily the thing. The presence of the appearance is beyond doubt; but the presence of the thing is a matter for caution. Thus *I have come* goes further than *It seems to me that I have come*, for *I have come* repeats the judgment of appearance while adding that the thing is true. Sganarelle, in his naïveté, is thus the dupe of an invalid inference: *If it seems to me that p, then p*.

True; but it is clear from this scene in Molière that the argument conceals a trap. Sganarelle did not invoke the invalid consequence for which Marphurius the skeptic reprimands him. He did not say *This must be so, since it seems so to me (= if it seems to me that p, then p)*. He said exactly the opposite, thereby drawing a different conclusion: *If p, then it seems to me that p*. What Sganarelle does not allow is that a thing might be true and not seem so to him. How could he have come to consult Marphurius without being aware of this? This is not the area of uncertainty. The real worry is that it seems to him he will be cuckolded—What conclusions should he draw?

The language of the description of appearances is not extracted or subtracted from a language ingenuously applied to the description of things themselves. It is not enough, however, to rest this case upon the greater graphic complexity of a formula such as *It seems to me that p*, compared with the simple proposition *p*. In that case we should also have to maintain that the negation of a proposition is logically posterior to it, since it takes longer to write (whereas we simultaneously understand the meanings both of a proposition and of its negation). In a passage rightly stressing the importance of Wittgenstein's argument, Tugendhat ventures the following explanation: the simple proposition *p* precedes the proposition *It seems to me that p*, insofar as it does not oppose it, for the proposition stamped by the subjective modification has as its antithesis *Really p*.[61] Tugendhat thus suggests that *apparently* and *really* should be treated as propositional operators: applied to a proposition, they give rise to a new proposition.

If this analysis were accepted, there would still be a loophole for the epistemologist. He can concede Tugendhat's opposition between the subjective proposition (*It seems to me that p*) and the objective proposition (*Really p*). Prior to this opposition, or profound schism (*Entzweiung*), we had only the simple or immediate proposition, consisting in a statement of the given, still lacking an appropriate determinant. Consequently, the immediate proposition precedes the subjective proposition that precedes the objective proposition. Understanding the subjective proposition is conditional on having understood the immediate proposition, but the latter does not yet bear upon either appearance or reality. It concerns what is given in any case, whether as mere appearance or as confirmed appearance, objective phenomenon. The epistemological argument asks no more than this.

But we have barely touched upon the question of grammar that arises here. The refutation of the epistemological tendency in philosophy—which elevates theory of knowledge to the status of dominant philosophy—must not itself invoke epistemological data. In this context, the question of order is a purely grammatical one; it is useful, therefore, to examine the grammatical category in which the phrase *It seems to me* should belong. If *apparently* and *really* are adverbs that can alter the sense of a proposition, they ought to have the same grammar as propositional adverbs of modality, like *possibly* or *necessarily*, or as the negative. *It seems to me that*, when applied to proposition *p*, ought to produce a new proposition. Among the possible interpretations of *p*, some will take the form *It seems to me that q*. By applying the operator *It seems to me* to this interpretation of *p*, we obtain *It seems to me that it seems to me that q*. Now this result is ill-formed and its structure incongruous, but an authentic propositional operator ought to be applicable to any proposition whatever. It should always be feasible to apply it twice. The double negative is perfectly meaningful, and in the same way anyone can distinguish *it is possible that p* from *it is possible that it is possible that p*. In place of *It seems to me*, let us apply *It seems*. Doubling is possible only if we take the sense *They say*. It is only legitimate to ask *What does it seem about what it seems?* in the sense of *What do they say about what they say?* But we cannot ask *What does it seem to you about what it seems to you?* Or again, let us use the phenomenological indicators of personal or universal subjectivity, *for me* and *for all*. *It is so for me for me* is meaningless. (Although it is worth noting that the possibility of a double *for me* is essential for a rigorous phenomenology: in order for me to declare anything whatever, it must appear to me that an appearance is an appearance, and also appear to me, eventually, that an appearance is reality itself.)

As a result, our adverbs *apparently* and *really* behave more like predicates or verbs, which can be applied only once, since the purpose of applying a predicate to a proper name is to obtain a proposition. *He comes* is congruous, *He comes comes* is not. And this brings to light the inherent complexity of phenomenological propositions. The insertion of a *for me* into the description of something does not pull us back from a discourse on the thing itself to a discourse on a kind of ectoplasm or omen of the thing, its appearance. This insertion exerts a predicative type of effect. The description of the thing now serves to describe a person. The itinerary is as follows: starting from an ordinary description (*it's red*), we apply an operator to this proposition, turning it into a predicate (*for . . . , it's red*), and finally we apply this predicate to a person, thus obtaining a new proposition whose logical subject has nothing to do with that of the initial description.

What are the consequences for the concept of appearance? How is it that there is no appearance of appearance, no phenomenon of the phenomenon, and no reality of reality? By giving priority to judgments concerning perceptible appearance, the epistemological argument distinguishes two subjects of predication, the phenomenal given—or appearance—and the thing itself. Its only problem is in discerning the respective validity of appearance and thing. How can the transition be made from the customer's word—*this fish looks fresh*—to the seller's *this fish is fresh*? This fish looks fresh, but is it? The skeptic needs a reason for applying the description of the appearance to the thing itself. Reality might thus be conceived as its appearance plus something in addition, the given plus some form of confirmation. Conversely, appearance is the thing minus something, the given reduced to itself. The appearance is not the thing, even though it may resemble it sufficiently to carry its predicates. This argument treats appearance as a kind of candidate for the status of Thing, which it will receive only upon passing an additional test. When fish looks fresh, it is not the fish but its appearance that is fresh. But how can an appearance be fresh? *This furniture looks solid.* How can an appearance be solid? We ought to state what it is that the various predicates apply to in the description of appearances. A naive theory of representation might encourage the reply: to our representations (conceived in the usual sense as images or depictions). But we should more readily say of a fish represented in a painting that it *looks* fresh, for the represented fish certainly *is not* fresh. The representative model is therefore inadequate. A subtler theory invokes the reduplicative proposition in order to find a subject for descriptive predicates when these are applied to appearances. *The fish as it appears to us* is fresh, although this does not entitle us to call it really fresh. The fish as phenomenon is fresh, but we do not know whether this goes for the fish as thing in itself. Such a solution is unsatisfactory from an analytical point of view, for the reduplicative proposition is not made up of a complex subject to which a predicate applies, as in the pattern *x as F* (subject) *is G* (predicate). As Aristotle observed,[62] the correct analysis runs *x* (subject) *is, as F, G* (predicate). Thus the descriptive predicate is always applied to the thing, and this is quite proper: only physical objects could be characterized as fresh or solid. We can see that the problem of phenomenological propositions is not, as the epistemological argument would have it, to find another, more archaic subject for the predicate that ordinary propositions apply to the thing. It consists in finding out how the meaning of the predicate is altered by introducing a restriction to appearances. This fish, as far as its appearance goes, is fresh. *The fish appears fresh* describes the thing, namely the fish. But it describes it as it appears, with a restriction: fresh or not, the fish looks the way it would if it were fresh. These additions to the proposition, that is, the necessary starting point if anything is to be understood, construct a new and more complex language. The obligation to start from a simple proposition is not based on epistemological proof (of the type found in theories of knowledge: sensible precedes intelligible, nonreflection precedes reflection, etc.), rather, it is based on reasons of grammar. To explain an enigmatic phenomenological statement (*this person appears blingbling*) necessarily involves an explanation of the direct application of the predicate. As for phenomenological alteration, this operates a transference from the physical description of things to the psychological description of our perception of them, the sight of them that is given to us.[63]

We can compare the two languages, that of the description of things and that of the description of their appearances, to actions performed sometimes in earnest and sometimes in play. The starting point is the simple description of what a policeman does. Then the opposition between play and earnest arises, corresponding to the phrases children use: *pretend* and *real*. If we were to apply the epistemological argument here, we should have to maintain that the cops pursuing the robbers are partners playing at cops and robbers who are, over and above these parts they play, cops and robbers respectively. Reality would be the game plus a measure of seriousness, the real cop a *pretend* cop plus the fact that he is a *real* cop. We can imagine situations where this would be the case— for instance, two actors rehearsing a love scene who are actually in love. Or crooked actors making a thriller who take advantage of location shooting to pull off a real heist, only to be promptly arrested by actors who are real policemen with a regular contract to play policemen in films. Such an imbroglio would make good entertainment in itself, another Sherlock Holmes story, with a stroke of genius from Moriarty foiled by the shrewd detective.

Just as this kind of situation is more complex than those described in the language we use to say what people do in earnest, so in the same way the language of the description of appearances is more complex than that of the description of things, because it is easier to say what things are than to say what they are to us. The difficulty resides in the impossibility of a direct description of self. Even in the attempt to describe intentional objects, we are forced back onto the language that serves to describe things. A form of reflection is indeed in order. But the reflection we practice is not the ecstatic reflection of a subject upon itself (the subject of the verb becoming, as that very subject, its own direct object: *I think myself*). It is rather the reflection of a language endowed with a new function, a new application. In the absence of any analysis of phenomenological propositions, we can suppose that this language movement is embodied in an exchange of the first subject of the predicates (the thing itself) for a new subject that is presented as both more original and distant, and more immediate and elaborate (the phenomenon). What we once said, naively, about the thing, we say now about its appearance. But the description of appearance is a description of self. The description of the spectacle that offers itself in a particular perspective is also the description of the *situs* having that particular viewpoint. Before long this draws us into the speculative coincidence of thing and self, of subject and object, but the grammatical analysis of phenomenological propositions destroys such an illusion. No identity of the subject of experience and its object operates in a phenomenological proposition because the description of self (which is the phenomenal description) does not take the form of an attribution of the thing's predicates to oneself. When the fish *looks* fresh, this is scarcely to say that the customer *is* fresh. In phenomenal description the predicates of the thing apply, quite properly, to the thing. The freshness always belongs to the fish, which may or may not be as fresh as it looks. But the descriptive proposition of the thing is integrated, as a direct object or a completive, within a phenomenal predicate made up of a verb (e.g., *to see* or *to feel*) and this complement. Whether the fish is fresh or not, it looks good as long as it is presented to the customer in such a way that he cannot distinguish it from a fresh one by sight alone.

3

The Present Interest of Transcendental Philosophy

The place reserved by philosophers for inquiries into the object is traditionally known as *transcendental philosophy*. The philosophical grammar I am elaborating here must therefore be a chapter of transcendental philosophy in its own way. Yet it bears little resemblance to what a reader with a French training would expect to find under such a title. However, I believe that the transcendental element in a grammar of the object can be quite easily explained.

The Critique of What Is

Today the term *transcendental philosophy* is historically well documented but remains a philosophical enigma. Historically well documented, because we have little trouble pinpointing the tradition perpetuated under this name: it is the philosophy that leads back to Kant and his "transcendental deduction," including along the way the neo-Kantian philosophies of experience, Husserl's transcendental phenomenology, and in our day, the recourse to a "transcendental argument"[1] in certain philosophies of language. It is also a philosophical enigma because the definition of its objective as the task of "transcendental justification" remains somewhat obscure for all but the initiated. What is transcendental about this philosophy? The contemporary accepted meaning of the word is the one raised to classical status by Kantians. *Transcendental* is used in the first place to describe philosophical reflection. A study is transcendental when it concerns those representations of an object which are prior to all experience and which must already be possessed as a condition for experiencing anything whatever. This produces a *transcendental aesthetics* and a *transcendental analytics*.

Above all, an appeal is made to "transcendental deduction" in order to justify our application of concepts that are not drawn from experience to objects given in experience. All this is well known but fails to explain the adjective *transcendental*. Since it is an erudite word, it ought to be definable by simple stipulation. What is transcendental about transcendental deduction? This is what everyone wonders on first encountering transcendental philosophy, before smothering their initial perplexity under a mountain of scholarship.

What belongs to the West is *occidental*. What belongs to the East is *oriental*. But what is the *transcendens* to which what qualifies as *transcendentalis* belongs? Representatives of the tradition will tell us that it is philosophy first and foremost that is transcendental. This philosophy must therefore bear some relation to something beyond. So we are led to ask: What is transcended in transcendental thought, and tending toward what beyond? The answer, apparently, is that philosophy transcends questions of fact in order to pose questions of right. It asks *Quid juris?* By what right? It does not bend its inquiry to what is given (*Quid facti?*) but asks what authorizes the given to be given, what allows it to be donated. In transcendental philosophy one asks not *What is given?* but rather *What may be given?* or *How is it possible that the given is given?* One would say, using the jargon of this school, that the question bears upon the "conditions of possibility." Now the conditions of possibility of the given are not given but belong to the reflection upon the given. It might finally be said that the conditions of possibility are "the transcendental," as opposed to what is merely offered, what gives itself immediately: "the empirical." (In what follows, I shall seek to avoid the phrase *condition of possibility*, for its substantive ring might encourage us to overlook the fact that a condition of possibility is what can serve as a consequence in conditional propositions: *You can walk to Mont Saint-Michel only at low tide.* By the same token, we are tempted to forget that the conditioned must also be signified by a proposition: what is conditioned is your access to Mont Saint-Michel, not Mont Saint-Michel itself. The same applies to the "unconditioned," which could never be, say, God, but rather his existence or his action. When we speak of the conditions of possibility of objects of experience, these "objects" can never be individuals, but only facts or events—whatever is to be signified by the propositional clause in a statement on the following pattern: *I am experiencing the fact that p.*)

The interest elicited by this philosophy is well summarized in the adjective *critical*, another word normally associated with Kant. Transcendental and critical are a pair. Transcendental philosophy answers the loftiest philosophical concerns, because the so-called transcendental question alone exonerates thought from a boorish confrontation with facts. Without this question, we would be at the mercy of the world as it is, of things that are what they are, of the *ens*. We would fall into positivism and empiricism, attitudes that for this way of thinking amount to an abdication of philosophical dignity—the dignity of an inquiring approach to the brutal evidence of what is.[2] We would not know what we were saying when making the judgment—as Hegel did apparently before the Alps—that *this is so*. Do we mean this is so, but it might have been otherwise? Or do we mean this was bound to be so? Or perhaps this is so, because it had to be one way or the other?[3] To illuminate our *this is so*, we must look to *why*. Such a *why*, however, is not the *why* of dogmatic metaphysics, which asked, Who did all this? For the dogmatic answer keeps us locked into the *ens*, shuttling us from one *this is so* to another, from one contemporary fact to another, more archaic fact. The transcendental question transforms the *why* by asking, Why do we judge that this is so? In other words, How do we know? How can we recognize that this is so?

The interest of transcendental philosophy understood in this way, then, is that it transcends the simple compilation of data in an impulse toward the possibility of criticizing these data, assessing what is necessary or arbitrary in them. Generally speaking, this school invests all philosophical questions with a canonical form that emphasizes the element of reflection upon "conditions of possibility"—upon what it is our right to expect from the given. (If we walked to Mont Saint-Michel, then the tide must have been out; similarly, if we experience objects, then our pure concepts must have "a connection with the object.") The philosophical problem of any specific kind of thing is the problem of the possibility for us of access to a thing of this kind (access in the sense of being able and permitted to have a look, as in access to documents on file or to shelves in a library). The philosophical problem of time, for example, will be reformulated as the problem of consciousness of time. The philosophical problem of number will likewise become the problem of the operations required to obtain different sets of numbers. The philosophical problem of the order of the world will be the problem of our consciousness of it, or the "problem of the justification of induction." The philosophical problem of God is the problem of whether our consciousness can eventually accede to anything we might recognize as divine. The philosophical problem of being is the problem of existential judgment, while the philosophical problem of good is the problem of value judgments, and so on.

Such was, until recently, the canonical form that all agreed was the proper form for philosophical questions. Since then, the concepts of consciousness and representation have fallen into disfavor, for it became clear that these notions remained dependent upon psychological data that also warranted a "critique." Contemporary transcendental philosophy too has taken its linguistic turn. Instead of consciousness, it speaks of language. Instead of asking, How do certain representations of our consciousness qualify as knowledge of an object? it asks, How is it possible for the language of science to be meaningful? For a given language (of science, of morality, etc.) to be meaningful, certain conditions need to be satisfied. To accept that a certain language is meaningful is to submit that these conditions have been fulfilled. What kind of conditions? The so-called *semantic* version of the transcendental philosophy of language imposes "ontological" conditions. It will debate, for instance, whether the fact of understanding a language that refers to sets requires us to admit, "in our ontology," that beyond the individual elements of these sets, there are abstract objects—namely the sets to which our language seems to refer.[4] The so-called *pragmatic* version undertakes to present certain ideals and certain rules as the "conditions of possibility" for a mutual understanding: for we would be unable to engage in linguistic communication, claiming (sometimes) to understand one another, if we had not already acquiesced to the validity of these ideals and these rules.[5]

My purpose in outlining the most familiar aspects of the transcendental tradition in modern philosophy[6] is to emphasize how misplaced and finally inexplicable the adjective *transcendental* appears, with its medieval, precritical flavor. The glosses above derive their inspiration from numerous statements in Kant, who repeatedly stresses that for him "transcendental" applies not to the knowledge of objects, but to the possibility of an a priori knowledge of objects.[7] But although Kant frequently makes this point, nowhere does he say that the reflection which transcends experience toward what must exist in order for experience to exist is called transcendental because it belongs to this movement of transcendence. Such an explanation is sooner found in Husserl and in the phenomenological school. There transcendental is defined (insofar as it is defined at all) with reference to what is called the "transcendence of consciousness," the movement whereby consciousness is necessarily in contact with something beyond itself.[8] For Kant the "transcendental" is not linked to a transcendence of consciousness; Heidegger opts to interpret it in this way only because he is committed to a phenomenological interpretation of the *Critique of Pure Reason*.[9]

The philosophy of conditions of possibility demands the attestation of all that is alleged, the confirmation of all that is presented, and the justification of all that is done. This preoccupation with unlimited testing explains why it is called critical. But we still do not know why critical philosophy must also be called transcendental; perhaps we have the wrong end of the stick. It is not that critical philosophy, upon reaching maturity, receives the title "transcendent." But transcendental philosophy that has already been defined as a transcendental study for other reasons turns into critical philosophy. Kantian philosopy is simultaneously critical and transcendental, but it is not critical by virtue of being transcendental, or vice versa.

To be called *critical*, a philosophy must never take *this is the way it is* for an answer, but must see in such a posture the starting point of its inquiry. It has often been said that this purely critical function of philosophy comes into its own when the positive sciences are so far advanced as to take care of all matters of fact. A division of labor is set up: if your questions are about what is, see a scientist; thereafter, if you still have unanswered questions, ask a philosopher. This explanation is too succinct, for it neglects to say why the question that transcends matters of fact should necessarily be the question of justification, of right: Why (by what right) is it so, and not otherwise?

Critical philosophy has striking affinities with the function a modern society assigns to those of its members known as *intellectuals* (by a *modern society* I mean one in which competition between individuals is accepted and can in principle expand indefinitely, its sole restriction being the measure of civility defined by the state of the culture). Most sociologies of the intellectual are disappointing because they seek out the social function of the intelligentsia in appropriately "intellectual" activities (handling "symbols" rather than the ax or the gun, the sickle or the hammer). The textbooks tell us that intellectuals spring from the educated and enlightened strata of the population. This rather complacent definition would classify as intellectual anyone who reads more newspapers than most before forming an opinion. But it is noticeable that those same newspapers rarely mention intellectuals, period—people whose trade it is to write, to read, or to speak. The word *intellectual* is usually accompanied by a sign of affiliation. There are no "intellectuals"; only party intellectuals, Catholic intellectuals, Jewish intellectuals, Polish intellectuals, and so forth. The lettered class is always a minority (the intelligentsia) within another threatened or enthralled minority (the militant party, the people of God, the subject nation), itself in the midst of a gigantic majority. The role of the intellectual is indeed to follow with passion the movements of ideas and things, but this is in order to know the fate the world holds in store for his tribe. Caught between the ongoing world and the goings-on within the tribe, he will diagnose whether the second is condemned by the first. *Are we doomed? Is it right that we should vanish?* The *nationalist* intellectual, addressing the nation (whose legend it is often his task to invent) proclaims that the nation will be reborn from its predicament because its disappearance would entail the doom of the whole world. The *revolutionary* intellectual betrays his own minority, which he views as justly condemned by a history yet to unfold, and joins the camp of the future masters. The current acceptance of the word "intellectual" dates from the Dreyfus Affair, when a group of pro-Dreyfus writers signed the *Intellectuals' Manifesto*. This exemplary case clearly shows that where there is a trial, there are intellectuals. But not all human iniquity amounts to an affair: there have to be grounds for a *J'accuse*. There would have been no Dreyfus Affair in Captain Dreyfus alone. The trial becomes the affair when everyone is implicated: the government, the judiciary, the army, the Jews, the fatherland, the enemy, and so on. It is through accusation that the intellectual participates. Indeed, the anti-Dreyfus intellectuals who tried to hit back could defend their miserable cause only by accusing the Dreyfusards in turn of all manner of crimes (against army morale and the interests of France, etc.). The intellectual's utterance is always *I accuse*; it can never be *I excuse*, let alone *I forgive* or *I give thanks* (for that, he would have to become a writer or a poet). The intellectual's function is thus to apportion blame. *Whose fault was it?* In the first place it devolves upon those who set the example for the crime—example, because a crime does not in itself amount to an affair, provided human justice is successful in punishing it by reestablishing a world order. The affair begins with an unpunished crime and culminates in the unpunishable crime, of which legal crimes or high-level coverups are the prototype. But those who count themselves just for having committed no crime are also to blame if they fail to oppose the perpetrators of unpunished crimes. Unlike affairs that hinge on one particular victim (the Calas Affair, the Dreyfus Affair, the Audin Affair), general affairs focus on impersonal faults committed in all legality (for no law needs to be broken to exploit the weak, to corrupt morals, or to lead minds astray). When both victims and culprits consti-tute a mass—as here—the accuser is better placed to file a universal lawsuit. Accusation becomes boundless, the victims innumerable, and likewise the culprits. Before long, each of us has to admit to harboring in ourselves a victim and a criminal, an exploited and an exploiter, a slave and a master. What is more corruptive than the already corrupted? What more misleading than the misled? To be epidemic or mimetic is a feature of evil.[10]

The more unfettered accusation becomes, the further it moves from a specific case, from the affair that takes the name of its prime victim. We understand affairs with names involved because they can be recounted with reference to people, facts, circumstances. By analogy, we understand affairs with collective protagonists (the oppression of a nation, the despoliation of a people). The transition to pure generality destroys the conditions for narration. In a universal trial, the crime can no longer be determined. The greatest sin of the accused is that they exist, but similarly the injustice suffered by the victims is that they too exist. Critical philosophy gives a voice to indefinite accusation, as if it were a matter of professionalizing the dramatic role of plaintiff in an affair (a role in a trial, in a drama with a beginning and an end). Ever since the theodicy of philosophers decided that God was too good to exist (for if he existed, he would have to be blamed for everything), the general fault has devolved upon those who do exist.[11] Critical philosophy demands of things as they are, By what right do you exist, instead of not existing? Later comes romantic resentment, expressed in the void: Why does nothing (satisfactory) exist, rather than something? You who do not exist, by what right do you not exist?

Ontology

The critical function—when it operates not in the drama of what some men have done to a particular man but in the drama of what has happened to all men thoughout history—can identify only suspects. Philosophy in its critical garb acts as justice on the trail of the ontological crime committed by that which exists without good reason. The philosophy that recruits intellectuals for an uninterrupted labor is the philosophy of history, reopening the file of God's cause, or theodicy. To this end, it mobilizes general metaphysics in order for the prosecution to be conducted in all its generality. Modern scholastic philosophy, from Suarez to the time of Kant, locates the height of universality in a kind of transgenerality it calls transcendental. Transcendental philosophy is *philosophia transcendentalis sive ontologia*, the doctrine of the *ens commune*, of the object in general, to which Kant still alludes in *The Architectonics of Pure Reason* (B873). As Heidegger so vigorously insisted, Kant's "transcendental philosophy" is no less a doctrine of being or of the object than is that of the so-called precritical writers (precritical like prelogical, as in the mentality of certain peoples, usually far removed from ourselves).[12] His philosophy is transcendental because it studies the object in general and because it aims to establish the conceptual system whereby we construe the properties that necessarily belong to an object, whatever it may be. His philosophy is critical because it strives to justify these concepts. Kant's philosophy is at once transcendental and critical, but what makes it critical (the attempt to deduce categories) is not what makes it transcendental. It may help to reverse the usual neo-Kantian explanation—what is transcendental is first and foremost philosophy with its movement of reflection, and only then what that philosophy sets in place (consciousness, objective correlation). Let us say instead that the transcendental is first and foremost the phrase *something in general*, or the concept of an object whatever it may be (if such a concept exists), and only then the study of this phrase (concept).

In contemporary usage, an *object* is any material item endowed with sufficient consistency for it to be moved in a single gesture. There is for example the lost and found office (*bureau des objets trouvés*), which accepts all sorts of objects besides umbrellas, hats, cases, and other possessions easily mislaid. Now this meaning of *object*, however indeterminate, remains restricted. The lost and found office does not take lost children, or even lost dogs with no collars, and certainly not lost quotations, opportunities, or bargains. Objects in ordinary language are thus far too determinate for the purposes of transcendental philosophy, which calls anything short of nothing an *object*. Everything is eligible for object status. Ordinary objects, which can be lost and found, are of a particular sort (consisting in fact of a material individual or agglomerate made or obtained by someone for some definite use). An object in the transcendental sense can be of any sort whatever.

Classically, *predicamental terms* are those that serve to classify. General terms in language are most often used to designate a group, as in the guessing game *animal, vegetable, or mineral.* Certain general terms, though, do not have this classificatory function. The word *being* does not classify, for what is not being is nothing. Thus the classical view is that being is not a genus. Indeed, a generic concept enables the factor common to several otherwise different things to be held in the mind. It can thus always be specified by means of differences. But the being of beings and the objectivity of objects are not factors shared by otherwise different things. If they were, then those things would be nothing at all. If things are distinguishable from one another, it is only through what they are, through their being.

Terms that are not apt to classify what they are applied to are called *transcendental.* General classificatory terms belong to predicamental lines such as those that feature in Porphyrian classification. Transcendental terms are those that ignore the difference between one predicamental line and another. The problem of transcendental philosophy is to determine the mode of signification proper to transcendental terms such as *being, one* (or *many*), *same* (or *other*), *something,* and so on.

Ontology sees the lack of classificatory value as the other face of an aptitude to transcend predicamental differences. It takes the transcendental for a higher kind of generality, a trans- or unlimited generality. Transcendental concepts can be applied even more extensively than the most exalted general concepts such as substance, quality, relation, and so on. They enable us to envisage properties that cannot fail to belong to any thing whatever, provided it exists. Ontology is the inventory of these properties. Transcendentals are so named because they transcend different predicamental lines. Thus the term *thing* is transcendental, because if I say, *You are forgetting one thing,* you cannot tell either which thing I mean or, more important, what kind of thing it is. You have no way of knowing what predicamental line it belongs to, whether it is a substance, a relation, or some other kind of thing. Ontology considers that transcendental terms transcend or surpass predicamental differences because they are more general than predicaments. The transcendental purports to be something exalted and sublime.

The Logic of Transcendentals

Until now we have looked at two senses of the term *transcendental*: the ontological sense and the critical sense that derives from it in fundamental epistemology. Transcendental philosophy is fundamental in both senses alike. Critical philosophy projects an ultimate foundation or radical justification of our pretensions to knowledge and our ways of judging. Transcendental philosophy properly speaking, as it still exists in Kant's work, is fundamental in the sense that it states the principles that hold good for all objects—the laws of being. For Kant there is the thing in itself, whose laws are irretrievably beyond us, and the thing as phenomenon. Insofar as the *Critique* offers "the complete ontology of the thing as phenomenon," it is already a phenomenology, as Beaufret makes clear.[13] It was precisely for this knowledge of the *ens in genere* that the word *ontology* was coined at the end of the seventeenth century. In ontology, the question of the *modus significandi* of transcendental terms is settled in favor of univocity. The meaning of the term *object* (and its equivalents *ens, chose, etwas, entity*) is such that by making it the predicate of anything, we attribute to that thing, whatever it may be, the property of objectivity.[14]

But just as transcendental philosophy need not necessarily be critical, so it need not be ontological. We have seen how the epistemology of critical philosophy is an ontology mobilized for the foundation of judgments. It may be that ontology is itself the transformation of a more elementary study, intended to found the laws proper to one or another kind of thing upon the universal laws of the object. Now there may be something primal attaching to an elementary study, but this does not make it fundamental. The logic of transcendental terms is doubtless elementary, inasmuch as no ontology can be contemplated until this logic has been grasped. Were the word *ens* (or the word *object*) not to constitute a univocal predicate, there would be no grounds for a science of the *ens in genere*. The question of the meaning (or the meanings) of the word *object* precedes the question of the object's objectivity (and, depending on the answer, makes or breaks the ontology).

What if the logic of transcendentals were to remain an elementary study, without founding an ontology that in its turn might inaugurate a limitless critique of that which is? We should then have to append to the first two a third conception of transcendental philosophy. Far from being a novelty, this elementary philosophy will revive the ancient alliance between the so-called question of being and the analysis of the *logos*.

We may protest of all ontologies that they fail to distinguish clearly between two manners of signifying—one proper to predicamental terms and another proper to transcendentals. The transcendental is regarded as an unlimited predicamental, making nonsense of the distinction. The classical explanation argues that a predicamental term adds something to the description of that of which it is the predicate (*white* adds to *man* in *this man is white*), whereas the transcendental term does nothing to enrich or complete the description but presents it afresh in the light of a new *ratio* (*being* adds nothing to *man* in *this man is being*).[15] Here is Aristotle's famous equivalence—origin of all the speculation about transcendentals—between one man, a man that is, and a man (if a man goes hunting, there is a man who goes hunting, and this humanity going hunting counts for one, if for example each hunter were to be allowed no more than one rabbit).[16] This equivalence shows that transcendental terms are used in apposition to predicamental terms. When we come effectively to deal with metaphysical questions such as *What is a being? What is a one?* we should not behave as if we were installed opposite something to be observed and described (the *object in general*). In Aristotle's example, *one* and *that is (being)* add nothing to the description that could be provided using only the word *man*; but they highlight something in this description.

Superficially, the grammar of *one* or of *identical* is that of any adjective such as *white* or *old*. It is tempting, therefore, to regard them simply as predicamental adjectives with a broader scope. The grammar of *being* appears to be that of a participle such as *singing*. The grammar of *object* seems to be that of a noun such as *journey*. If no grammatical difference can be detected between these pairs, we shall have no cause to deny transcendentals their univocal meaning, and we may continue to invoke with confidence the transcendental properties of that which is. The word *identical*, for instance, enables the property of identity to be attributed. But in what sense can identity be the property of something? *Everything is identical to itself.* For this "ontological law" to have any content, however, a property must effectively be attributed in this statement to everything, causing us to invest the logical concept of identity with a certain descriptive capacity (identity might, for instance, be a state of good repair). Similarly, in order to give a univocal content to the onto- logical *ens* we might look to verbs of state (*to be*, as in *to be part of something*, part of the group) or to verbs of action (*to be* would be to act, to survive, to resist the forces of destruction).

If we take it that the word *entity* serves to attribute "beingity"[17] and the word *object*, objectivity, are we to say that two things to which beingity has been attributed are distinct as entities, or that as entities they are not distinct? Is a fork distinct from a knife insofar as the fork is— objectively—and the knife also is, just as they are distinct in terms of cutlery? At first sight, things that are can be distinguished if one is what the other is not (the knife and the fork are two items of cutlery because this piece of metal is cutlery and this *other* piece of metal is another sort of cutlery). Such things are therefore not distinguished from the point of view of beingity or of objectivity. From an ontological standpoint, there is no more than one object (which will always and in all circumstances be "the transcendental object = x" of theory of knowledge). But if there is one and only one object, then there is no other. Scarcely have we uttered *no other* than we hear the inevitable rejoinder, *No other what?* To answer *no other object, no other being* is to acknowledge that our previous affirmations were worthless. We cannot speak of another object or another being unless we know when there are two beings (two objects) and when there is twice the same being (the same object). It is reasonable to demand some criterion to apply each time there is a choice between identity and alterity. Are you reading the same book as you were reading yesterday? The matter must be clarified. For instance, what separates two copies of one text is that this text is printed on materially different sheets of paper. It may also happen that a single page bears two separate texts at once (as in the case of a coded message). Similarly, two persons are distinct individuals if they are materially different (if it takes two arm- chairs to seat them), whereas the picture of a child and that of an old man may be pictures of the same person (but not of the same child or the same old man) if certain conditions of personal identity are fulfilled—these being harder to specify than we might think. Therefore it is not a case of standing in front of something and saying: Let's ignore the genus to which this something belongs, let's keep to the properties hypothetically attributable to it and draw up a list of these ontological properties. The moment we overlook the kind of object we seek to confront, we are no longer faced with anything identifiable.

The objections that demolish ontological ambitions can also be made to the explanation furnished by the elementary logic of predication. According to the textbook, simple attributive propositions have the pattern "Fa" ("F" standing for the predicate to an argument and "a" for a proper name), from which we obtain by existential generalization, "(∃x)Fx" (commonly transposed as "There is an object x such that x is F"). Now these simplistic concepts already founder on the attribution of properties of the generic type to individuals, which does much to reveal the interest inherent in a logic of transcendentals. Wittgenstein notes the oddity in Russell's transcription of the ordinary sentence *I met a man*.[18] According to Russell the logical form of this proposition is:

There is an x such that I met x and x is a man.

This reading is open to challenge on two counts. First, it includes as an element of the conjunction the strange declaration *x is a man*. But the predicate *man* is not used like this, to assign a property to an individual, except in very particular circumstances. Only in textbook logic do we find *Socrates is a man*. This sentence is actually absurd. *Socrates* is a man's name, at least in its most common acceptation, and barring special circumstances it will already have been understood that Socrates is a particular human being prior to any assignation of an authentic predicate such as *a philosopher, bald, in bed,* or whatever. To understand the proper name *Socrates*, you have to understand that it is a proper name. To understand this, you have to understand that it refers to a particular individual, and to understand this reference, you have to know how this individual can be identified in accordance with his genus. If Socrates is the philosopher's name, then this name, used in the same sense, must designate the same man. (Thus *x is a man* is plausible only when there is doubt: what you saw was not a statue, or a robot, or a god, but a man.) The properties that define the kind of thing an individual is cannot be attributed by the scheme "Fa" (or "a is F").[19]

Second, the use of the letter "x" remains unexplained in the logician's works. According to Russell, the sentence *There is not a human being on this island* should be transposed as:

There is not an x such that x is a human being on this island.

This notation, says Wittgenstein, suggests that we review one by one all the things on the island until we reach the conclusion that none of these is a human being. Such a review is manifestly impossible. Where shall we begin? How shall we know whether we have already inspected *this thing*? And if we cannot know this, how shall we know what we meant to designate when we said *this thing*? The flaw in Russell's transcription is thus to regard the concept of thing as a generic concept, and the generic concept in its turn as a property that might be attributed after thorough scrutiny to an individual already identified elsewhere. The concept of thing is not generic, however, since it does not provide any criterion of identity.[20] And the generic concept is not that of a property that might be discovered to belong to an individual, since an individual is identifiable only with regard to its genus.

It is not uncommon to consider ontology (or the science of the being of being and the thinghood of things) as an outworn illusion. To call it outworn or superseded seems premature. This is why transcendental philosophy is at present interesting as a means of proceeding to the reduction of ontological propositions.

4

The Grammatical Reduction of Ontological Propositions

The Problem of Reduction in Philosophy

Several programs of reduction are known in philosophy. The most famous is doubtless the *nominalist* reduction of uselessly postulated entities to indispensable entities alone; it is the reduction of universals to names, that is, the reduction of all words to names.[1] *Entia non sunt multiplicanda praeter necessitatem*. Although we speak of multiplying or reducing the number of beings or at least of classes of beings that must be admitted in order to account for the meaning we attach to our signs, these operations, strangely, are performed without fertilization or contamination by reality itself. Ockham is not Malthus.

More recently, the phenomenological reduction was defined as a reduction to the effectively given, the absolutely present. By virtue of Husserl's "principle of principles," everything that offers itself "in flesh and blood" by means of a perceptual presence in consciousness must be received just as it is given and understood to be exactly as it is given within the strict limits of this perception.[2] The phenomenological reduction and the empiricist reduction of the "content of experience" to "immediate sensory data" are only variations on the great *epistemological* reduction of modern philosophy: the reduction of science to method and of the thing to its donation within experience.

Earlier, however, we sketched out the program for a third kind of reduction: the reduction of grammatically misleading turns of phrase (misleading because of their appearance of incongruity) to overtly congruous phrases. This reduction is not based upon the nominalist assumption that all words are names, any more than it is based upon the epistemological decision that only what is given beyond doubt may be considered effectively given. When we speak of "philosophy of language" as a well-constituted specialism, we affect belief in a single thought line running through contemporary philosophy. In reality, this denomination is an umbrella for highly divergent undertakings. What distinguishes them from one another is the type of reduction attempted in each: nominalist, epistemological, or grammatical. It is true that the semblance of a common goal is created by the tactical alliances formed between one school and another; between, say, nominalism and empiricism. But the grammatical program is as alien to the intentions of fundamental epistemology (epistemology as heir to ontology) as it is incompatible with the postulates of nominalism. Its earliest model is to be found in Aristotle, for whom the Platonic theory of forms is not so much an erroneous doctrine as a misleading manner of speaking, calling for reduction rather than refutation: "But to say that the ideas are patterns and that other things participate in them is to use empty words and poetical metaphors" (*Metaphysics*, $3.991^{a}.20–22$). The Platonic manner of speaking is inadmissible because it obliges us to say what we may not understand in order to say what we mean. We may be trying to say that Socrates is a man. We certainly do not mean that Socrates is the only man, or that he is only a man, or that he is what all men are, namely a man. Platonic turns of phrase enable us to avoid such awkwardness, but only at the price of this theory of Models whereby we are to understand the meaning of our predications. Aristotle's critique says in effect that the Platonic manner is acceptable provided it is viewed in spite of itself merely as a metaphor rather than as an illuminating theory. *Socrates shares in Man* is acceptable so long as this working means simply that *Socrates is a man*. We have come full circle, and it only remains to concede that *man* in this sentence means whatever the sentence says that Socrates is (but not a Model, a "one man" that Socrates is not).

Our aim is not to reduce certain things to other, less contestable ones (universals to individuals), nor derived objects to primary ones (objects fully constituted in their subsistence and mutual order to immediate objects of the senses). We wish to reduce manners of speaking about something to other manners of speaking about something. While this reduction has a critical dimension, it is not negative. Its critical virtue is to eliminate the false impression of having said, in the sentence undergoing reduction, something other than the statement to which it is reduced.

Let us now consider various philosophical propositions about the object. Grammatical reduction has a powerful critical potential in this respect. But it is already apparent that it does not constitute in itself a critique of the language of philosophy, but rather—and this is different—constitutes a philosophical critique of language. The kind of examination we propose is foreign to the preconceptions of a "language of philosophy," let alone to those of a "*langue* of philosophy," whose use would forcibly impose upon philosophers various assumptions about identity or permanence. In any case, the critique of the "language of philosophy" tends to confine itself to problems of vocabulary, not to say etymology. It is the critique deployed by minds that have been shaped by translation, in particular the translation of ancient texts. It requires its followers to be quick on the dictionary. There the most common question is not, How could all this be said another way? Rather it is, Did the Greeks have a word for this? How would it go in German? We need only think of the endless debates over whether the word *being* exists in such and such a language, or about the great significance attached to its decline, along with other equally dangerous items (such as *subject, concept,* etc.). In schools where this mentality prevails, little time is spent on the problems of the construction of propositions. Yet the real difficulties arise not from words in isolation (from the fact that *subject* irresistibly suggests a hidden substratum or that *concept* always evokes some kind of grasp or purchase), but rather from particular uses of these words, in which the *modus significandi* remains elusive.

I shall now examine three discourses: first, upon the object in general, second upon the object of consciousness, and third upon the object of knowledge.

The Ontology of the Object in General

Transcendental philosophy is the study of the grammar of terms endowed with a transcendental function in language. As we have seen, the word *object* has this function when it is used as the equivalent of *something, aliquid, etwas, quelque chose,* and so forth.

Now ontology has been defined as the science of the object or the being. What object? Any whatever, since ontology considers only the quality of objectivity. It does not study what is (being) but examines the properties of what is taken as such, in its being as being. Thus there is something to be said about the object as such—namely that it is an object. There is something to be said about the being as such, namely that it is a being. This is the founding axiom of all ontology. The problem is now, What is predicated of the object by saying that it is an object (or that it is objective)? What are the ontological properties of the object?

It is this sense of the object that gives rise to Leibniz's question: Why is there something rather than nothing? To ask this is to admit that there is something to be said about something. "For Nothing is simpler and easier than Something" (*The Principles of Nature and Grace,* 7). That there should be something leads in itself to a question (Why?) and to a conclusion (because there is a necessary Being).

Our first access to the goal of ontology is thus to see it as the study of the property necessarily possessed by whatever is not nothing—a property denied to whatever is nothing. Ontology is the study of being and nothingness. This is indeed how the discipline was introduced by those who initially formulated or adopted the word *ontology*, which, however hellenized, is not Greek. In this sense, ontology is a recent field, and one Aristotle had proscribed when he wrote: "And, since being [*to on*] is not a genus, it [*being, to enai*] is not the essence [*ousia*] of anything."[3] According to Aristotle, being (in the sense of what we say of a thing by saying *it is*) is not part of what the thing in question is (of its *ousia*, its essence or substance), because there is no genus of things that are (opposable to the genus of things that are not). There is no genus of being as there is a human genus. Nor, therefore, is there a property of being (of beingness or beinghood) attributable to the thing of which one says *it is*. That a thing should be does not, for Aristotle, amount to a property belonging to that thing.

To ascertain whether there is a transcendental property attributed to any object whatever by virtue of referring to it as an object, we may start from Wittgenstein's question: "Does it, for example, make sense to say 'a, b and c are three objects'?"[4] Is it possible to view what are simply objects and distinguish them as object a, object b, which is also an object but not the same as object a, and yet another object, c? Do these objects, taken together in this way, have any transcendental properties? It might, for instance, be said that each object is the same as itself (it has identity with itself), but each is other than the others (it has difference from the other). These properties are lacking in whatever is nothing: nothing is distinct from nothing because nothing is identical to nothing. We have thus defined *idem* and *diversum*, two ontological properties that belong inevitably to anything whatever and that we know a priori to be verified.

All this reasoning is worthless, for it is impossible for anything to be "simply an object"—precisely because here the word *object* has a transcendental rather than a predicamental meaning. It is conceivable only if we are mistaken about the concept of number, another transcendental term. We imagine that number is a property of a set, so that we might say that in the set defined by the enumeration "a, b, c" the set totals three elements. Hence the illusion of further properties where all properties have been dismissed. Since I have not mentioned any property, my objects are whatever they may be. But since they are grouped into a set that is a set of objects, they are objects possessing objectivity, which allows the possibility of identicality to themselves and distinction from one another. It is, however, a mistake to assume that a set may be defined by a list of its component members.[5] A set is not a collection, or an assembly, or a grouping. The word *class* as used in mathematics encourages this misapprehension. Class CII at the Charlemagne School can be defined by the list of its elements (the pupils) because this class is a collection. *Class CII* denotes not a set, but a complex concrete object made up of *pupil* objects that do possess a common property: they have been registered in such a way as to belong in the same classroom. Objects a, b, and c in Wittgenstein's example can likewise form a set (assuming that the names "a," "b," and "c" represent objects) if it is agreed that I have drawn up a list, for whatever purpose, in which certain names feature together. There is a confusion here between two operations: first I compose a list grouping certain names on a piece of paper; this sequence of names is a collection, that is, a complex object (name "a" heading the list, then "b" one line below, and "c" one line below that). This by no means constitutes a set. Next I can consider the list: it is made up of written names. Only now do I have a set of written objects. Suppose it is a guest list for a party. We might easily confuse the gathering of guests and the set of guests, but not so easily the set of people who—much to their displeasure—were not invited and a gathering of those people in a protest meeting outside the host's windows.

There is no point in hunting for what might be said of something about which nothing has yet been said. There is no concept of the object in general. Each time we think we have found one, each time we make intelligible use of the phrase *an object whatever it may be*, the transcendental term will have been replaced by a predicamental term; for example, that of a material body endowed with a certain physical homogeneity: a game of French bowls is one object if the bowls are all in the box, and three objects if they are separate. The illusion of a "transcendental object" in classical ontology is the belief in a significant use of the formula *something* $= x$—a powerful formula, in which abstraction adopts a quasi-algebraic precision. In this text, for example:

All our representations are, it is true, referred by the understanding to some object [*auf irgendein Objekt*]; and since appearances are nothing but representations, the understanding refers them to a *something* [*ein Etwas*], as the object [*der Gegenstand*] of sensible intuition. But this something [*dieses Etwas*], thus conceived, is only the transcendental object [*das transzendentale Objekt*]; and by that is meant a something $= x$, of which we know, and with the present constitution of our understanding can know, nothing whatever.[6]

What does the letter "x" correspond to, and the sign "$=$"? The letter "x" is certainly not the symbol of a variable, as it would be in a function equation, precisely since it cannot be given a determinate value so that, on the other side of the equation sign, we could substitute for the word *Etwas* (something) some appropriate description or the name of a transcendental object. This pseudoequation thus invites us to identify the transcendental object with what we do not know, with we know not what. But since *we know not what* eludes all possible identification, nothing can be equated with it. It might be said that the formula is designed to drive home this very failure: the impossibility of saying what the transcendental object is; of equating it with anything whatever. The transcendental object is not something (i.e., one thing or another, a thing of one kind or another). But then the transcendental object is not "something = x," but rather "x = not something." We do not know what it is.

The formula *something in general* = x springs from the same philosophical teratology as Locke's definition of substance: the *we know not what* that we invoke as the support of visible accidents.[7] Substance, for Locke, is the ultimate indeterminate support: just as the world rests upon the elephant, which rests upon the tortoise, which rests upon we know not what, so accidents are supported by we know not what.[8] Indeed, Kant takes up this reasoning and endows it with a "transcendental" value: "It has long since been noticed that in all substances the subject proper, namely what is left over after all accidents (as predicates) have been taken away and hence the *substantial* itself, is unknown to us."[9] But a word that means I know not what is a word whose meaning I do not know. It does not mean *something, but we know not what.* It means, *we know not what thing.* In other words it means nothing.[10] Consequently, the transcendental object is not something, but something unknown. We should say instead that *transcendental object* is a phrase to which no meaning has been allocated.

It is striking that the paradoxes of classical ontology are so often exposed by the presence of an equation sign in its attempts at formulation. *Something* = x is as meaningless as the notorious "principle of identity," or A = A. Not only is the equation of A with A posited quite without any criterion of identification; worse, we are not told how to interpret the letter "A" (as a proposition? a predicate? a name?). Classical ontology and transcendental epistemology share the assumption that it is sufficient to equip oneself with a mental correlate in order to identify this as the "intended," the vis-à-vis, or in Husserl's words, "it the object, it the selfsame, it the x taken in abstraction from its predicates."

The Ontology of the Object of Consciousness

Another way of understanding the word *object* in the ontology of modern philosophy is embodied in the adage of transcendental idealism: *no object without a subject.* The concept of object is far from being empty, incorporating as it does an essential relationship not only to thought but also to the subject of thought. There cannot be any knowledge of the correlative object of thought, this logically possible object. This does not, however, apply to the correlative object of a thought referred back to the thinker.

Now this subject can be understood as the subject of consciousness (based on the *cogito*) or as the subject of knowledge (based on the *I think* that accompanies all my representations). The first sense—the object is the object of the subject of consciousness—is the broader. It is found in Husserl's expression of the intentionality of consciousness. We read in the *Fifth Logical Investigation*: "In perception something is perceived, in imagination, something imagined, in a statement, something stated, in love something loved, in hate hated, in desire desired, etc."[11] A comparable series of examples is to be found in *Ideas*:

> We understood by intentionality the unique peculiarity of experiences "to be the consciousness *of* something" [*Bewusstsein* von *etwas zu sein*]. . . . Perceiving is the perceiving of something [*etwas*], maybe a thing [*Ding*]; judging, the judging of a certain matter [*Sachverhalt*]; valuation, the valuing of a value; wish, the wish for the content wished, and so on. Acting concerns action, doing concerns the deed, loving, the beloved, joy, the object of joy.[12]

Thus the object is equivalent to *something*, as in the phrase, *all consciousness is consciousness of something.* On each occasion we are to consider as the object of consciousness whatever will replace the indefinite *something* (*etwas*). The perceiving consciousness is consciousness of something perceived, the imagining consciousness is consciousness of something imagined. The judging, the evaluating, or the loving consciousness is consciousness of something judged, evaluated, or loved. The doing consciousness is a consciousness of something to be done. If we are more explicit we shall bring to light the differences between these various types of consciousness. The perceiving consciousness is the consciousness of something perceived, perhaps a thing: a house, or an apple tree in bloom. The judging consciousness is the consciousness of something judged; namely a state of affairs. These differences between forms of consciousness and types of corresponding object are in every instance respectful of the correspondence itself, the correlation of the object and of consciousness. Therefore we can say what the object in general is: it is the correlative object,[13] the perceived of a perception, the wished of a wish, the loved object of love.

Unfortunately this correlative object is only a bad dream of language. It is quite impossible to form a concept of object such that it would enable us to speak unequivocally of the object perceived, imagined, loved, evaluated, or done. The invention of such an object is in no way a discovery made by dint of purely descriptive research taken to greater lengths, as Husserl rashly suggests in *Cartesian Meditations*.[14] It is a philosophical construction, which is to say a postulate entertained by phenomenologists so as to preserve their right to speak of the correlation of two terms, consciousness and the object of consciousness. Using this construction, it is certainly possible to say that consciousness as a kind of knowing must be understood as a relation between what is meant by *ego cogito* and what is meant by the corresponding *cogitatum* in the canonic formula of phenomenology: *ego cogito cogitatum*.[15] But all this is merely a construction, for the general thesis of correlation coheres only provided abstraction is made of examples or applications. The examples advanced by Husserl are not really applications of *all consciousness is consciousness of something* but are plain, familiar turns of phrase marshaled together so that we may distill the notions of a consciousness in general intending an object in general. We fancy that we understand *all consciousness is consciousness of something* because we think that the phrase says nothing beyond what we readily grasp in the examples. The phenomenological dictum appears to state in general what the examples show in particular cases. The fact is, however, that what we grasp from the examples does not apply to the dictum in general.

In each example we understand a grammatical construction. Each illustrates a rule of grammar. This is more striking in the passage from *Ideas* quoted above, for there Husserl uses articular infinitives, hard to render in translation: "a to perceive" (*ein Wahrnehmen*), "a to judge" (*ein Urteilen*), "a to evaluate" (*ein Werten*), and so on. Then we have nominal infinitives: *to act, to do, to love*. But *a to perceive* equals *a perception*. In other words, the abstract nouns that feature in the text of the *Fifth Logical Investigation* mentioned above are also verb derivatives. We understand all these examples, therefore, only because we grasp their grammar and are able to revert to the corresponding verb. Between *in perception something is perceived* and *a to perceive is a to perceive of something*, the sole difference resides in the manner of signifying. The *modus significandi* may differ, but it is neutral with respect to what is signified. The corresponding turn of phrase that best expresses the *modus essendi* should of course contain the verb in verbal form: *If one perceives, one perceives something*. What is the value of this statement? Needless to say, the point here is one of grammar, not psychology of perception (although a psychology that ignored this point of grammar, persisting in its use of the verb *to perceive*, would be absurd or unintelligible). It amounts to saying, the verb *to perceive* is transitive and requires a direct object. The same applies not only to the other verbs listed by Husserl, but also to the Latin *cogitare* and the idioms whereby we express the Cartesian *cogitatio* in living languages: *to be conscious of, to have consciousness of*, and so on. So long as we leave it at that, thought or consciousness is merely one grammatical example among others: the verb *cogitare* requires a *cogitatum* just as the verb *to perceive* requires a *perceived*. All these verbs need a direct object or (as Ryle put it when, in 1932, he introduced British philosophers to phenomenology) an "*accusative*."[16] This term, noted Ryle, is more helpful than either object or *Gegenstand* because it removes the temptation to think of a subject of attribution, an entity, unequivocally presenting an *object-of. . . . Accusative* is clearly a grammarian's term—another appreciable advantage. There is, however, one serious snag, which is the possible suggestion, contrary to Ryle's intentions, that the direct object must be a noun— which would exclude complementation by an infinitive or a subordinate clause.

Husserl loses sight of the fact that transitive verbs do not form a homogeneous class. Some of the verbs he cites can take several constructions, others only one. If we look at these examples, we will see that they fall into three classes.

1. Certain verbs take a noun or pronoun as their direct object: *to perceive, to love*, and *to hate*, for instance.
2. Others find their complement only in a completive proposition. For instance, *to declare, to judge, to wish, to contrive, to be glad, to desire*.
3. Others, finally, appear to take both constructions: *to imagine*, for instance, and also *to consider*.

The existence of this third class seems to cast doubt on the wisdom of the classification, which now becomes purely idiomatic. Furthermore, it is easy to find uses of verbs in the first class where something other than a noun is the complement: *I love traveling, I love to hear you say that*. But the crux of the problem is whether the difference in grammatical construction reveals a logical (and not merely an idiomatic) difference in meaning. Let us look at the second class. To declare is to declare that; I cannot declare Peter or Paul. To judge is to judge that. The word *judge* in *I judge Paul* clearly has a different meaning than it has in *I judge that Paul is the man we're looking for*. We cannot say that a judgment and an object of judgment exist in each case. When I judge Paul, I bring a judgment (whether just or unjust) to bear on Paul, who is therefore the object of judgment. When I judge that Paul is the man we're looking for, what I judge is not Paul, but rather that he is our man. I cannot be of the opinion that Paul; nor can I condemn or approve that Paul is the man we're looking for. In one, *to judge* has the sense—and therefore the grammar—of *to hold the opinion that*; in the other it has the sense—and therefore the grammar—of *to condemn*. There is only a relation between myself and the object in the second sense. *To wish* is clearly *to wish that*. ... *To contrive* is *to contrive that*. ... *And yet we can contrive a meeting*, or *contrive a solution*. True, but we must not be led astray by the superficial grammar, which in this case encourages us to see some relation in "contrivance" between a contriving subject and an object that is contrived. This is the relation we find in *to chop wood*: when someone chops wood, there is wood being chopped by someone. If someone contrives a meeting, there is not a meeting being contrived by someone, because the agent in this case is not in a relation to something, an object, the object of his contrivance. *To contrive a meeting* should be paraphrased not as:

For a certain thing x, I contrive this thing x

but as:

I contrive that, for a certain thing x, this thing x should be what I have contrived.

If to contrive a meeting were to enter into a relationship with a possible thing in order to bring it into existence, then the meeting would already be accomplished prior to any operation. It would suffice to unveil its existence, to make it public, to produce it in the world. To avoid this absurdity, one is sometimes tempted to make of the *operatio* a *creatio ex nihilo*, stressing that the result did not exist before it was produced. But this solution is equally deceptive, since the act of contriving or making something involves a relation not to the result itself, but to the material of which it is to be made (in contrivance, events are manipulated; in making, say, a pot, the clay is manipulated). Might it be possible to say that we distinguish two relations, that of the worker to the work he produces, and that of the same worker to the materials out of which it is produced? The worker's or agent's relation to this material is a physical, active one (the material is what the agent manipulates to obtain his result). The relation of the agent to his goal is intentional, teleological; it is his relation to that possible outcome which gives meaning to the first relation. So there are two correlations, one linking the agent to the object that is the material, the other linking the intelligent agent to the object that is the possible result or work. But what indeed is this object that we can identify as the possible work? The worker can have a relation only to individuals. But the possible work is precisely not a possible individual; it is the possibility of an individual (namely the possibility of an individual derived from the material). There is a possible work because it is possible to transform this (individuated) material, to make something of it. The possible work is not one that lacks only the final touch or the ultimate precision—the "actualization," as they say. The possible work is nothing at all. There is only the material with its possibilities of transformation, and the doer with his skills; there is nothing that could be described as the result the agent might contrive. There is a more or less capable worker, and a more or less malleable material. (In the wake of Heidegger,[17] lengthy debates have ensued about the relevance of concepts of form and matter to the apprehension of works, especially works of art. I do not consider these controversies to have been very enlightening, since they omit to posit the problem of individuation, or of identification, which arises out of any discourse on the process of becoming, or production.)

Similar observations apply to the verb *to appreciate*. We do not find the same grammar in *appreciating someone, appreciating travel,* and *appreciating that. . . . Appreciating that* is always *understanding that* (in the sense of understanding a handicap). This kind of appreciation is expressed in a judgment, whereas appreciation of a person may influence the judgment we make about him or her but does not find expression in a judgment. *To appreciate traveling* is to appreciate the activity in general; no particular journey is intended here. However, to appreciate a person involves a relation to some individual, at least in intentional terms. To say that all appreciation or love pertains to a beloved amounts here to positing that love is signified by a relative term. Saint Augustine's famous *Nondum amabam et amare amabam* ("I was not yet in love, yet I was in love with love," *Confessions* 3.1.1), clearly shows that the verb *to love* has two different meanings according to the construction. If this were not so, Augustine would already have found an object of love when, loving no one, he loved love.

The fake ontology of intentionality maintains that all love is love of a beloved. If Augustine's beloved is love, then he is wrong to say that he lacks something to love. For he goes on, *Quaerebam quid amarem, amans amare* ("I sought something to love, in love with love"), thus demonstrating that for him love is not a suitable object of love.

The transcendental word *object*, in crossing predicamental boundaries with such ease, preserves none of the important logical differences that make of the construction with a nominal direct object and the completive construction two distinct logical categories. We can quite well say: all love is love of something, all belief is belief in something. There is thus an object of love and an object of belief—but are these the same type of object? Phenomenology would classify them as different species of object that nevertheless share a crucial property: correlativity, the fact of being the object with which a consciousness is in relation. Let us now look more closely. In love, something is loved, and this object of love may equally well be the object of hate. The same kind of object (an object of the same genus), indeed the very same object, can "correspond" to these feelings. If I love something, then something is loved. Suppose that a declaration of love turns out to be false. I said *I love you,* but in reality *I don't love you.* The negation of love is not hate but indifference: *I can't stand you* grants more than *I don't love you.* There is a logical difference between these nuances in our feeings. If I love something, then something is loved; if I do not love something, something is not loved, which is not to say that it is hated. Now if there is something I love, that thing is the object of my love. But the negation of this is not *there is not something I love,* but *there is something I do not love.* For *I don't like anything* is stronger than *I don't like everything.* If we turn now to the verb *to believe,* we shall soon realize that its grammar is very different. In belief, something is believed. To believe is to believe something. An object of belief is hereby introduced, and since all belief has an object of belief, we might assume a correlation of the believing consciousness with the object believed. But can belief be analyzed through a relation of the believer to the object, as of the lover to the beloved? Suppose a given profession of belief were to be a lie—that the alleged believer claiming to believe something is an unbeliever who believes no such thing. Are we to say that a certain object is believed by the believer while it is not believed by the unbeliever? We should indeed be obliged to, if we sought to establish a relation here between a consciousness and an object. If I believe something, something is believed. For instance, I believe that things will sort themselves out. What if I do not believe this? I do not become indifferent (as in the case of *I do not love*) but unbelieving. If I do not believe that things will sort themselves out, then I believe that they will not sort themselves out. To say that *I believe neither one nor the other* says more than simply *I do not believe it.* If I do not believe this thing, I believe its negation. Don Juan can say, I don't love Mathurine, I love Charlotte. But Charlotte is not the negation of Mathurine, and if Don Juan does not love Mathurine, this is not sufficient to make him the lover of Charlotte. This is why he can get away with loving both. The unbeliever, on the other hand, is not in a position to believe one thing (that better days will come) and also another thing (that they will not come).

In short, the correlation to be found between love and the object of love is such that two attitudes or relations are possible with regard to this object: to love or to hate. The negation of the existence of either of these is the assertion of the absence of relation, or indifference. Between belief and the object of belief, the correlation is such that the absence of this "relation" to the (propositional) "object" is the existence of the very same "relation" toward another "object," namely the negation of the first "object." The attempt to construe belief or unbelief as a relation is, finally, a futile endeavor. No sooner do we erect belief into a relation to something or someone than we obtain something else: faith. For we can say: *I believe you, I do not believe you*—two opposite relations to a single object, just as we saw earlier with love and hate. Here, then, is another verb whose grammar requires a nominal or pronominal object. Such a verb signifies a particular kind of relation—the relation between the person who loves or believes (has faith in) and the person he or she loves or believes. To love is a certain correlation, or at least relation, between individuals who can be named or at least denoted, whereas the verb requiring a completive signifies something altogether different from a correlation to a special object. It invokes the state of things. It is not a correlation with some other kind of object, for it is not a correlation at all. Let us suppose that the verb *to believe (that)* establishes a relation between one term (the *ego* of intentional consciousness) and another (the correlative object, in this case a state of things). If a relation really exists, it should be possible to say between what and what. On one side of the relation, we find someone: the subject of consciousness. On the other side, we require an object. Someone says *I believe (that) it's going to be fine*. The object of this relation must then be the state of affairs *(that) it's going to be fine*. Is it legitimate to treat this nominalization *(that) it's going to be fine* as a designation, as a way of denoting something? Assuming that it is, let us give this object a name, always with the proviso that it will have the same reference *(Bedeutung)* as the designation *(that) it's going to be fine*. We shall call it Hector. Now, since to believe is always to believe something, it might be *to believe Hector*. Where the object of belief is Hector, there will be a particular relation between the believer and Hector. Not to believe is a contrary relation to the same object. The unbeliever who disbelieves what our believer believes has an inverse relation to the same object: what for the believer is an object of belief is an object of disbelief for the nonbeliever, who does not believe Hector . . . but all this is pure verbiage, for the expressions *to believe Hector* or *not to believe Hector* already have meaning in the language, as we have seen. He who believes that it is going to be fine does not have faith in *that it is going to be fine*. It is grammatically impossible to make of the belief that . . . a relation to an object, since any attempt to signify this relation inevitably borrows the grammar of verbs taking a nominal object, with the result that we say something other than what we meant. It transpires that we do not know what we meant by a relation of belief to an object of belief. Another aspect of this impossibility: the unbeliever who does not think that it is going to be fine does not fail to be in a relationship of belief to Hector (just as Don Juan, ceasing to love Dona Elvira, is not automatically drawn to hate her). The unbeliever is not without relation to Hector, for he believes that Hector is false. To express this, he must be placed in a relation of belief to another object (that it will not be fine). We should have to call this object not-Hector. But it is nonsense to apply the negative to names.[18] All efforts to find some relation, not to say correlation, which this class of verbs might signify, are doomed to failure. There are beliefs and there are things believed, but there is no object of belief or any relation to be sought between a believing consciousness and a thing believed.

These grammatical observations throw light upon the difference between *loving* and *desiring*. The verb *to love* takes a nominal or pronominal object wherever it signifies the feeling of love. Once the loved one has been named, there is nothing more to say. *To desire* is not employed in this way, for although we can say we feel a desire for someone, nothing has been said until we specify what would satisfy this desire, and to this end it is not enough to name the person. I feel a desire for someone, but what do I desire? (That he should pass his exams? Submit to my whim? Go to the devil?) *To desire* calls for a completive clause: *I desire that*. There is a relation between lover and beloved, but none between desirer and desired. There is no relation to what is known as the "object of desire." This object cannot be designated; it must be spoken, as is unmistakably clear in the everyday use of the phrase *object of desire*. The object of desire may perhaps be someone else's cooperation, but not the actual person. For such cooperation might come from whomever is willing to grant it: in that case no specific person, *him* or *her*, can be identified as the object of desire. Theories of desire tend to overlook the fact that the object of desire belongs to the order of the sayable (and of the unsayable), not to that of the nameable (or the unnameable) in the sense of naming an individual by a proper name. They evoke the object of desire as if it were divorced from any verb. We are told, for example, that the first object of desire is the mother's breast (although in fact the first desire is that the mother should offer the breast). More sophisticated doctrines hold that desire reaches toward desire. In the words of Hegel's adage, often cited by neo-Hegelians, desire is *desire of the desire of the other*. Grammar obliges us to paraphrase this genitive by a completive clause: for instance, we desire that the other should desire our presence. Or we desire that the other should desire to possess what we have, to become what we are. A very different example would be to desire that the other's desire should be fulfilled. Suppose the other desires to be rich. According to the first construction, I desire to be rich myself because the other desires it. According to the second, I desire that the other should grow rich (which is indeed the only way I can literally desire what he desires). In any event, the important point is that no denotable object (individual) can ever be appended to the subject's desire (to the verb *to desire*) by the "desire of desire."

Let us now examine the grammar of the word *consciousness*. This abstract noun is understood to be another way of saying what could be said by using a verb phrase incorporating the verb *to know* (French *savoir*, Latin *scire*) or an equivalent. Now the French verb *savoir* clearly belongs to the class of verbs that are to be completed by a propositional clause. One may *savoir que Pierre est là* (*be aware that Pierre is there*), but not *savoir Pierre* (*be aware of Pierre*). The French verb *connaître*, despite appearances, is actually a member of the class of verbs that takes a completive: for the sense in which *connaître* can be followed by a name is always one in which certain relations are invoked. For instance, *Je connais Pierre* implies that I have had relations with him. But I could not say *Je connais que Pierre est là*, since Pierre's presence is not an object with which I could entertain relations (when Pierre is there, it is not Pierre's presence that is there).

The first consequence of this is that verbs which take a nominal object are not forms of consciousness—are not, in idealist jargon, "consciousnesses." Love is not a form of consciousness, precisely because I love someone. On the other hand, I may or may not be conscious of loving someone. Likewise, to recognize someone is not a form of consciousness: consciousness would be to recognize that it is he. And to see something is not a consciousness, and there is no consciousness of the house before me or of the apple tree in bloom in the garden. No one can be conscious of an apple tree in bloom in the garden, because the paraphrase of such a "consciousness of the object" is "I know that I the apple tree in bloom." A verb is missing from the completive clause. Because it is unfinished, an object—a direct object—is missing from the alleged consciousness of a blossoming apple tree in the garden. But I can, of course, be conscious of seeing this famous apple tree, because it is possible to say *I know that I see the apple tree.*

The "consciousness of the apple tree in bloom" of phenomenology is philosophically barbaric. Let me emphasize the point of this remark. It is not to contest one psychological theory in favor of another. No precise thesis is being disputed or amended here, no criticism leveled at phenomenology for endowing man with too much lucidity and mastery, overlooking drives or energies, ignoring social conditioning, overplaying this and underplaying that. We are all too familiar with such demystificatory critiques. Often fascinatingly ingenious in certain applications, they are not the most philosophically trenchant. The critique of false consciousness leads to the proliferation of occasions for uncertainty (the meaning consciousness claims to find can always be the wrong one, merely a screen obscuring the true meaning). Thus it has a profoundly clerical effect, persuading us to mistrust ourselves when we carry out our own examinations of consciousness. The more we internalize the possibility of false consciousness, the more we depend on our spiritual tutors. Its philosophical effect, meanwhile, is limited. Wittgenstein's critique of consciousness has no clerical effect. But it is philosophically weighty, denying as it does the existence of any phenomenological thesis. Wittgenstein claims that no such thesis has yet been stated, and so there is nothing (yet) to discuss. A Cartesian spirit persisted in the demystificatory critique, in that it aroused fresh doubts. The phenomenologist lacks the means to distinguish between authentic and false consciousness. We can never tell whether this or that was indeed what we wanted, sought, desired. To doubt relies upon the appearance, at least, of knowledge—yet none of us knows the object of our will, no one is conscious of the apple tree in bloom. This is not a fine psychological point, but a comprehensive grammatical point.

A correct expression of the intentionality of our acts, therefore, should not be ontological but grammatical: their common factor is to be signified by verbs, all of which require a direct object. The transcendental term *something* (*etwas*) stands for this object, which will sometimes be a name, sometimes a proposition, sometimes a predicate (*I like traveling, I like red*, etc.). The phenomenological dictum says nothing more than this:

All consciousness is consciousness of a direct object.

Strange dictum indeed, if viewed as anything other than an auxiliary formula whereby the philosopher indicates that certain expressions require a direct object. It does not mean: "all consciousness is consciousness of something = x, and formal ontology sets out the properties of this object to be derived from the correlativity of any object possible for consciousness." Rather, the formula should be interpreted as follows: "a consciousness is consciousness of (insert here a direct object)."

All consciousness is consciousness of something makes good sense, provided it is seen as a comment upon the verb *to know* or the predicative locutions *to be conscious, to be aware, to realize* (and even, returning to the conspiracy latent in the etymology of *conscientia, to be in the know*). The gist of this comment is that absolute use of these predicates (*x is conscious*) logically presupposes some transitive context in which the direct object features explicitly. This direct object necessarily adopts the form of a completive (*x is conscious that* . . .). The object of knowing is not some thing, an object, in the sense in which the knowing subject, by virtue of knowing, is projected onto something other than himself (the "other of consciousness," as idealists call it). In fact, having no relation to this other, the knowing subject is not even thrown into contact with an object that would be himself. Consciousness is not a relation to an object, even if the verb *to know* is associated with a grammatical object. By the same token, consciousness of self is not a relation of the subject of the verb *to know* to an object identical to it. It is not the relation to an other-than-oneself that is the same as that self, or to oneself posited as another, nor is it the identity (to oneself) declared through the mediation of difference (between subject and object), or difference (between oneself and the object) suppressing itself as difference.[19] The noun *consciousness of self* corresponds to those uses of the verb *to know* that assign the subject of the verb *to know* to the verb in the completive clause, as in *I know that I V* ("V" standing for an appropriate verb).

Taken by itself, the phrase *all consciousness is consciousness of something* emerges as incongruous or at least indeterminate. Yet it is likely to be invoked in an explanation of the necessity for a direct object. *All consciousness is consciousness of something,* just as *a soldier's feet are the object of something* when the training officer is testing the men on the handbook. (*Of what are a soldier's feet the object? Of his utmost care and attention.*) In both instances alike, an auxiliary formula inadequate in itself is successfully invoked to elicit completion of another sentence.

The Ontology of the Object of Knowledge

How are we to comprehend the Kantian concept of object? Let us consult the celebrated text that states what is usually called "the critical problem," in the Preface to the second edition of the *Critique of Pure Reason.*

Hitherto it had been assumed that all our knowledge must conform to objects. But all attempts to extend our knowledge of objects by establishing something in regard to them *a priori*, by means of concepts, have, on this assumption, ended in failure. We must therefore make trial whether we may not have more success in the tasks of metaphysics, if we suppose that objects must conform to our knowledge. This would agree better with what is desired, namely, that it should be possible to have knowledge of objects *a priori*, determining something in regard to them prior to their being given. (B16)

What are we to understand here by the word *object*? Dogmatically, it was assumed that consciousness should take its cue from objects, whereas the contrary hypothesis is envisaged here. But what are these objects? Does Kant mean objects of knowledge, or objects whose properties are known to us? Certainly not both, for they are separated by grammar. An object of knowledge is the grammatical complement of a phrase equivalent to *I know that*. This verb can be completed only by a proposition. Grammatically speaking, an object that we know and can identify is the designation of a thing to which the knowing subject has a relation enabling him to know it or to know something of it.

   Since Kant speaks of knowledge and object, we are initially tempted to interpret this as knowledge and its object. Here the object is the object of knowledge. According to this reading, Kant is positing the problem of the foundation of truth, nominally defined as "the agreement of knowledge with its object."[20] Knowledge is knowledge because it is true, and it is true if the proposition expressing it, whereby the knowing subject says what he knows, is in agreement with the object corresponding to this proposition. To take Aristotle's old example, *you are white* is a true statement if you are indeed white. Here, knowledge is knowledge of the fact that you are white; the corresponding object is (the fact) that you are white. The problem presented by Kant, then, concerns the foundation of this consonance of the true proposition with what is actually the case. But it is a problem that genuinely arises only with regard to a priori knowledge, and not in Aristotle's example. The agreement occurs either because the proposition derives its validity from the fact, or vice versa.

   We can express the two hypotheses on the foundation of knowledge as follows:

1. Dogmatic hypothesis: *You are white* is true if you are white; *the museum is open* is true if the museum is open. *Everything that happens has a cause* is true if everything that happens has a cause. Notice that on each occasion what is said would be false (if it were false) because the fact or the state of things alleged in the proposition would not be consonant with what is the case: because you are not white, because the museum is closed, because there are events without a cause.

2. Critical hypothesis: *You are white* is empirically true if the fact that you are white depends on the (transcendental) truth of the judgment *you are white*; *the museum is open* is true if the fact of its openness depends

on (or is based on) the truth of the judgment *the museum is open*. *Everything that happens has a cause* is true if the fact that everything has a cause depends on the truth of the synthetic a priori judgment which esteems that *everything that happens has a cause*. And if it were false, it would have to be so in each case because the object was not consonant with the judgment. Indeed the museum can open without someone's saying *the museum is open*, and it can remain shut in the face of that same statement. The same goes for the other examples. The critical hypothesis invites us, then, to distinguish empirical truth—that of the proposition corresponding to the fact—and transcendental truth: that of the proposition with which the fact itself must agree. Among the examples above, the first two lay no claim to transcendental truth. If it should happen that the fact of the museum opening depends upon the utterance of "the museum is open," this statement would have to be considered in a practical rather than a theoretical sense—an inaugural speech, or a command issued in the indicative. The causality principle, on the other hand, invests itself in Kant's view with transcendental truth, since that is the only truth to which it can lay claim.

Now the correspondence between the true proposition and the known thing is by no means a relation. If truth is defined as the consonance of the proposition (rather than of knowledge) and the thing, we should bear in mind that this consonance cannot be a relationship between a certain proposition and a certain thing, if by that we understand an identifiable individual. The *res* of *adaequatio intellectus et rei* is anything whatever, any topic of discourse whatever (in the sense of that which we speak about). There need not be something (this individual or that) embodying the *res* of which we speak. If I say that an automobile breakdown is the cause of my delay, the *res* I invoke as my excuse is the breakdown, and if my excuse is true, this is indeed the case, and the proposition will have stated matters as they stood. But it does not follow that there is a certain thing that is a breakdown; there is only a car that has stopped working. *Adaequatio* is not a relation, because we cannot specify between what and what it is supposed to be established. It is impossible to designate what should correspond *in rebus* to the proposition without simply repeating it. The proposition is true if it is consistent with what it says, or again if what it says is as it says it is. Hence the measure of disappointment we feel with the common explanation of the correspondence that *you are white* is true if you are white. Those who are unhappy with this were probably expecting some other means to indicate the *res* that corresponds to a discourse—evidence that they had taken this *res* for a thing that could be named.[21] But we must stand by Wittgenstein's

doctrine in *Tractatus*: the gulf between names and propositions cannot
be bridged. Propositions do not designate; they describe. Names designate but do not describe. What can be named cannot be described. What
can be described cannot be named.

   Up until now our reading of this passage, in search of the propositional
object, has remained consistent. We are concerned not—once again—
with Kant's solution to the problem he raises, but with the very statement
of the problem ("the problem of pure reason"). It may be understood
that the objects of knowledge, for the examples given earlier, are: the fact
of the museum being open (but not the museum), the fact that events
have a cause (but no particular event), and the fact that you are white
(but not yourself in person). Not only is this reading possible, it is
required by what the text proposes. Individual objects cannot be aligned
to propositions. The fact that the museum is open can agree with *the
museum is open*; but the museum cannot. Both hypotheses, the dogmatic
and the critical alike, have a bearing on the meaning of a consonance
between a proposition and a fact. We can say that the proposition *the
museum is open* is true because the museum is open. But what follows the
conjunction *because* in that sentence is precisely that with which knowledge agrees in the realist hypothesis, namely the object. The known
object cannot therefore be the museum, because the substitution, *salva
congruitate*, cannot be made, any more than in the dogmatic hypothesis:
It is true that the museum is open because the museum, or in the critical:
The museum because the museum is open. We can say, *This event has a
cause because it is transcendentally true that all events have a cause*. Here
we cannot substitute *this event* for *this event has a cause*. We might want
to put things another way and say that *the museum is open* is true by
virtue of the museum. But either this form of expression differs merely
by its *modus significandi* from the more legitimate form (*by virtue of the
museum* being a way of saying by virtue of what the museum is), or else it
alters something in order to maintain a philosophical pseudothesis,
accurately paraphrased in the illegitimate construction above.

   The following result has been obtained: knowledge is what is
expressed in a judgment, and a priori knowledge of objects is expressed
in a priori synthetic judgments. Known objects are propositional. The
object whose principle of causality expresses knowledge is *that there are
causes for everything that happens*. The dogmatic hypothesis holds that
the principle is true because such is the case; the critical hypothesis
maintains that such is the case because the principle is true.

   This result must be extended to the justifying principle of a priori
synthetic judgments: "The conditions of the *possibility of experience* in
general are likewise conditions of the *possibility of the objects of experi-*

ence, and for this reason they have objective validity in a synthetic *a priori* judgment."[22] The objects of experience are objects of knowledge—facts.

Perhaps, but the alternative sense of the word *object*, meaning the reference of a singular designative term, is certainly necessitated by other passages in Kant's work. The Introduction to the *Critique* contains an example designed to illustrate the difference between a priori judgments and judgments of experience: "Thus we would say of a man who undermined the foundations of his house, that he might have known *a priori* that it would fall, that is, he need not have waited for the experience of its actual falling. But still he could not know this completely *a priori*. For he had first to learn through experience that bodies are heavy and therefore fall when their supports are withdrawn."[23]

What are the objects here? They are of two kinds. The scatterbrain in this example was unable to know something in advance. The object that he could not know was *that the house would collapse if its foundations were undermined*. To say that he might have known (this object) a priori means that he had no need to undergo this particular experience since it was predictable. Here Kant evokes objects of knowledge: we say that he might have known a priori (*er Konnte Es a priori wissen, DASS es einfallen würde* = he might well have known *it* in advance, *that the house would collapse*); and yet he could not have known this (*dieses*) a priori. It is something he could learn from his first experience of heavy bodies. Thus the proposition *bodies are heavy* is empirical, and therefore synthetic. But it is synthetic in that the predicate cannot be gleaned from the concept of body by applying the principle of contradiction. Kant again uses the word *object* to mean the individual about whom or about which judgments are being made. The concept that may or may not yield a predicate is the "concept of the object."[24] Analytic proposition: *This house is extended* (for it is a body). Synthetic proposition: *This house is heavy* (for it is a body that happens to be heavy).

In the first concept of object, the object is what the proposition says. In the second concept it is the house itself. The first case holds a known object to be that which one knows (*that bodies are heavy*). The second case holds the known object to be that which one knows something about, that of which a predicate is true (the house, of which it is true that it is heavy).

We find that the word *object* is to be taken now in one sense, now in the other—a harmless oscillation, provided it is clear which one is intended.[25] But it becomes problematic when both readings are required simultaneously, as in our extract from the Preface. The earlier interpretation, according to which Kant speaks of knowledge and the object of knowledge, not of the object about which knowledge exists, can be upheld only if we ignore the opening lines: "Hitherto it has been assumed that all our knowledge must conform to objects. But all attempts to extend our knowledge of objects by establishing something in regard to them *a priori*, by means of concepts . . . have ended in failure." *In regard to them*—objects the dogmatic hypothesis takes as the standard from which knowledge derives its cue. These objects appear, indeed, as individuals.

Kant goes on to break down the critical hypothesis into two separate hypotheses, one concerning intuition and the object of the senses, the other concerning the concept and the object given within experience. Neither intuition nor the concept alone amounts to knowledge. These representations fall short of truth and therefore fail to furnish an object of knowledge (fact) with which the true proposition may be consonant. Earlier, it was possible to maintain that the object is the correlate of truth, in that there is some fact by virtue of which the proposition is true. We can no longer say that an object given in intuition is the fact that there is an object given in intuition (in the same way as the fact represented in *you are white* is the fact that you are white). The object given in intuition is the intuited object. Since for Kant, intuition is the immediate, singular representation of the object, the object of intuition must be the represented version of this representation: a house, for instance (or more exactly its facade). So when Kant ponders whether intuition agrees with the "constitution of the object" or whether it is the object that conforms to "the constitution of our faculty of intuition,"[26] he no longer has in mind the coincidence of what the proposition says with the way things are; he is thinking of the connection between the subject of knowledge and an object of knowledge that is no less individual than the subject.

In the Preface, Kant finds a precedent in Copernicus. The change of method he advocates is comparable to the transformation wrought by Copernicus in astronomy. This analogy has led to the description of Kant's work as a "Copernican revolution." Perhaps it can tell us what object the knowing subject is dealing with.

If the analogy with Copernicus was intended merely to illustrate the potential fecundity of new hypotheses, the comparison would be clear but brief: Copernicus, realizing that a particular hypothesis was incapable of explaining certain observations, decided to test another. Similarly, faced with the failure of one hypothesis (the dogmatic) to explain something (the fact of a priori knowledge), we too may benefit from trying another.

If this is the analogy, it hardly amounts to a Copernican revolution. There are grounds for comparison only between one epistemological situation in which the trial of a new hypothesis turned out to be seminal and another with potentially similar results. It is unnecessary, then, to go further and compare the meaning of the Copernican change of course with the meaning of the same maneuver in Kant. Nor need we be concerned with what makes the two peculiarly comparable in order to believe that what worked for one case might also work for the other.

Since Kant never actually said he was contemplating a "Copernican revolution," we might leave it at that and press the analogy no further. However, he himself compared not only the change of hypothesis in general, but also the content of the four hypotheses involved. Returning to Copernicus further on, he writes:

the invisible force (the Newtonian attraction) which holds the universe together . . . would have remained for ever undiscovered if Copernicus had not dared, in a manner contradictory of the senses, but yet true, to seek the observed movements, not in the heavenly bodies [literally "in the celestial objects," *in dem Gegenständen des Himmels*], but in the spectator. The change in point of view, analogous to this hypothesis, which is expounded in the *Critique*, I put forward in this preface as an hypothesis only. (Bxxiin)

The analogy must after all be developed to the full, for not only the change of hypothesis but also the hypotheses themselves are being compared. Kant is not simply suggesting that our endeavor is to metaphysics what Copernicus's endeavor was to astronomy, that is, an attempt to explain what the traditional conception could not explain. He is making the more precise point that his hypothesis is analogous to that of Copernicus; in other words, the critical hypothesis is to the dogmatic hypothesis what the Copernican hypothesis was to the Ptolemaic. This is why the analogy permits us to speak of a Copernican revolution, and it has generally been understood to do so.

Let us therefore consider these hypotheses. No grammatical difficulty is presented as far as the astronomical hypotheses are concerned. The Ptolemaic hypothesis explains the movements observable in the sky by a real movement on the part of the sky; more precisely, it explains the fact that we observe such a movement by the fact that this movement exists. The Copernican hypothesis also explains a fact by a fact. The inversion consists in saying that there is apparent movement of the sky because there is real movement on the part of the spectator, rather than, as in the past, that there is apparent movement of the sky because there is real movement of the sky. In all these sentences, we find a proposition on each side of the conjunction *because*. The phenomenon requiring explanation to the left of *because* is propositional. The fact that explains it, to the right of *because*, is also propositional. Furthermore, the hypotheses bear upon objects in the individual sense; on one side the stars, the "celestial objects," and on the other the earth and the observer placed on the earth. The observer's relationship to the stars is not that of truth or falsehood linking a proposition to a fact, but that of an individual to one or several individuals.

The other half of the analogy concerns the two epistemological hypotheses. Dogmatism is to Kant what Ptolemy is to Copernicus, and dogmatism is to Ptolemy what Kant is to Copernicus. The explanation for what demands to be explained can be sought either in objects or in the subject. In astronomy, this means either in heavenly objects or in the observer; in epistemology, either in the objects of knowledge or in the subject of knowledge. The analogy taken as a whole can then be rendered as follows: in the Ptolemaic hypothesis the objects of the heavens are to the movements observed in the heavens what in the dogmatic hypothesis the objects of knowledge are to a priori knowledge of these objects. In the Copernican hypothesis, the observer is to the observable movement of the sky what in the critical hypotheses the subject of knowledge is to a priori knowledge of objects. This general comparison consistently locates epistemological objects in the same position as astronomical objects; they are the equivalent of stars, confirming that here Kant sees them as individuals. The known object is indeed the house, not *that the house is an extended body*. Yet we know that we must say *the house is an extended body* and not merely utter the designation *the house*, if we wish to complete the formula . . . *because a certain principle of understanding is a priori true*. Is there any way of reconciling these contradictory demands regarding the object?

What does the analogy with Copernicus tell us about the "Copernican revolution"? Inverting the relationship between the static and the mobile in the determination of the sky's apparent movement, Copernicus declared that the motion we observe as being of the sky belongs in reality to our own position on the earth. Kant was to echo: "We can know *a priori* of things only what we ourselves put into them" (B18). By turning method on its head, Copernicus explained the observable movement of the stars and Kant explained a priori knowledge of things. The motion of the earth is responsible not for the appearance of stars, but for the fact that from our point of view celestial objects appear to be mobile. The same goes for the critical hypothesis: the appearance is not that there are things, but that these things are in themselves as we know them a priori. Is this not precisely what critical philosophy seeks to maintain? This is what we have always assumed, and we have preserved the distinction between the object as phenomenon and the object as thing in itself. Kant is reproached by some for preserving the thing in itself, while others admire his audacity in doing so. Consequently, the Kantian distinction between the two meanings of the object must hold the key to the problem of what the word *object* means in the passage we are concerned with.

Where does the analogy locate appearances? Astronomically speaking, the appearance is of a host of stars revolving around the observer. *Appearance*—or *phenomenon*, as it is commonly called—signifies whatever corresponds to a statement of observation. From our point of view, we observe the sky moving. Whatever we subsequently make of it, that remains the phenomenon: the sky appears to revolve. From now on, everything seems to fall into place: the subject is in relation with individual things (like the astronomer with heavenly bodies), and the phenomena given him through experience correspond to propositions. It is the phenomena, and not things in themselves, of course, that take their cue from the subject's a priori knowledge. And this is just what we had sought to say.

Since everything in the analogy fits, we may suppose that our reading was correct. The objects (with which the knowing subject has a relationship analogous to that of the astronomer with the stars) do not obey that subject, any more than the stars actually revolve simply because the astronomer is in a position to see them do so. The subject has an a priori knowledge of phenomena, not of things in themselves. If, for example, the house appears bound in advance by the necessity of being a particular extended body, this is due to the subject's mode of representation. Only the phenomenon of the house is bound by our necessity. The subject legislates for nature, the realm of phenomena. If we pursue the analogy, the change of method prompts us to say that the house is not really an extended body, just as the stars are not really on the move. As soon as we say this, we sense that it is impossible. The solution we seek cannot be that the stars are to things in themselves what observed movement is to phenomena. To opt for this reading is to have Kant say the opposite of what he claims. If things in themselves were to stars what phenomena are to the apparent motion of the sky, we should have to grant that the house is a thing in itself while the fact of its inevitable extension is the phenomenon. And if this were the case, we should effortlessly attain to the truth about things by asserting whatever was the opposite of appearance. Copernicus achieved this when he rejected the appearance of the sky, as seen from the earth, in favor of the truth of the sky as seen from the sky. Appearance suggests that the sun moves; truth reveals that it is stationary. This discovery of the truth comes about because the sun itself is not an appearance. In supposing that the sun does not move, Copernicus adopts the determinate negation of the Ptolemaic hypothesis. The sun must be stationary. But by saying that the house is not what it is qua phenomenon, we obtain an indeterminate negation that leaves us with nothing: the house that is not an extended body is the transcendental object, still unknown.

We have been led astray by our desire that the subject be in relation to the thing itself, and that the phenomenon act as the apparent fact corresponding to a judgment of perception. This reading made us mistake the phenomenon for a thing in itself and the seeming, mere appearance (*Schein*) for a phenomenon (*Erscheinung*). We have confused a phenomenon in the Kantian sense with the fact, say, that the subjective apprehension of a house is necessarily successive: first we see the front, then the back, and so on. The house itself possesses all its parts at once, and we justly say that the house, always successively apprehended, is not itself successive.[27] We do not, for all that, know the house in itself.

Correction: the subject is in relation to phenomena, as Kant indicates. But what phenomena? Hitherto, phenomenal objects corresponded in the analogy to what the astronomer's statements of observation described relatively truthfully (for it is true that from our standpoint the sky appears to move). Phenomena were those states of things by virtue of which certain judgments were true. The subject of knowledge can have no relation to phenomena of this kind. The impossibility is grammatical. The subject has no relation to the "object of knowledge" (taken as the counterpart of the proposition expressing a knowledge), any more than the Copernican observer moves relative to the fact of the sun's immobility. It is not the fact of the sun's appearing to revolve around the earth that appears to revolve around the earth; it is the sun itself. And what turns upon itself is the earth, not the fact that the earth appears to be motionless.

If the subject is to be in relation to phenomena, these must be individuals; phenomena, then, ought to correspond to the "celestial objects." This ultimate solution imposes itself by default, given the impossibility of all others. Yet it is also "the most impossible of all," as Plato would have put it. For this solution is the one we began with and instantly rejected by reason of its impossible construction (*the museum because the museum is open*).

We are left with the conclusion that the "Copernican revolution" is based upon an incongruous hypothesis.

5

The Inn of the Emancipated Signifier

The Inn of the Emancipated Signifier is a Franco-Swiss establishment where you will find somewhat mixed company. The Swiss side of things is largely confined to a portrait of a respectable-looking gentleman whom they say was the first owner. The guests hail from far and wide, and if they are here it is doubtless because they could find nowhere else. You will soon discover that refreshment amounts to a concoction of whatever you had the foresight to bring. Here all meals are prepared with food supplied by the guests.

Semiology and Ideology

There will be no question of linguistics in this chapter, any more than elsewhere in the book. Various doctrines of the signifier claim descent from Ferdinand de Saussure, but I shall examine not Saussure's teaching itself, in linguistic terms, so much as the teaching it engendered. As originally published, the *Course in General Linguistics* gave rise to a philosophical doctrine, and it is philosophy I would like to consider. We are thus free to ignore all the controversy surrounding the editing of the *Course* along with the debates about what Saussure really thought. We shall be dealing with no more than a few catchphrases, slogans, and sayings that make up the breviary of semiological philosophy.

The linguistic sign is arbitrary. (*CGL*, p. 67)

There are no pre-existing ideas, and nothing is distinct before the appearance of language. (*CGL*, p. 112)

A segment of language can never in the final analysis be based on anything except its non-coincidence with the rest. (*CGL*, p. 118).

In a language there are only differences *without positive terms*. (*CGL*, p. 120)

It must be said that these formulae are hardly greeted with the same enthusiasm today as they aroused ten or twenty years ago. Ancient history? Far from it. Semiological philosophy has nowhere been refuted or revised, or even properly discussed. The thesis of the arbitrariness of signs may no longer be a burning topic, but this is only because it is now taken for granted. Semiological philosophy has deserted the headlines and entered the textbooks, upheld as the indispensable koine of those who share a certain attention to language—anthropologists, literary critics, cultural sociologists, communications specialists, philosophers of language in the French mold, Parisian psychoanalysts, and so forth. In any case, even if I were suddenly informed that no one cares a hoot any more about the semiology of the signifier, this would not absolve me of the need to examine it. We are in the business of elucidation, which eschews a number of procedures on grounds of inefficiency: histrionic rejection (*No! Never again!*), compulsive recantation (*No, no, we don't believe that now*), or polite evasion (*Oh, don't let's talk in those terms*). The only way to cast off a dogma is to expose its shortcomings.

Semiology is the study of sign systems. I do not intend to look at any one system, and so I am not concerned with semiology properly speaking. Semiological philosophy (or, to cut a long story short, the semiology I deal with here) is a philosophy of language that displays more strikingly than any other the characteristic ambiguity of this expression. Semiology sees itself as having triumphed over the traditional conception it criticizes. This conception asks, What is a sign? The question in this form encourages us to believe that a sign can exist in isolation. The reply to such a question offers a definition of the sign as standing for something else (for an "object," say some; others, for an "idea"). According to this reply, there is a sign if there is something to which whatever performs as sign is in a relationship of signifying thing to signified thing. The semiological concept of the sign abolishes the subordination of the sign to something else. The very notion of a sign system necessitates the definition not of a sign but of an element in this system. Whenever the question of the sign is put in the singular, the pre-Saussurean answer resurfaces even from the most Saussurean of writers. Here is an example from Benveniste: "The role of the sign is to represent, to substitute for something else, evoking it at one remove."[1] If we were to espouse this definition, we would have to concede the priority of the thing to be represented over the thing that replaces it.

Linguists with a Saussurean background inform us that the semiological starting point of the *Course* is decisive. In it, linguistics is relieved of the inappropriate task of studying the relation between signs and things and therefore of studying things (which are "extralinguistic"). If signs are

arbitrary and form themselves into a system, the linguist has no further
need to dally with reality. This declaration of independence was not lost
on philosophical semiology, which advocated a further step. For reasons
which will later become clear, it was considered that the independence of
the sign (from the thing) was no more than a dry run preparing for the
independence of the signifier (from the signified). The signifier precedes,
dominates, and finally dispenses with the signified—yet it affects to be a
mere "substitute," replacing something else in order to evoke it. To the
semiological philosopher, this paradox indicates that the limits of traditional thinking have been reached. It inaugurates a new intellectual
regime.

In my opinion the reverse is true. Philosophical semiology, with all its
paradoxes, is far from pioneering some intrepid breach of the limits that
constrain traditional thought. On the contrary, it is exquisitely regres-
sive. The day the signifier was officially absolved of its responsibility to
signify a thing, the "structuralist" or "poststructuralist" school of
thought saw the lifting of a prohibition. Once again it was permissible to
bask in the delights of ideology, always a familiar exercise to French
philosophers—and here I mean the ideology of ideologues, in Destutt de
Tracy's sense. At the turn of the century it was thought necessary to
renounce this kind of inquiry, the associationist school having been
discredited (in its attempts to explain thought by the laws of "association
of ideas"). The new philosophies of the time made their way at a cost,
relinquishing the dream of a mechanics of the mind that could explain
thought formation by phenomena of attraction and repulsion. In the
wake of Bergson and Husserl, ideology seemed decisively vanquished. It
was duly renounced, until semiology found a way of being ideological
without appearing dated. Like semiconverted peasants reverting from the
Mass to their ancient rites, semiology transgressed full circle. Or rather,
like cannibals abruptly rejecting civilized steak and chips to devour the
missionary who had weaned them away from human flesh, semiology
put paid, in one gulp, to the phenomenology that stood between it and
the ideological tradition dating from Locke's invention of the word
sēmeiōtikē.

Ideology can be defined as the fullest development of the idea that
people have ideas. For instance, they have ideas of sense qualities (smells,
colors, textures), ideas of individuals (self, kin), ideas of natural species
(cat idea, dog idea) as well as more abstract ideas whose source is harder
to explain (the idea of a right to property, the idea of liberty). The idea
that people have ideas is not included among the ideas they have. In the
preceding sentence the word *idea* is understood in two ways, as grammatical construction shows. Descartes was the first to have had the idea

that we have ideas of things. *Idea* is followed now by a propositional complement (*to have the idea that* . . .), now by an individual designation (*to have the idea of* . . .). The first use, which is the most common, presents no problem. The idea is a thought, one that usually occurs to us through a kind of visitation or illumination: the possible solution, the seductive theory. It has a more banal version in the shared opinion (as in "the history of ideas"). The ideologue's idea, on the other hand, is representative: its complement will be a name or a singular designation. Thus for a thinking being to have an idea presupposes a relation of the thinker (the subject of representative thought) to the designated individual (the object of the representation, in the sense that there is an individual of which this representation is the representation).

How are we to know what ideas we have? The procedure runs as follows. Do I have the idea of a seahorse? I must think of a seahorse and see whether anything comes to mind. What I am thinking (the object of my thought in the sense of the direct object of my thinking) as I think about this thing (the object of my thought in the sense of that of which I am thinking) will be my idea. I conclude that if I can think of a certain thing, I necessarily possess an idea of that thing. Otherwise I have not thought of anything; I have thought a word without understanding it. If I understand *seahorse*, I have an idea of the seahorse. But where did I acquire this idea? Ideology investigates the origin of the ideas we have. From Locke to Nietzsche, ideology is a genealogy, and like all genealogies it seeks to discover what descends from what. Despite appearances, the genealogist is not a historian. History records filiation; genealogy establishes it. In other words, the genealogist is always at the service of the antagonists in disputes of legitimacy. The positivist historian, armed with his precious objective facts, misses the point that the documents were designed to swell the dossiers of litigation. Genealogy exists because of contestations, rights to be reestablished, usurpations to be condemned. At least these may always arise, which is enough to show that no research into origins can be altogether disinterested. The account of origins always serves to endorse some authority. In epistemology as in politics, the question is whether the present incumbents of high office are entitled to the respect they demand of us. Conservative genealogical philosophies invoke sources in order to confirm the propriety of the status quo. Any crisis of confidence in authority is surmountable so long as a *continuous* genealogy can be shown to link today's tottering rulers to the ancestors, to the founder of all authority. In epistemology, the absolute source of authority is I myself; more exactly, the possibility of my appearance before the court of my own attentive mind. Subversive genealogical philosophies research sources for purposes of demystification: the sources, they say, have been betrayed, corrupted, disfigured. Authority is not derived from the lineage it claims; filiation is discontinuous. Or perhaps the compilation of the genealogical tree uncovers appalling skeletons—shady deals, a disreputable forebear, an unworthy marriage. Why stir up all this ancient history? asks the alarmed chorus. Because it must be done, the hero replies. Everything must be revealed; only justice can halt the epidemic ravaging our city. Of course the first victim of the ensuing scandal will be the hero himself.

Within the context of legitimist thinking, any research into the past is hermeneutic, in the proper sense of the word. The relics of the past contain the ancestral word upon which all my expectations are pinned. Who am I? If I am indeed the heir I claim to be, everything I have is mine by right. But if my shameful origins leave me nameless and stateless, there is no place for me, and I may as well camp at the city gates between the forest and the town, in the twilight zone where vultures and wolves fight over the bones of men. The hermeneutics of allegiance knows that our forebears were founders, worthier than ourselves: witness the decline from them the sowers to us the reapers, the latecomers. It is enough to make us wonder whether they were really as exemplary as legend has it, as irreproachable as their reputation suggests. Is the ancestral gallery perhaps nothing but a meretricious collection, fraudulently acquired from some junk shop by an unscrupulous great-uncle? For the hermeneutics of suspicion, our lineage is a patchwork chronicle of fabrications. We are not the latecomers of history, but parvenus who have clambered up from our sordid beginnings.

Beyond the context of legitimist thinking, ideology becomes somewhat academic. Napoleon took no notice of ideologues, regarding himself as seminal.[2] The moment we accept that origins are the source of all greatness and majesty, any inquiry into the origin of ideas ceases to be the result of curiosity directed at the past and becomes a lawsuit, for the purposes of which all plausible family trees are traced. The modern reader, of course, will associate the word *ideology* with Marx's *German Ideology* sooner than with *Elements of Ideology* by Destutt de Tracy. But that is irrelevant if we recall that the Marxian and post-Marxian acceptation of the word evolved directly—and legitimately— from the ideologists' sense. There is only a marginal difference between ideology as an analysis of the ideas we have by rights and ideology as the totality (even system) of collective representations available to human agents enabling them to recognize one another, enter the cycle of rights and obligations, formulate transactions, and settle differences. The two are divided only by the shift from an individual repository of ideas (the person making the inventory of his ideas, both innate and acquired) to a collectivity (the group carrier of ideology).

Ideology rises from its ashes in a new, subversive shape, by courtesy of the semiological thesis of the primacy of the signifier over the signified. It is acceptable once more to maintain that words are signs for ideas (now that along with the phenomenological missionary we have done away with his intolerable "referent"). But words are no longer signs for ideas, as if signs were created to communicate ideas, themselves already received or acquired (received from the ancestor, the God, if we are of good family; acquired by the sweat of our brows if we are parvenus). Words are signs for the ideas they afford us by dividing up the field of the signified, or of thought, as dictated by the "laws of the signifier" (we are neither heirs nor nouveaux riches, but beneficiaries, grant holders, and future employees). By the same token we keep our ideology free of individualism or psychologism. For as long as words were signs for ideas, these ideas were necessarily the representative ideas belonging to someone who had acquired them prior to signifying them. But if it is to be language that distinguishes between one idea and the next, then ideas belong to no one. The origin of ideas is no longer a matter of sensation, and as such a private matter. It is signifying difference. Formerly it was epitomized by a sentient statue turning into the smell of roses when a rose was nearby. Now the story endlessly retold and reelucidated is that of the little boy who hides his toy and makes it reappear, with the words *Fort! Da!*[3]

Language, *Langue,* and *Parole*

The *Course in General Linguistics* names the object of linguistics as language minus speech (*parole*), which leaves *langue.* "*Langue* is *language* minus *parole.* It is the whole set of linguistic habits that allows an individual to understand and to be understood" (*CGL,* p. 77; amended translation).

The *Course* concedes that this distinction is a deliberate choice and remarks that it will be difficult to convey in other languages. When the Egyptologist Sir Alan Gardiner attempted to present the Saussurean distinction in English, he decided in his turn to oppose *language* and *speech:* "The sentence is the unit of speech (*parole*) and the word is the unit of language (*langue*)."[4] Gardiner's treatment is actually more specific than the explanation given by the *Course: speech* is a social act (*act of speech*) accomplished by an individual agent addressing a listener whose role is not that of a purely passive receiver; *language* is not only the speaker's capacity to speak but also the listener's capacity to understand. The difference is nicely put in Gardiner's example.[5] James to Mary: "Rain!" Mary replies, "What a bore!" James's contribution is confined to a single word, and yet it functions as a complete sentence (hence the exclamation mark in the transcription). Thus the signifier *rain* features in the English language as a word, but also in certain instances of discourse as a one-word sentence.

Gardiner's distinction persists in the writings of the masters of "philosophy of ordinary language." Gilbert Ryle refers to it explicitly, adding that philosophy of language is concerned not with language (= *langue*, i.e., linguistic inaccuracies, solecisms, misspellings) but with *parole* (what statements are saying, in any language).[6] Austin introduces a slight variation in his own distinction between units of language and units of speech.[7] It happens, however, that the French word *langage* as it occurs in *philosophie du langage* overlaps the distinction made by the *Course*. In his *Dictionary*, completed by 1877, Littré detects a nuance as follows: *langue* is the means, *langage* the use of this means. If we consult the nine entries listed under *langage*, we find that this term subsumes the entire range, from *le langage romain* (= Latin tongue or *langue*) to speech: *Maître Renard par l'odeur alléché / Lui tint à peu près ce langage* (*Master Reynard, when he smelled the cheese / spoke in more or less these words*), via modes of expression (*un langage obscur, le langage de l'amour*). What is true of the French word *langage* applies equally well to the German *Sprache* and the English *language*. Where Wittgenstein writes "Die Gesamtheit der Sätze ist die Sprache" (*Tractatus*, 4.001), translated by Pears and MacGuiness as "The totality of propositions is language," it comes quite naturally to Klossowski to translate as "La totalité des propositions est le langage." It would be impossible here to take *Sprache* and *language* in the sense of the French *langue*. Had the English translators wished to abide by Gardiner's convention, they should have written "The totality of propositions is speech." "Language," as far as analytic philosophy of language is concerned, is plainly taken in Wittgenstein's sense. Philosophy, he says, seeks to illuminate the "logic of language," that is, the logical form of the proposition. If so, what "philosophy of language" may be gleaned from the *Course* when it is so firmly committed to *langue*? Either semiological philosophy of language, unlike its analytic counterpart, is interested neither in propositions nor in discourse, or else it follows every philosophy of *logos* since Plato in dealing with propositions—ignoring the fact that Saussurean doctrine concerns language minus speech, language minus the totality of propositions.

What we have is the second option. Semiological analysis has focused not on the language of myths (if such a notion has any meaning) but on mythological narratives. It has studied the text of the dream in preference to its code, the fictional text in preference to literary convention. It analyses the image, the canvas, or the film, but not their respective languages within which the iconic, pictorial, or cinematic discourse is produced. There are sufficient examples of this curious quid pro quo to quell any lingering idea that this is due to an exceptional lapse or a blunder on the part of a few inept advocates of the theory.

The misunderstanding might have been more readily avoidable had the word *signifier* not been caught in a similar indecision between *langue* and *parole*. To signify is to be the sign of something; that is the linguistic or dictionary meaning. Such and such means such and such: "The word *lupus* means wolf in English." But if *lupus* means wolf, it does not mean anything to me; it has nothing to tell me and does not constitute a discourse (as when someone cries "Wolf!"). There is thus another sense of *to signify*; it means to declare, to make known, to notify, *signum facere*.

Et je vous viens, monsieur, avec votre licence,
Signifier l'exploit de certaine ordonnance.

I am here to tell you, sir, with your permission,
Of a writ that has been served.   *(Tartuffe)*

When we hear of signifiers, we may understand the term either in the Saussurean manner (to me they signify nothing, signifiers though they be) or in the manner of speech acts that, once accomplished, affect both sender and receiver alike, as in the quotation above. The difference is not a material one; it is not reducible to degrees of complexity. The signifier *land,* an English word, is not the same as the signifier *Land!* called by the lookout; but we cannot say that they are different signifiers, as *water* differs from *land* and *Man overboard!* from *Land!* The *signifier* is equivocal, which is manageable so long as we remember this and do not change course in midstream. The difference between the two is a matter of logic. To use Wittgenstein's comparison, it is the difference between placing a piece on the chessboard in order to set up a game and moving that piece in the course of play. Only the second gesture constitutes a move in the language game. A word can declare nothing; it signifies something but says nothing. Conversely, a *parole* or speech act cannot be the sign of anything; it signifies something, but it is not the sign of one thing or another. Unable to specify a preference, we subject ourselves to the mental contortion of treating *langue* as *parole* or *parole* as *langue*.

The first alternative consists in supposing, for instance, a dictionary of the English language to be a discourse, like a book written in English.

While there are indeed discursive elements in a dictionary, these serve to comment on each word, in a language that does not have to be English. Let us bracket off what must necessarily be in English for an English dictionary: English words, normally found in alphabetical order. The list of words, even when each is supplied with examples of possible meanings, tells us nothing. Conceivably it could help us to make a statement; for instance, *The following words* (and here insert the list from *a* to *zymotic*) *are all English*. Or it may be useful in formulating a discourse, by becoming the logical subject of a predicate. In the context of a proposition, the list signifies something to me. In isolation it tells me nothing. What could it say? No one can tell. Let us suppose, however, that it says something. Will this be the same as the list of words in another language, or something else? If the English language says something, is what it says closer to what German says than to what Finnish says? To deny what a list of Russian words says, must we establish a counterlist of Chinese words or words in some other language? Far from being absurd, all these questions would have to be asked if we seriously accepted that languages signify. In particular, the notion that languages are vehicles for a "world view" or a "thought" should enable us to assign to each language another (even if potential) language denying what the first asserts.

We can immediately conceive of the reverse fallacy. To treat *parole* as *langue* would be like approaching a book as if it were a dictionary. The signifying whole is now a text, and the appropriate semiological treatment would be to search through it for a sequence of signs, a list of the propositions contained in the text, drawn up in a particular order (like the alphabetical order of words in a dictionary). Of course, if the signifying differences discernible in the text operate at the level of the words, I am no longer analyzing the text, since I have exchanged the totality of propositions for the totality of the words used. But we had meant to analyze the text. Imagine that we are reading an episode in a newspaper serial. The first sentence we encounter in Monday's paper is *The duchess went out at five*. This is a "signifier" bringing an alleged event to our notice, what literary criticism calls in the fashion of certain linguists a "referent." Let us consider, for the purposes of the demonstration, that a signifier in this sense is also a semiological signifier, signifying what it does by means of its signifying differences within the system to be found. At this point our reading is interrupted by an unwelcome visitor; we lose Monday's paper and cannot pick up the story until the following day. On Tuesday the episode begins: *The duchess went out at five*. We have here a new "signifier" bringing an alleged fact to our attention, but the inconsistency of our previous reading leaves us guessing. It may be the same duchess on another day, or another duchess on the same day, or perhaps another day (duchesses always go out about five o'clock). It could be the same duchess on the same day, either because the story is starting again, or because another character is retelling the first scene, or because the newspaper has simply reproduced Monday's episode in Tuesday's edition (by mistake, or because it was illegible on Monday). All in all, we are bewildered. Could this reading problem be solved by resorting to a dictionary of the narrative statements in the story? It would be conceivable if the statements were the sign of something, signs for signified referents (and here I am not introducing an "extralinguistic" element—I have introduced nothing; the serial is fictitious; neither a duchess nor anyone else is involved).[8] One would consult this dictionary to establish whether the two signifiers are the same (having the same fictitious referent as their signified) or whether, in the contexts that by chance escaped us, this sentence constitutes two separate signifiers: *the duchess went out at five$_1$* and *the duchess went out at five$_2$*). This is the usual procedure when encountering difficulty in understanding a proper name, either through ignorance of the fact that someone has two names (Is Buonaparte the same person as the Emperor Napoleon?) or because there are ill-distinguished homonyms in the same context (Is this Poincaré the same as the Poincaré we know of?). Yet this procedure cannot be applied to statements. Statements are not signifiers of any "referent," they are "something-signifiers," so to speak. It would be meaningless to constitute them into a list of signifiers corresponding to as many signifieds. In our situation, the only solution is to reconstruct the context so as to know not whether *The duchess went out at five* is a single signifier within the textual system of signifying statements (i.e., whether there is a signifying difference between it and all the others) but whether *the duchess* is used for the same character throughout and whether *five o'clock* refers to the same afternoon. In other words, the answer to the problem is quite naturally to analyze that logically complex sign, the statement. Such an analysis will enable us to differentiate between whatever is already determined by the (identical) statement and whatever is not. Wherever we read it, the statement says that a certain person is a duchess and that at a time when it was five o'clock in that part of the world, that person went out. This is what the statement means. Identifying the duchess and dating her excursion require us to know more. In the meantime, all the possibilities reviewed earlier are acceptable. If once a duchess went out at the stipulated time, then matters stand just as the statement signified them to us. If this duchess goes out every day at five, the statement is still true. If all duchesses go out at five, together or by turns, this too would endorse the statement. Now, is this the analytic procedure to which we resort in order to solve the problems of reading peculiar to the semiological signifier? When confronted with a signifying difference between two signs, the semiological analyst is in his element. There is a discrepancy between *Bonaparte* and *Buonaparte*; there is a signifying difference between them in the French language system, which leads to a signified difference, that is, two different ways of presenting the same person: once by his surname and once by a nickname with a kind of sneering exoticism that is itself semiologically explicable. Let us now take a case with no visible signifying difference. *Poincaré was elected to the Academy of Sciences* and *Poincaré was elected president of the Republic.* We do not analyze the surname *Poincaré* to discover in the signifying elements *P-o-i-n* and *c-a-r-é* the possibility that this name denotes both the mathematician and the politician. The statement *The duchess went out at five* is a general proposition concerning all women, stating that among those who are duchesses, at least one went out at five. But the name *Poincaré* is not a general name covering a variety of individuals, Henri, Raymond, and the others. There is no lowest common denominator of meaning between *Poincaré (Henri)* and *Poincaré (Raymond)*, whereas one exists between *The duchess (of Argyll) went out at five* and *The duchess (of Windsor) went out at five.*

Semiotics and Semantics

Before we go any further, I should answer the obvious objection that at least one writer, Emile Benveniste, firmly emphasized the divorce between the study of signs and the study of discourse. In his 1966 lecture he opposed the semiotic and the semantic in linguistics[9]—a long-standing preoccupation, as evidenced by Lacan's allusion in the *Seminar* of 1954.[10] Might this opposition be the remedy for any temptation to confuse semiological and propositional signs? Semiotics studies the sign, which always implies the membership of a sign within a system and its potential to combine with or replace other signs in that system. A spurious semiological philosophy of language is attempting to take root by extending semiotic processes to language as a whole—an error rectifiable by the prudent demarcation that allocates signs to the semiotician and statements to the semanticist.

It is striking, however, that when Benveniste observes the incongruity of a semiotics of discourse, he finds no better way of avoiding the fallacy than to add to the semiotics of *langue* a semantics of *langue*—not of language, as one might expect, but of *langue*. This is what dooms his effort at clarification to failure. The difference between semiotic and semantic is assigned to *langue* and lies between two "modes of signification"[11] operating within it. The semiotic mode pertains to signifiers that form a "signifying system"[12]—Saussurean signifiers. The semantic mode consists in signifying something, referring to things outside language.[13] The two modes belong to *langue*. Thus Benveniste follows Saussure's decision, which he justly describes as "the reduction of language to *langue*."[14] Such a reduction is highly fruitful for linguistics, or so linguists say, but it is useless in philosophy, since we would find ourselves confined to *langue* alone, robbed of our crucial material, which is the totality of propositions. In his philosophical address on language (for the lecture entitled *Form and Meaning in Language* does not deal with one or several languages [*langues*] or with "linguistic data"), Benveniste endorses the reduction of language to *langue*, attempting belatedly to mitigate its disastrous consequences by locating within the reduced object a fresh distinction between "*langue* as semiotics" and "*langue* as semantics."[15] Language is only a *langue*, but the latter must not be reduced to a sign system. Doubtless these formulations can be explained with reference to the model of a linguist at work upon a corpus of assembled material (recordings, inscriptions, texts). To study this corpus through the segmentation and extrapolation of paradigmatic classes is to study a language (*langue*). The formal object of the linguist studying a certain discourse is then a language, even though his material object consists of a sequence of statements. But if the scientist should ask himself what these statements mean now that he has deciphered the language, he will have to renew his analysis of the same material, only this time as a "*langue* in use and in action."[16]

A primary drawback, in this conception, emerges in what might be called the paradox of the signified.

In semiology, it is unnecessary to define what the sign signifies. For a sign to exist, it is necessary and sufficient that it be received and that it connect in some way with other signs. Does the entity under consideration signify? The answer is either yes or no. If yes, no more need be said, it is registered; if no, it is rejected, and no more need be said either. Does *borrow* exist?—Yes.—*Barrow*?—Yes.—*Berrow*?—No.[17]

Semiology, then, is not bound to give the meaning of signs. Perhaps it can accomplish its aims without this, but would it be able to provide meanings? Is it unnecessary or rather impossible for it to do so? The ideas above have encouraged certain readers to believe that signs can signify without signifying anything in particular. Of course I may be ignorant of the meaning of a sign, but I take it to be a sign because I credit it with a determinate meaning that is unknown to me. Here I do not know in what sense the sign is used, which is not the same as saying that it is used to mean I know not what. Broadly speaking, an indefinite sense would not really be a sense at all.[18]

As we found earlier with the duchess's outing, a vague or general meaning is wholly determinate: what it permits is thoroughly distinct from what it excludes. If I promise to stop by your house sometime tomorrow, my statement is vague yet quite determinate. If two days later you berate me for not coming, for not doing as I said, I could defend myself only with a "sophistical refutation" invoking the vagueness of my suggestion. (How can you charge me with not doing as I said, when what I said was vague and indeterminate?)

The semiotician contends that the meaning of a sign is irrelevant to our earlier inquiry whether the sign exists in the language and is recognizable to those that speak it. *Borrow* is recognized, *berrow* is not. How does recognition operate without some criterion of identity? *Berrow*, for instance, is admittedly not recognized as English (as being a word other than *borrow* or *barrow*), but it might be accepted as a phonetic and graphic formation that looks English. If we came across *berrow* in a text, would we think that it was a misprint, an unknown word, or the semblance of a word that had been mischievously slipped in? The question therefore is how we decide a sign's identity. Yet we are given no criterion: "Taken in itself, the sign is pure identity to itself, pure alterity to any other."[19] There is something fantastic about such an entity. A sign claims to be the sign that it is, itself and none other, by being other than all others. But what others? The same *what*, another *what*? Semiotics draws its criterion neither from the material ("phonic substance") nor from the meaning. Each sign is thus the same as itself and other than all the other signs. To quote the Saussurean image of the sheet of paper cut into pieces, each piece is the same bit of paper as itself and another bit of paper than the others. We understand that two bits of paper (exhibited at different moments) may or may not be the same piece. When are two signs the same sign, and when are they two separate ones? Semiotics uses a pseudocriterion, holding that two signs are identical if they are acknowledged by the speaking community as being the same, even though we do not know what criterion of identity the community applies.

A further disadvantage of the division between semiotic and semantic is the impossibility of launching any semantic analysis of the proposition on such a basis. The line is drawn between the sign and the sentence, not between the word and the sentence.

Against the notion that a sentence can constitute a sign in the Saussurean sense, or that by mere addition or extension we may graduate to the proposition and thence to a variety of syntactic constructions, we maintain that the sign and the sentence are two different worlds, calling for different descriptions. We etch a fundamental division *within langue*, quite different from that which Saussure attempted between *langue* and *parole*.[20]

A very different division indeed, for it inhabits *langue*, to the exclusion of a *parole* that the semantics of *langue* altogether fails to recover. The incision passes between the sign and the sentence. Both sentence and word are situated on the side of semantics, with the result that their mode of signification is the same: both the word, which is the semantic unit, and the sentence signify things in the same manner. According to Benveniste, not only the word used but also the sentence uttered must be accorded meaning and reference.

In semantics, "the meaning of a sentence is its idea and the meaning of a word is its use."[21] Thus the difference between the pseudomeaning of semiotics and authentic semantic meaning is that whereas semiotic meaning is unspeakable (there is signifying that signifies nothing), semantic meaning can be explained or elucidated. Furthermore, semantic meaning introduces the concept of "referent." The referent of a word is a "particular object," the referent of a sentence is a "situation," a "state of affairs." Here we are hard pressed to follow the semanticist's thinking. The referent of a word is "the particular object to which the word corresponds in concrete terms of circumstance and usage."[22] As for the sentence, its referent is given as "the state of affairs that occasions it, the factual or discursive situation to which it alludes."[23] In both cases the "referent" or "reference" is viewed as that which corresponds *in rebus* to the semantic entity in question, the correspondence being established by the circumstances surrounding each use. As the context shows, Benveniste has in mind all the words whose meaning hangs upon the fact that the referent is a function of the condition of enunciation (such as demonstrative pronouns). Now let us take as an example, *My grandfather was a fine man*. We understand what *grandfather* means in any story that begins like this, but we are unable to apply the word to a person until the circumstances of use have been specified—or so semantics teaches. Yes, but what about the words *was a fine man*? Since we are engaged in semantics, we must show how they signify with regard to the *res significata*. If the referent of words is inevitably "the particular object to which the word corresponds in concrete terms of circumstance and usage," we should say what the remaining words apply to. Setting aside the fact that there are several words, let us simply take *a fine man* as one semantic unit. According to the above, this unit should apply to a particular fine man, just as *grandfather* applies to the person whose grandchild is the speaker of the sentence. So the sentence means that someone's grandfather is identical to a certain fine man, or a certain fine man is identical to someone's grandfather. Since words have particular corresponding objects as their referents, the proposition must be analyzed as the identification of two designations (this grandfather = that fine man). Alternatively it may be explained that *my grandfather* has as its referent a certain person (whose grandchild the speaker is, forgetting that this description may obtain for two people), while the referent of *is a fine man* is a class, the totality of fine men. The proposition would thus establish as a link between these two "objects" the membership of an individual to a class; but having already set up the class of fine men, we must already have included the individual in question among its members, and thus we already understand the sentence that was to be semantically explained. Furthermore, if we now begin the story with *My grandfather was not just anybody,* we must ask who this just anybody was, that the speaker's grandfather was not? Or again, where is the list of those undistinguished anybodies that does not feature the grandfather's name? In short, we find that the "referent" or "reference" involved here is quite unrelated to "reference" in the sense of Frege's *Bedeutung,* whereas it exhibits a striking affinity with the old "extension" described by the logicians of Port-Royal. Indeed, it shares this term's shortcomings: in the "extension" of the idea of a fine man, there is the speaker's grandfather. For Frege, on the other hand, the reference or referent of the predicate *is a fine man* can never be taken for a "particular object" (an identifiable individual); it is the *Begriff,* or the attribute, of being a fine man.

The semantics of the sentence does not fare any better. What is the referent of a sentence? Sentences not only have a meaning (the "idea"), they also have a referent because they apply to an ever-particular situation in the particular circumstances of their emission. The sentence refers to a situation; ignorance of the circumstances in which it was produced entails ignorance of this referent. We may as well say that the semanticist treats sentences as names or designations. For every name actually used, there is an individual to whom or to which this name belongs; for every sentence actually emitted, there is likewise a situation to which the sentence corresponds. If we do not know to whom a name has been given, we do not know its referent; if we do not know in what circumstances a sentence was emitted, we do not know its referent. Such parallelism is deceptive. Who is the bearer of a certain name? We can communicate this only by designating him in another way. To what situation does a statement apply? We can explain this only by describing it in another way. Names designate, propositions describe. Our example

The duchess went out at five is not a singular proposition. Although the verb appears in the third person singular, it is a general proposition, in that it applies to at least one duchess (if there are any) but not to any one in particular. To maintain that the proposition is singular, we must turn to the writer's intention, to whatever he has in mind—to the fact that he means a specific person. For his statement may well be attended by a mental focus upon one duchess to the exclusion of all others. Crucially, however, none of this is discernible in the statement as it stands (otherwise, to say *Introduce me to Smith* when in fact you meant Jones, whom you mistakenly thought was called Smith, would be to refer to Jones, whom you meant, and not to Smith, whose name you uttered).[24] In Benveniste's semantics the correspondence of semantic units to things is likewise tied to the intentions of the emitter, that is, to the mental acts and processes that attend his discourse.

The same objections can be made to the position adopted by Paul Ricoeur in *La métaphore vive.* Here he correctly insists upon the difference between the analytic concept of language (analyzing a discourse) and the theories of the signifier generated by Saussure (analyzing the workings of a sign system). He shows that a statement cannot be treated as a sign; the *Course* erroneously held that the difference between *langue* and *parole* was psychological, residing in degrees of freedom, whereas it is a logical difference.[25] Unfortunately Ricoeur goes on to endorse Benveniste's distinction, trading off the difference in analytical philosophy between complete signs (names, propositions) and incomplete signs (predicates, logical operators) against the inoperative difference between the semiotic signifier (signs) and the semantic signifier (words and sentences). This confronts us once more with the difficulties of assigning such a distinction to *langue.* For example, we read: "The semiotic recognizes nothing but intralinguistic relations; only semantics is involved with the relation of signs to what they denote, that is, with the relationship between the language [*langue*] and the world."[26] But there is no face-to-face relationship between the language (English, for instance) and the world. Things are not "extralinguistic," as if they were outside the language, for the language is a thing in the world. Languages exist because there are people to speak them. Likewise, there are no grounds for wondering whether a language is adequate to the world.

In the last analysis, the Benveniste brand of semantics leads us back to Husserl via the concept of the speaker's or writer's intention. For Husserl, a proposition points to something, to an "object": the state of things intended by whoever animates the sentence with a "semantic intention" ("*une visée sémantique*"), as Ricoeur puts it. Ricoeur justly detects Husserl's intentional object in the reference of the semantic entity as seen by Benveniste. Strangely enough, however, he also links this reference to Frege and Wittgenstein. We read, "Thus the opposition between Benveniste and Frege is not irreconcilable. For Frege, denotation is communicated from the proper name to the entire proposition, which then becomes the proper name of a state of affairs. For Benveniste, denotation is communicated from the whole sentence to the word, by distribution within the syntagm."[27] In fact, the gulf between Benveniste and Frege could not be wider. For Benveniste, each use of a sentence refers to a particular situation. For Frege, propositions are complete signs and therefore have a *Bedeutung*, but this is never the particular fact being signified. For him, all true propositions are the proper names of a single object, the True, and all false propositions are those of another, the False. Wittgenstein explicitly rules out this reference for the proposition (*Tractatus*, 3.144). But the important point for us is not that Frege and Wittgenstein disagree with Husserl and Benveniste, but that Frege and Wittgenstein should be correct. It is the business of the proposition to advance a true or a false thought. If we think that the proposition is the sign, or name, of a referent, we shall say that the proposition is true when something corresponds to it in fact or in reality. But what? Its referent, the fact it names. But then the false proposition is one whose referent is nonexistent. A false proposition corresponds to nothing outside in the world; it designates in a void, it is a hollow name. This leaves us defenseless against the sophistical trap: *logos* is the *logos* of something, error is the *logos* of nothing; therefore error is impossible. The false proposition says nothing, much as an unallocated telephone number is nobody's number (although it is not exactly the number of a nonperson, the number of Nothing). Naturally Ricoeur condemns such sophism. But no semantics that assigns a referent to propositions can argue against it— unless the solution lies in adopting the idealist version of phenomenology, as other authors have done.

This version itself exists in two forms: multireferential perspectivism, and ontology of the unsayable referent. Let us start with the fact that phenomenological doctrine cannot draw the line at sentences. If the sentence, like the name, possesses a referent, then so must the totality of sentences. Ricoeur is aware of this. If we call *text* or *work* the semantic entity that is to the sentence what the sentence is to the *name*, we can say that the *world* (the referent of the work) is to the *state of things* (the referent of the sentence) what the latter is to the individual *object* (the referent of the name). Since all sentences have a referent, all works will deploy or delineate a world.[28] Every work has a reference, whether it be science or fiction, prose or verse, journalism or literature. For this reason an identification problem recurs here. Just as we can always inquire whether two names designate the same thing or two distinct things, so we should be able to ask whether two works are designations of the same world or of two distinct worlds. Is the world of Newtonian physics the same as the world of Cartesian physics? Does the world of *Hamlet* merge with the world of *Othello* to constitute a single Shakespearean world, or are the two as distinct as the two works themselves? If one work is presented as the refutation of another, is its world a nonworld, namely whatever the refuted work is not? All kinds of oddities transpire until we realize the phenomenologist is not saying that a work presents a world, but that it presents *its* world, the world that is its own. So the phrase *the world of the work* hovers between two meanings. To say that the work presents a world (i.e., the world it presents) is not quite the same as saying that there is a world the work presents, that there is a world that is the world the work presents. To invoke some "world of the work" does not amount to a guarantee that every work has a reference. In fact, what is here called a "referent" may not be a reference at all, since phenomenology does not divide the world from the work whose world it is. The referent remains intentional, the correlate of the speaker's or writer's intentions, or perhaps the correspondent to the intentions of the statement. What we call world remains an object, the direct object of an intentional verb. Not every portrait of a woman corresponds to a woman whose portrait it is, and similarly not every work delineating a world points to a world being delineated by the work. A relation of reference would require the world to be detachable from the work or from the worker, so that it is possible to show which individuals are the poles of this relation (but although I can designate the worker or the work, I have no way of denoting what should correspond to it other than "the world of the work").

Abandoning the view that decrees one world whose regions are all the worlds of all the works, we enter the school of perspectivism. This is a wise move in some respects, for it dispenses with the formidable difficulties of reconciling all these worlds on a single map. We need no longer worry about which worlds are identical, adjacent, disparate, or opposed. Above all, we no longer need to fit the referent of an affirmative proposition onto the same map as the referent of its negation. Thus we need no longer appeal to a dubious dialectic. The price we pay for all these advantages, however, is that the world constituted by works is the only world. The "world of the work" is still the direct object of delineation by the work, but the work itself is identifiable. The world is thus a monadology in which the monads are texts or works.

Other phenomenologists have been reluctant to do away with all reference—all authentic relation between discourse and something other than discourse. Behind the intentional object (the apple tree in bloom) lies yet another intentional object, intended through the first (the "something = x" that reveals itself to me under the aspect I attribute to it of a blossoming tree). The authentic referent to which we relate is thus the indeterminate subject of determinations, "it, the selfsame." We are now in the ontological school, which posits that discourses refer to something, even if we cannot say what. If a world of reference exists, there is one world for all discourses; in their conflicts they venture descriptions of this world that *by rights* are reconcilable at the end of an infinite labor. This world is unique and unsayable in itself, otherwise it would be identical to the world of a work, and other works would lose their referents. The world named by every name is unnameable, distinguished from all else by its very indistinguishability; it is the thing without being any thing, the only topic of all time, the prepredicative. It is never what we say of it, precisely because saying what it is involves speaking of it. It is the destination of an infinite journey that culminates in its name; it retreats when approached and is distorted by observation. It is itself, the selfsame, the identical that is identical to nothing; and it is also itself, the other, which nothing distinguishes from anything else.

What we speak of, precisely because we speak of nothing else, is never what we say about it (it, "the selfsame"), whatever we say. This paradox has the same shape as another more familiar one: what appears, precisely because it is what appears, is precisely what fails to appear. Now and then we affect to project our thoughts toward something ("it"), but halfheartedly, always postponing the problem of identifying this reference—the problem of the individuation of this thing. We are better off without a semantics that demands such impossible feats of us.

The Mystery of the Left-hand Box

The transition from the old to the new concept of the sign begins on page 65 of the *Course in General Linguistics*. This passage has become a classic. The sign was traditionally conceived as a simple entity; now, consequent upon the semiological view of language, it must be forged into the unity of signifier and signified. These pages have a propaedeutic role in the *Course*. The real issues for general linguistics are broached only later, with the problems of describing a state of the language (synchronic linguistics) or an evolution of the language (diachronic linguistics). Linguists as such will find little to interest them in these pages. Yet semiological philosophy describes no particular language and traces no linguistic evolution. It merely comments upon the change in the concept of the sign. It is based entirely upon these linguistic preliminaries.

Here is the beginning of the chapter entitled *Nature of the Linguistic Sign* (reproducing only part of the table, which I have also squared out):

Some people regard language, when reduced to its elements, as a naming process only—a list of words, each corresponding to the thing that it names. For example:

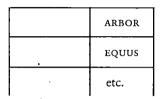

This conception is open to criticism at several points. It assumes that ready-made ideas exist before words. . . . It lets us assume that the linking of a name and a thing is a very simple operation—an assumption that is anything but true. But this rather naive approach can bring us near the truth by showing us that the linguistic unit is a double entity, one formed by the association of two terms. (*CGL*, p. 65·)

I have supplied this lengthy quotation in order that Saussure's familiar, much revisited text might be seen *without* the figurative part of the example. For, of course, the two boxes I have outlined and left empty normally contain a picture of a tree and one of a horse, much as they used to feature in the old pictorial ABCs. Opposite the words ARBOR and EQUUS, the reader could easily be instructed to place the pictures that correspond to the words in the original *Course*. But according to the same *Course*, these drawings are not the things to which the words correspond. If, for instance, typesetters settled on the names *arbor* and *equus* to stand for these two emblems, it might be possible to say, I want an arbor on the cover and an equus between these two paragraphs here. But the example clearly sets out to illustrate a certain traditional concept we have of words, of the words *arbor* and *equus*, for example, taken in the usual sense to mean the same as the English *tree* and *horse*. This conception is open to criticism, says the *Course*. It is too simplistic. Yet however far it may be from the truth, it can serve as a starting point and lead us, once corrected, to a more satisfactory conception. The transition from the traditional to the semiological attitude toward the sign will be achieved by bringing the necessary amendments to the crude but widespread view, which we must first examine in order to grasp the scope of these corrections and their raison d'être.

Some people regard language as a nomenclature, or a list of names. In the case of Latin it might be *"arbor, equus,* etc." In a nomenclature, designations are devised in order to be applied to things. The simplistic aspect of the traditional conception, then, consists in thinking that the sign is created by the assignation of a particular thing (a specific sound or graphism) to another particular thing, whereas in fact it is created by its position within a system. This is what the *Course,* at any rate, proceeds to say, and what semiologists have repeated since. Before we reach that point, however, we must still grapple with the mistaken conception, so as to modify it as required. Until now we have understood only half of the explanation and the example. The notion of nomenclature is easily grasped, and it is not hard to detect what is simplistic in the reduction of a language to its nomenclature (all words become names). To see this example in its entirety, we must complete terms by things. A nomenclature is "a list of words, each corresponding to the thing that it names." We know what a list of names is. In the simplistic notion of our example, it must correspond to a collection of things. There will be as many names as there are things. If, for example, there are two names (*equus* and *arbor*) on our list—plus the possibility of adding to it indefinitely ("etc.")—the collection of corresponding things will consist of two items. What are these things? To what things does our basic conception make the two words *arbor* and *equus* correspond?

Already we can see that the conception we need to correct is not only one of simplistic linguistics (a language is composed, in this model, of designative terms); it is also one of simplistic semantics, in other words, a doctrine of the way words signify things. We know that Saussurean linguistics excludes semantic problems from its field of study. The "referent," to use an expression that came later, would be bracketed off. However, what holds for semiological linguistics does not hold for semiological philosophy, which, if it wishes to correct the simplistic conception, must first state it and then indicate its shortcomings. In so doing, it will simultaneously correct the simplistic semantic conception and improve upon it. We are thus entitled to ask: What is a thing? Semiology of language recognizes only the word *thing*; semiological philosophy of the sign, for its part, must be able to explain the concept of the thing.

The simplistic conception believes that a language is composed of as many terms as there are things. Surely the thing corresponding to the word *arbor* is a tree (any tree) and the thing corresponding to the word *equus* is a horse (any horse)? Thus the example on page 65 of the *Course* should be interpreted as:

Here plant a tree	ARBOR
Here place a horse	EQUUS
etc.	etc.

The right-hand boxes are designed to contain inscriptions. The left-hand boxes are respectively a patch of garden (for the tree) and a paddock (for the horse). Our four boxes are full. The order followed in the example—things on the left, signs on the right—signifies that the left-hand boxes were filled first. To place a thing (the inscription *arbor*) in the right-hand box is to institute a thing (a certain inscription) as a sign of the thing in the box to its left; this procedure is reproduced in an explanation by means of the ostensive definition of the term *arbor*. To explain the meaning of what is written in the right-hand box, we are invited to look at what has been placed in the corresponding box on the left.

The left-hand boxes were filled first. What do they contain? In opting for a Latin nomenclature, the *Course* deflects the problem of the article. If the terms of the nomenclature were in English, what would we put into the first box on the right: *tree, a tree, the tree,* or *trees*? In this conception, there is one term per thing. In every right-hand box, there is one term and one term only. We know how to count the terms. But do we know how to count the corresponding things, the alleged "referents"? Suppose that we translate *equus* by *horse*, as the dictionary does. The inscription is now *horse*, and it counts as one term. But do we, by placing a horse in the box to the left, supply this inscription with the thing of which it is the sign? If we herd several horses into the paddock, must we modify the inscription? Do several horses count as several things or as one thing only? We do not know. But then the conception is not simplistic—merely unintelligible and as such impossible to correct. We cannot use it as our starting point.

To extricate ourselves, we must return to the notion of nomenclature. If our list is a nomenclature, we will be able to imagine a situation in which it might have been drawn up. What, in such a situation, would be the collection of corresponding things? The list "*arbor, equus*" could have been drawn up by the curator of a natural history museum (Mr. Adam). A small town decides to assemble a collection, but so far there are only two exhibits. In such a modestly stocked museum, only two plaques are necessary. The simplistic conception of a language consists in imagining that words are forged one after another, in the same way that the keeper of our museum has a new plaque struck for each addition to the collection. The right-hand boxes are plaques. The left-hand boxes are display cases. The curator mounts his first plaque, marked *Tree*. What do we find in the corresponding display case? One tree or several? Something else entirely (but what)? Page 65 of the *Course* does not tell us, because it does not happen to be a natural history museum. Page 65 presents words "in person" but not the things to which they correspond (it is like an even more impoverished museum, with no collection at all, reduced to filling its cases with representations). The *Course* says that things, according to the simplistic conception, are given prior to the terms of nomenclature, but it does not say what these things are. As far as we are concerned, the example amounts to this:

Here insert the corresponding thing	ARBOR
Here insert the corresponding thing	EQUUS

According to the example, the left-hand boxes were filled first. Then the plaques were put up to accompany them. The reader of the *Course*, however, does not know how the left-hand boxes were filled. He is like an employee at this rudimentary museum whose job it is to put the exhibits in the cases already marked by plaques, but without understanding what they say.

The *Course* is a text, containing only signs. In the Botanical Gardens in Paris, however, there is a magnificent cedar planted near the entrance to the maze. The plaque assigned to the cedar bears the following inscription.

> CEDAR
> OF LEBANON
> —
> (*Cedrus libanotica*)
> Brought from England by Bernard
> de Jussieu in 1734.
>
> Grown from seeds of Lebanese origin.
> Presented to de Jussieu by the
> English doctor Collinson.

Cedar of Lebanon is the name of a species. At the same time, the plaque details the history of this cedar of Lebanon. So what we see is at once the cedar of Lebanon (a tree belonging to this species) and this particular cedar of Lebanon (this particular tree belonging to the species). There is only one thing presented, but it may be regarded in two ways: as a species of tree or as a tree belonging to a species. What is presented to us is a certain tree; but a certain type of tree (a tree belonging to a particular species, like the cedar of Lebanon) is always a tree of a certain type (for example, this cedar, the cedar that has this history).

Even though only one cedar of Lebanon is presented in the inscription, the name affixed is not a proper name for this individual of the species. Otherwise the correspondence of word to thing would be comparable to that which obtains between Mount Hollywood and the name *Hollywood* written in vast white letters across the side of Mount Hollywood for the edification of tourists. A museum curator does not distinguish between a tree and this tree, this horse and a horse, any more than Noah did on the ramp of the ark. In the zoological section of the gardens I found neither horse nor horses. But I was able to admire some splendid creatures in two separate enclosures, one marked POITOU DONKEY (I counted five of these) and the other POITOU ASS (I counted three). Suppose for simplicity's sake that a Poitou donkey is the same species of beast (a beast of the same species) as a Poitou ass. For zoological purposes, these eight animals constitute a single POITOU ASS. There is only one thing here: an endearing sort of donkey with long, slightly frizzy hair and strangely splayed legs. (This is a fair description of the POITOU ASS.) But from the administrative point of view, there are eight beasts to feed and tend. Now the gardens do not display individual animals on the one hand (eight asses, three American bison) and species on the other (POITOU ASS, AMERICAN BISON): that is, a grand total of thirteen objects. It displays things that can be enumerated in two ways—eleven living individuals belonging to two distinct species.

Although the inscriptions appearing on the plaques are not proper names for the samples in captivity, neither are they, as is sometimes held, names "denoting" or "referring to" *the totality of individuals belonging to the species.* For one or several Poitou asses may be exhibited, but not the totality of Poitou asses. This is not merely because it would be impossible to make room for them all (in fact the Poitou ass is an endangered species and it may not be long before all Poitou asses can be held in a single enclosure) but because, logically, a set is an abstract entity: it can be constructed but not presented in an ostensive definition.

We have managed to state how the left-hand boxes were filled. Whatever the number of donkeys, the curator will always print POITOU ASS on the plaque. Naturally he can tell the difference between one donkey and two. But used in this way, the word does not need to be pluralized. The inscriptions that appear in the right-hand boxes are not words, therefore, but propositions. To print POITOU ASS on the plaque by the enclosure full of beasts is like saying: *Behold the Poitou Ass.* Consequently, the traditional conception examined here describes not a language but rather one possible use thereof. And in this use we find not words corresponding to things, but words used in order to name things.

The error of the simplistic conception, then, is not that its notion of the relation between words and things is crude. After all, it is possible to establish nomenclatures in a language. It would simply be a mistake to imagine that the only possible use of a language is nomenclature. But the illusion of the traditional concept of the sign—if it consists in taking language for a nomenclature—is to believe that we are describing a language when we describe the construction of nomenclature in that language. Thus the conception at issue appears not so much simplistic as confused. If it were merely simplistic, it could always be made more sophisticated. If it were partial, it could always be completed. But it is based upon a confusion of logical categories: the words of a vocabulary are part of the language, whereas assigning these words to things belongs to the use of language. If we espouse the idea of language as a nomenclature, we would have to hold that a language is composed of things that operate as signs (words) and things that correspond to them. The horse and the tree would then be part of the English language. But if this is the case, the traditional conception is beyond salvaging. We cannot use it as a point of departure.

The semiologist will object that everything we have said so far is grist to the semiological mill. "So," says the semiologist, "you maintain that the conception of language as a nomenclature is incomprehensible? Why that is exactly what the *Course* requires you to accept. It is out of the question for a sign to be able to link or unite a signifier and a thing [its 'referent,' as certain semiologists would say later]. We are not looking for our point of departure in such a coarse theory; we seek it only in the presentiment that a sign is composed of a signifier [the right-hand box] and something else [the left-hand box]. But in no circumstances can this something else be a thing."

We read in the text: "This conception is open to criticism at several points. It assumes that ready-made ideas exist before words." Here, then, the correspondence is no longer between a list of words and a collection of things; it is between that list and a totality of ideas. The naïveté lies not in the correspondence thus established but only in the belief in an empire of ideas already separate from one another, already distinct, which require nothing more than to have terms in the language assigned to them.

According to this new version of the example, the left-hand boxes are not destined to contain things. Nor will they contain signs (all words go into the right-hand boxes). And so we should look again at what on page

65 of the *Course* act as indicators of the things signified. The example will now look like this:

Here, the picture of a tree	ARBOR
Here, the picture of a horse	EQUUS

In the naive conception (no longer absurd; merely in need of amendment), the museum curator has already installed his cases. His samples will be arriving any day now. The staff members who handle and arrange the collection in the cases do not know the language of the museum. They must be taught the terminology. Along with the name on the plaque, therefore, the curator has included a likeness of the item (itself still absent). This is the procedure of certain zoos that have put several species into the same enclosure: the plaque carries the name and the picture of the animal exhibited.

Our understanding of the example has been considerably modified. It is no longer a question of the thing, the referent. Nothing has yet been exhibited; nothing has appeared. The right-hand boxes stand for that part of the plaque that bears the inscription of the species' name. The left-hand side carries the corresponding descriptive image. The example on page 65 of the *Course* is analogous not to a miniature natural history museum, but to the plaques alongside its cases, since it shows next to the actual word, the actual image of the appropriate species.

By amending the naïveté of this theory of language, we will attain to the semiological conception. The simplistic theory supposes that "ideas" exist before words, as if the curator of our museum, before receiving any exhibits, already had a twofold stock of labels: first a series of images to be distributed on the basis of one portrait per case and then a series of names, distributed in advance to the things represented by these portraits. But we are constantly alluding to a curator of designations, a legislator of language. In reality, the staff must work in the absence of any omniscient director. One arrival succeeds another, and the staff must house each exhibit without knowing in advance which classification to apply. Although the number of cases in the museum will not be infinite, it is such that a new plaque can always be added to those already in place. The plaques are drawn from an anomalous stock of quite different signals. It is just as if an improbable scrap merchant had sold the museum a bulk order of signs that usage was now to endow with meaning: *Tree, Horse, Information, Poitou Ass, Cardholders Only, American Bison, Ticket Office, Cedar of Lebanon, Exit,* and so on. In the empiricist model, the staff are supposed to begin by inspecting the contents of each consignment, noting the similarities and differences before putting everything that looks the same into one enclosure and mounting a plaque beside it. In the semiological model, each consignment remains a muddle of similarities and dissimilarities until the signifying differences between the plaques have been used to settle the differences between the descriptions. The staff would begin by distributing the plaques among the cases, before putting the exhibits in place. Each time a consignment of items has been distributed to the various enclosures, a difference is noted between the occupants of distinct spaces and a character common to the occupants of the same space is acknowledged. Each completed placing process is a synchronic state of the language; each delivery of items precipitates the diachronic movement from one state to another.

Here then is the correction brought by semiology to the common view of language. It is normally believed that "ideas" are given before any conventional signs have been agreed for them (as if our curator, already equipped with the descriptions of each item in his future collection, proceeded to find designations for them). In reality, the signified of a signifier (the way of filling a display case, or the left-hand box) depends upon the state of the system. This is the semiological conclusion:

> A word may have different forms (e.g. *chaise* "chair" and *chaire* "desk"). Any nascent difference will tend invariably to become significant but without always succeeding or being successful on the first trial. Conversely, any conceptual difference seeks to find expression through a distinct signifier, and two ideas that are no longer distinct in the mind tend to merge into the same signifier. (*CGL*, p. 121)

We might as well say that if two enclosures have different labels, a reason could always be found for perceiving a difference between the objects they contain; but if by any chance the plaques on two separate enclosures were to lose their signifying difference, a reason could always be found to combine the contents of the two.

The museum analogy, however, has obliged us to reintroduce the thing, which was to have been left aside. To describe the language is like describing the state of the museum before the gradual delivery of the collection. This language is made up of signs: in the right-hand boxes are signifiers, and in the left-hand boxes, signifieds. The descriptions (or instructions for the classification of items) are not given in advance. So long as nothing has arrived, the left-hand boxes remain empty. On the left stands a place for the possible depiction of the awaited objects. The semiological signified is completely indeterminate; it is impossible to say what pictures should be put beside the words. Semiologists are quite content with such a signified in its virtual state, with such a possibility of description. They maintain that determinate meaning will emerge as soon as the objects are in place. As for how they are to be placed in the absence of any instructions, this is unimportant. Any classification of a consignment will enable an inventory to be made. Whenever the same signifier is used (whenever any newly delivered items are housed in the same case), a determinate signified will be obtained (an identical description may be made of the contents of that case).

I have just said that before using signifiers to classify things, the left-hand boxes remain empty. We saw earlier that it is impossible, in the absence of any criterion, to know what thing had been placed opposite a term. Whatever the occupants of a left-hand box may be, we do not know what things they are so long as it is not specified whether the inscription on the right applies to a proper name or a generic name, a name or a predicate, and so forth. So long as the grammar of the word remains obscure, we cannot talk about its relationship to the thing. But the semiologist's signifying differences do not recognize grammatical differences. We must therefore conclude that the doctrine offered here as a starting point is, in all its versions, finally irredeemable.

For instance, Benveniste's famous article discussing the Saussurean notion of the arbitrariness of the sign picks up the case of a word such as *mare*.* This word is a sign made up of a signifier (ma()r) and a signified (the concept of mare). When we speak of the arbitrariness of the linguistic sign, we may mean—to follow the *Course*—that the signifier ma()r is arbitrarily associated with the concept of mare. Benveniste amends this view: "What is arbitrary is that this particular sign rather than another should have been applied to this particular element of reality rather than to another."[29] As for the two component parts of the sign, these are necessarily linked together. "Between signifier and signified the link is not arbitrary; on the contrary, it is *necessary*. The concept ('signified') 'mare' is necessarily identical in my consciousness to the phonic whole ('signifier') ma()r."[30] But once the sign is applied arbitrarily to an element of reality (once a mare is placed opposite the box marked *mare*), is this as a completely constituted sign or merely as a signifier still bereft of its signified? If the linkage of signifier and signified is necessary, the concept of mare would already be "identical in my consciousness" with the signifier ma()r before the sign is applied to anything at all. How is this possible? The concept of mare, then, must itself be severed from the connection it is commonly thought to have with mares. Before the boxes

---

*Benveniste uses the example *boeuf* (ox). Descombes extends the phoneme through *oeuf* and *veuf* (egg, widower) to find an ambiguous homophone in *neuf* (nine, and also new). [TRANS.]

designed to contain things are filled, the concept of *mare* is only the concept of something that is neither a *fair* nor a *hare*. All well and good; the concepts of mare, fair, and hare are purely differential. But let us continue the sequence: a *bear* is that which is neither a *mare* nor a *fair* nor a *hare*. Thus the concept of bear is identified in my consciousness with the phonic whole ba()r. Next we apply the sign *mare* to mares and the sign *hare* to hares. But to what do we apply the sign *bear*? Is it to the animal bear, or to the action of putting up with something? The ursine concept and that of bearing something are logically distinct. One is the singular designation of a certain species; the other is a verb describing the action of toleration. There is no context of usage where the word bear can be understood as equivocal. If I say *I can't bear bears*, everyone will understand the first *bear* as the verb and the second as the animal, and not the other way around. Grammar precludes any confusion. Yet there is no signifying difference between *bear* and *bear*. Thus the gap in the left-hand box should be seen not as an indeterminate signified, but as the indetermination of a signified. What is associated with a signifier is not a "purely differential" signified (such that *mares* would be *hares* for us, and vice versa, if we had exchanged the respective applications of the two signs to reality); it is any signified whatever. The differences between one signified and another have yet to be produced.

A Case of Linguistic Idealism

I will now turn to the didactic exposition of this question as it is found in the *Encyclopedic Dictionary of the Sciences of Language*—an exposition with the merit of deigning to provide an example.[31] The entry "Arbitrariness" presents the common doctrine of signifier and signified according to Saussure and Benveniste. (I hasten to add that since this is a dictionary entry, there is no point in attempting to identify the author's own personal views, only the *status quaestionis*.) We might call it a doctrine of linguistic idealism[32] to hold that if we did not have such and such a language we would not have the particular ideas we have, and that if we did not have these ideas we would not have this experience of things, the world, the "referent." Things would not be what they are to us. According to a traditional image, the classification of things is like the perpetual sectioning (*découpage*) of a continuous body, with as many visions of the world as there are possible cross sections. Behind all these cross sections it is necessary to identify the sectioning of "phonic substance" into signifiers.

The entry takes up Benveniste's amendment to the Saussurean notion of the arbitrary aspect of the sign. The link of signifier to signified is necessary, but the link of the sign to its referent is arbitrary. The theory of the sign need not concern itself with this referent but only with the relation within the sign between two indissociable constituent parts. Since signifieds are concepts, they are dependent on the language. And now for the example:

There is no general idea that could subsequently be indicated by the word *courage*: it is the use of this word that concentrates and unifies a multitude of different moral attitudes, although there is no reason whatever why they should be subsumed under a single word. It is thus an artifice of linguistic thought that leads us to envisage an intellectual unit corresponding to the word *courage*.[33]

In this example, the first point to note is the appearance of the *general idea*. This is nothing less than an ideological genealogy, detailing the origin and formation of "general ideas." The ancients believed that general ideas were ideal things, entities actually visible in some ideal domain (and here we will recognize the "essences" against which empiricist ideology always strove, denouncing the projection of human language into things). The moderns wisely repatriated these "ideas" to the thinking individual in order to constitute them as representative ideas. But they were wrong to infer a psychologistic genealogy from this (on the basis of sensations and an experience of the "referent"). Semiology, then, subjects general ideas to the signifier. It is a doctrine of constitution: the use of the word *courage* constitutes something like courage, something like courageous. The use of the word produces a concentration that in turn encourages the illusion of an intellectual unit existing before language.

But before understanding the causality invoked here (because we have the word *courage*, we have the general idea of courage and the idea that there is such a thing, through a play on the equivocal nature of the word *idea*), we must clarify the terms that are linked: word, concept, and referent.

If we did not have the word, we would not have the concept. This is too hasty. If there is a word, there is a concept. Granted, inasmuch as the fact of regular use attests to our possession of the concept (such that the best definition of this mental capacity known as the concept is to call it the capacity to make signifying use of a word). If a vocabulary contains no word for a certain sort of thing, then there is no proof that the intelligent subjects whose vocabulary this is actually possess the concept in question. But if we can paraphrase a certain concept we have proved ipso facto the possibility of explaining that concept in that vocabulary. For example, there is no special word in our language (or therefore in our culture) for certain conceivable forms of courage: *courageous in great things but not in small things; courageous like a woman in labor*. These differences are not lexically defined for us, but we can see how they might be—and as soon as we imagine this, we have a concept to match, though we cannot use it in the prevailing state of our culture.

According to the normal semiological conception, it would be erroneous to posit a "general idea" or an "intellectual unit" independent of language that the word *courage* might serve to indicate. In fact, this word is used to cover "a multitude of different moral attitudes." Here, apparently, is an allusion to Plato's *Laches*.[34] The courage of the infantryman, for example, consists in remaining fast at his post, while that of the cavalryman consists in executing perilous maneuvers. One shows courage by not moving (to safety), the other by moving (to the attack). The various moral attitudes are not concentrated in themselves, but only if they are subsumed under a single term. What, then, are these moral attitudes grouped under the term *courage*? Are they types of behavior (to perform or not to perform certain sets of movements in such and such a situation)? In that case, there would be species of courage. But if the moral attitude known as COURAGE is an artifice of linguistic thought, the same must be true for species of courage. For example, there is a kind of behavior known as FLIGHT. This "intellectual unit" would not exist if we did not subsume under the same vocable various behaviors that "have no reason whatever" to be concentrated in this way. Thus we have to understand that the various types of behavior grouped together are the actions and effective gestures of certain agents. Paul is a brave soldier because he does not flee; Peter is a courageous entrepreneur because he takes risks. A general pattern emerges: x is an A because he is an F; y is an A because he is a G. We apply the word "A" to the being-F of x and to the being-G of y. And it is by this use of the word "A" that we constitute x as A and y as A. Without this common application of the sign "A," we would not have the "idea" that x and y possess something in common. Let us assume that this is the case. The "referents" x and y have nothing in common except that they are characterized in the same way by a certain use of language (i.e., in a certain culture). In this case the word "A" is equivocal and can be eliminated in favor of the words "F" and "G," which are not. For example, we might decide to scratch the equivocal word *courageous* from the vocabulary and use other words in its stead: *bold*, in one case, *enduring*, in another, *mettlesome*, in another. Of course the word *courage* is not equivocal in this sense and only appears as such in the distinctly sophistical discussion by Socrates in the *Laches*. What happens if we turn to a genuinely equivocal word like the adjective *good*? Here is a case where the constitution of the "intellectual unit" by the word used seems to be a more apposite doctrine. What is there in common between a good wine, a good drill, and a good father? Nothing at all. It is no use answering, *nothing, except that all three are good*, for we would then be hard pressed to explain this property of goodness that all three are recognized to possess. Nor is it of any use to say that the adjective *good* is used to form statements which, while purporting to describe things by attributing properties to them, are actually of another kind: instead of describing things, *good* would describe our own relationship to them (these three things are desirable), or alternatively it would prescribe a certain relationship to things. Univocity, which cannot be found in the description of things, becomes accessible elsewhere, in the description of our mental state (something is good if it is the object of our aspirations) or in the prescriptions we make (*this wine is good* means *I recommend this wine*). Let us try to analyze *this wine is good*. What, in this sentence, is meant by *good*? Choosing not to put the question to a connoisseur, we reply that the assessment of this wine by means of the pseudodescriptive adjective *good* conveys that it is desirable. Or perhaps it lays down a prescription (I expressly recommend that the whole of humanity drink this wine, provided there is enough to go round). And so to the second example, *this is a good drill*. If we are emotivists, we will understand *this drill gives satisfaction*. If we are prescriptivists, *I recommend this drill*. But perhaps we have no idea what a drill is. It could be a form of medication (like *pill*), a variety of herb (like *dill*), or an item of sartorial adornment (like *frill*). According to both of the preceding theories, this should not matter in the least. Since the adjective *good* is univocal, a single meaning is mobilized by the assessment. This is patently absurd: *Here is a thing; I have no idea what it is, but it gives me satisfaction. Or I recommend it to all and sundry*. It is quite clear that the meaning of the adjective *good* cannot be separated from the meaning of the general term with which we describe the thing being assessed. It turns out that a drill is a kind of tool. We now understand that the judgment *this is a good drill* can be followed by justification (*it gave me satisfaction*) and advice (*I recommend it*). Yet if a drill were an intestinal parasite or any other kind of affliction, we might well judge it in the same way, but we would base our judgment upon the opposite justification (*it was very unpleasant*), giving wholly different advice (*avoid it!*).

   It could now be argued that the equivocity of the concept of goodness is irreducible because it is transcendental. That the wine, the drill, and the father are good does not mean that there is a property common to all three. It means that for each of them there is a certain property which, in each case, founds the judgment. The wine is good by virtue of character-

istics A, B, and C; the drill by virtue of characteristics X, Y, and Z. To say
that the wine is good is to say it is A, B, C. To say that the drill is good is
to say it is X, Y, Z. The concept of goodness is therefore equivocal.
Nonetheless this equivocity is not accidental (reducible) but transcendental. What is common to the wine and the drill is not some shared
property but rather a relation of each of them to certain properties. Not
all wines are good wines. Not all drills are good drills. What we find in
common between the good wine and the good drill is thus the presence in
both cases of a sum of properties (different in each case) that has the
same relation to the predicate describing the kind of thing under consideration. For instance, if this wine is a good wine, it is a proper wine, as
wine should be; if this drill is a good drill, it is a proper drill. To echo the
medieval authors lately followed by Geach, we say that the predicate of
goodness adds no new property to those already signified by the descriptive term *wine* (as though we were saying *this wine is a rosé*); rather, it
presents what has already been said (this is a wine) according to a new
ratio.[35] The words *wine* and *rosé* are predicamental terms, *good* is a
transcendental term. What *ratio?* One of confirmation, apparently (in
saying that this bottle contains wine, we are assigning to these contents a
characteristic behavior, a set of natural or habitual ways. In saying that
this is a good wine we are judging the extent to which this beverage
behaves as we would expect of a wine).

   According to the "Arbitrariness" entry in the *Dictionary,* the signified shares the fate of the signifier to which it is indissolubly linked. Were
it not for a certain use of the signifier *courage,* there would not be a
certain signified of the word in the prevailing state of the language. Use of
the word gives rise to a particular "intellectual unit" (in which we shall
not be surprised to recognize the "sense unit" of phenomenology). The
unit engendered by the use of the signifier can thus never be independent
of the language. Semiology gathers from this that it has successfully
demonstrated the arbitrariness of the signified. For the demonstration to
have been conclusive, however, it should have subjected the referent, not
the signified, to the signifier. The arbitrariness of the signifier is shared
here not by the signified attaching to the signifier *courage,* but by the
thing itself, the virtue of courage. The article should have established the
following distinction: when we say that Achilles, Alexander, and Paul
Revere are courageous, we are not saying there is anything that Achilles,
Alexander, and Paul Revere are (namely courageous), but simply that all
three are held to be courageous in a linguistic context where the word
courage exists. The article should in fact have shown that the predicate
. . . *is courageous* has no referent. If Foot Soldier Calchas takes to his
heels while Foot Soldier Callias steadfastly mans his post, there is cer-

tainly something that Calchas does and Callias does not do (namely, flee); but the example as it stands does not show that Callias possesses a virtue lacked by Calchas. And so even if the example given had been conclusive its value would have remained limited, for it cannot seriously be claimed that all predicates are devoid of reference.

If the signifier is arbitrary with respect to the referent and if the signified is necessarily linked to the signifier, the signified must also be considered arbitrary. Philosophical semiology attempts to draw ideological conclusions from this. Signifying differences elicit conceptual differences. Since the differences between signifying forms cannot be explained by the need to reflect the world order—the signifier is autonomous—the signified obeys the law of the signifier. This ideology can hardly be termed psychological; it has little to do with anybody's idea of mares or of courage.[36] It is sociological; it inventories the ideas of the English speaker at a given period.

Yet the semiological demonstration does uninentionally bear upon the referent. It engenders the referent. The *Dictionary* chooses an abstract noun (*courage*) to illustrate a thesis it presents as generally valid. This thesis verifiably offers the formula for a semiological constitution of the objects of possible experience. Take a word I shall call "W." We can understand this word in its various senses, because repeated use provokes a concentration of the various things to which "W" is applied, leading to the presentation of these diverse things as cases of a single kind of thing, the W kind. Next we succumb to the inevitable illusion that the W kind of thing is really given, independent of our use of the word "W." The formula is a general one and can be applied to categories of words other than abstract nouns. Each time we rehearse it, we are enacting the constitution of the referent, not of the concept. First we interpret the letter "W" as a proper name, for instance, *Socrates*. By applying the formula, we express the constitution of Socrates, not that of the "concept of Socrates" (if such a thing exists). We shall be saying that repeated use of the word *Socrates* on various occasions condenses the variety of referents to which the word is each time applied into an ideal entity, the man Socrates. This is why we believe, forgetting the function of language in the constitution of the identity of this ideal entity, that all these referents are really one Socrates: Socrates here, Socrates there, Socrates yesterday, Socrates today. By applying to each of these elementary data the same proper name, we constitute them into slices of Socrates (as if we were constantly saying, here is some Socrates and here is a bit more Socrates). In this way ideological semiology applied to proper names offers a theory of the constitution of the individuals in question. The signified that is engendered in the process (the idea of Socrates) is precisely the referent (Socrates himself), since the use of the proper name Socrates is not for Socratic phenomena, apparitions, or slices, but for Socrates himself, who figures in all these unnamed manifestations. Similarly, if we interpret the letter "W" as the name of a species such as *horse*, then by applying the formula we propose a doctrine of the constitution of the equine species. Note the ambitiousness of the semiological formula. It does not support the fairly plausible thesis that our concept of the species is acquired by regular and repeated use of the word *horse*. It claims that by repeated use of the word *horse* we become convinced that certain animals are horses. It ought to add that by reiterating the word *animal* we concentrate different living creatures into a single class; this in turn gives rise to the ideal unit of an animal kingdom. Likewise, the use of the word *living* gathers individuals into a single order of the living. (And at this point the doctrine of constitution breaks down, for no one is quite sure what should be assembled in order to yield individuals.)

What is arbitrary, then, turns out to be the referent. This unexpected and undesirable outcome results from the failure of semiology to specify precisely what should be added to the signifier in order to constitute a sign.

The Structuralist Misunderstanding

In the preceding sections of this chapter, we dealt with a range of semiological analyses of the linguistic sign. These applications to language of the semiological concept of the sign are supposed to develop the hitherto neglected distinction between the signified and the referent. Unfortunately we were unable to sever one from the other in our efforts to grasp the examples illustrating the theory. It became evident that we were constantly shifting from the description of the system to which a sign belongs to a use of that sign (from *langue* to *parole*, language to speech). If this is already the case where linguistic signs are concerned, how much more intractable are matters likely to become when we extend these analyses to nonlinguistic signs. Semiology, generally speaking, studies the signifier. Now, there are two types of signifier—that of the linguist and that of the sociologist. The linguistic signifier answers the question: How many dictionary entries would it take to describe the state of the language at a given date? But there is nothing lexical about the sociological signifier; in sociology signifying occurs when a behavior indicates the status or position of the agent within the group. From this point of view, *to signify* is *to state*; it is always to state the case, make a claim, draw a distinction, proclaim one's membership in an elite. The sociological signifier is the utterance of a statement. The first signifier is the province of the typographer or the crossword fanatic, whereas the second belongs to the headwaiter, the couturier, or the diplomat. The linguistic signifier poses problems of identification. (Is there a signifying difference between these two utterances?) The sociological signifier poses problems of recognition. (With whom am I dealing?) Borrowing the names of Proust's characters, I shall call the first the Brichot-signifier and the second the Norpois-signifier.[37]

Sociological semiology looks for signifiers in fashion, consumerism, tastes, forms of expression, types of discourse, or the arts. The snag is that a Norpois signifier tends to be treated as if it were a Brichot. This quid pro quo is flagrantly apparent in Roland Barthes's first semiological essay, entitled "Myth Today." The opening sentence asks, "What is a myth, today?" To which the second sentence replies, "Myth is a type of speech."[38] The fourth sentence, alas, prescribes a method for the study of modern myths as follows: "But what must be firmly established at the start is that myth is a system of communication, that it is a message." Is myth a Brichot-signifier or a Norpois-signifier? If it signifies as a function of its differential position in a system comparable to a language, it must be a Brichot. Or perhaps it is the system itself, within which mythic units or "mythemes" might be discernible, whose signification would be of the Brichot kind. But we read: it is a message, a type of speech. So it is a Norpois-signifier after all. For example, the sentence *Quia ego nominor leo*, from a Latin grammar, is "addressed to me" and signifies something to me. It is a Norpois-signifier, saying, *I am a grammatical example*.[39] "Take a bunch of roses: I use it to *signify* my passion."[40] There is no room for doubt. The roses signify my passion if I send them. To signify, then, is unmistakably to make something known to someone. The very same roses when on the florist's shelf will "signify" that they are for sale (and not that the florist loves me madly), but if I give them to someone they will signify my passion.

The Brichot-signifier and the Norpois-signifier belong to logically distinct categories. For the semiologist, the Brichot-signifier is part of a system. If we follow Barthes's definitions above, the Norpois-signifier (the myth) is itself a system. A mythic narrative may be a system, but it is certainly not a tongue. There is nothing semiological in its analysis therefore, in the Saussurean sense of the word, until the signifying difference between this and a series of other narratives within the mythological system has been identified.

If this faux pas were simply a momentary lapse on the part of the author, it would not be worth mentioning. But since it recurs again and again, we are forced to conclude that the semiological burden deforms the gait of all those who bear it. The entire analysis is crippled. In *Elements of Semiology*, a work with more technical ambitions, we read: "To wear a beret or a bowler hat does not have the same meaning."[41] This example of the semiology of headgear is patently concerned with a Norpois-signifier. The signification attaches to the beret, if worn—the wearing of the beret. But *Elements of Semiology* claims that the opposition of beret and bowler belongs to "the language of clothes" (whereas we should say that wearing a beret, in the contemporary code, constitutes a definite message because this choice is inevitably loaded with meaning: the man might have opted for a cap, a Stetson, or nothing at all). The beret itself would be a Brichot-signifier. But the elements of a language exist for the purpose of building sentences, whereas the wearing of a beret is already a statement in itself. Comprehension of this statement should evolve from an analysis of beret wearing, not from the opposition of beret, cap, and bowler.

Barthes is not alone here; the example is set by an even higher authority. A famous passage by Lévi-Strauss[42] on the "floating signifier" encourages a confusion between Brichot and Norpois, extending to statements the analytical principles laid down for the study of languages. Language, says Lévi-Strauss, could only have arisen at a stroke. There is language once a language has appeared. Since a language is a totality, the persons who acceded to language could immediately avail themselves of the entirety of the signifier and—since signifier and signified are indissoluble—of the entirety of the signified. Yet the emergence of language does not endow mankind with knowledge of the world. The acquisition of language occurs through mutation, the acquisition of knowledge through a slow progression. This is how we can speak of the world before we know of it. So far, it is not hard to follow Lévi-Strauss's (speculative) demonstration. Our difficulties begin immediately, however, when human potential is seen as having been realized and possibilities are treated as actual resources. The gap between the sudden acquisition of language and the laborious acquisition of knowledge is explained semiologically: from the beginning the entirety of the signified is given together with the entirety of the signifier, but this signified is "given as such without, however, being known."[43] So there is a given signified, as yet unknown, to which the "floating signifier" will correspond, flourishing in discourses that are alien to science (art, poetry, myth, religion, etc.). What is given is, of course, no more than possible. Whoever can understand one sentence is thereby capable in principle of understanding all sentences, and whoever pronounces one sentence can always utter others. In Lévi-Strauss's analogy, this human potential is treated as actuality:

It is as if mankind had all at once acquired an immense domain and a detailed map to go with it; mankind had the notion of the mutual relationship between the two but had spent millennia learning which symbols on the map represented which different features of the domain. The Universe signified long before it began to be known what it signified—this, no doubt, is obvious. But it also follows from the above analysis that it signified, from the beginning, the totality of what mankind can expect to know about it.[44]

Language is like a map, and the things signified are like the territory the map represents. This is an ancient comparison, still as suggestive and as deceptive as ever. The map is the entirety of the signifier, the domain is the entirety of the signified. Both are given to us simultaneously, but we only gradually learn to understand which symbols on the map apply to which parts of the territory. Meanwhile, those symbols whose representative value remains unrecognized constitute the floating signifier. This little fable does much to illuminate the bizarre side of the conception of language that it is designed to illustrate. Mankind does not learn about its domain by reading the map; it learns to read the map by visiting the domain. Would a tourist go to Rome in order to understand his Blue Guide? But there is another paradox inherent in the cartographic conception of language. Does the map represent the domain, or does the domain represent the map? Lévi-Strauss's parable assigns a signifying function to the universe: as soon as there is language, the universe signifies, even if we do not know what. It signifies what is written on the map. The map is not a language; it is a discourse. The symbols are analyzed not like elements of a linguistic system, but as the elements of a system that is the discourse on the universe of an infinite scholarship. The entirety of the signifier is the entirety of true propositions. The entirety of the signified is omniscience. Thus, even when anthropological semiology speculates about the linguistic signifier, it hastens to move from the fact of language to the fact of speech. This fable would have us believe that the appearance of language was the gift to men of an infinite but self-sufficient library in which everything possible is written. The library is the "divine understanding" referred to below.[45] But primitive man is bewildered by this gift, for he cannot read. In reality, if we wanted to express the sudden appearance of language in terms of maps and territories, it would be more accurate to depict man as receiving a gift in the form of the domain and a blank sheet (tabula rasa) on which to draw the map with the aid of a finite, self-sufficient series of symbols. Everything that can be said can be said on the sheet of paper, everything one wishes to say about the domain must be said with the aid of the symbols provided. Consequently the first man, having acquired language, has simultaneously acquired the possibility of saying everything. The moment Adam is capable of speech, the following proposition becomes true:

Now, Adam has the power to say everything that is sayable.

For it would be a *fallacia compositionis* to state:

Adam has the power to say *now* everything that is sayable.

By exchanging the capacity to form sentences for a rather suspect totality (all the true propositions of which we are capable), Lévi-Strauss's image leads us surreptitiously from language to discourse. Language is now the Book of all truths, and knowledge is the reading we can achieve of certain passages from this Book. Thus signifier and signified have changed places along the way, as the result of a perfectly semiological manoeuvre. *Everything in the world exists to culminate in a book*, wrote Mallarmé. In the analogy, language is that book. The world has gone topsy-turvy. In Mallarmé, the Book for the sake of which there is something rather than nothing was not an account or a narrative. But in the analogy it is a map. Thus we learn to find our way about the world as we explore it only in order to find our way about the map. Mallarmé's Book is an absolute because it does not speak of the world, or does so only in a few incidental references. But the map is purely a representation of the territory; and yet the world is what signifies. The universe has always signified. The Book of all truths tells us what the world signifies. Once we have learned to read a chapter of the Book, we know what one part of the world means. As for the chapters we do not understand, we must approach them as though they too applied to the parts of the world we already know. If the world has always signified the totality of what mankind will ever know about it, the world is a kind of signifier. But what kind? Needless to say, it is a Norpois-signifier, not a Brichot-signifier. After all, here the world is not a language; it is the domain represented by the map, by a discourse. To say that the world signifies is to say that human beings proceed by inference: *if there was this, then there will be that*. In other words, the world signifies by signifying to us. If the wild geese fly past early, then it will be a hard winter. If a farmer cultivates a field several years in a row, the land will become exhausted. Finders keepers. Red sky at night, sailors' delight. Such are the signifieds that events in the world afford us. Some of these signifieds may feature in the chapters we are able to read. Others belong to chapters we cannot read, although we can utter them: if someone draws a losing number, he is unlucky. If the king is king, it is because he is the Lord's anointed. A gift must be returned, because the gift has mana. All these signifiers are

Norpois-signifiers: to us, they signify that. . . . But we cannot say what they signify without breaking away from the language of positive knowledge and speaking of *luck*, of *consecration*, or of *mana*.

The Signifier of Desire

Un mou de veau et je suis sauvé.
(famous signifier)

The most acclaimed doctrine of the signifier is surely that of Jacques Lacan, from whom I have borrowed the term *doctrine of the signifier*.[46] Nonetheless, the interest of Lacan's earliest publications is in no way diminished by the absence at that time of any such doctrine.[47] This interest centers upon the manifest concern to return psychoanalysis to history, linking the "Oedipus complex" to the evolution of the patriarchal family and associating individual neuroses with the global malaise of civilization. The psychoanalyst's prey is the "'emancipated' man of modern society"[48] who unwittingly contradicts the great humanist doctrines of the modern age by proclaiming "in all his troubles as by all his acts: God is dead, nothing is any longer permitted."[49] This man suffers from irrational feelings of guilt, which cannot be explained by philosophies of consciousness. At this period Lacan does not separate the spread of the psychoanalytic "plague" and the decline of the great traditional orders in the West. There would be no psychoanalysis if individuals were not at the mercy of themselves or if they had found, once liberated, the satisfactions humanism had promised them. Was Lacan's diagnosis meant to imply that psychoanalysis could remedy these disorders, or that it was the vehicle of some new order? The obscurity of his writings makes it impossible to tell.

During the same period, philosophers readily discussed the concept of the unconscious, taken in its strictly psychological, Freudian sense. The unconscious was a certain state of the *res cogitans*, a peculiar state that could elude the examination of consciousness undertaken by this *res*. A person's unconscious (= what is unconscious to him) is thus composed of thoughts (*cogitationes*) and representations (ideas, *Vorstellungen*) of which he is unaware. Belief in such an unconscious would hinge upon a belief in such a consciousness. For there to be an unconscious in the sense of a state of something represented to oneself without one's knowledge, there must be consciousness in the sense of the capacity to observe one's own representational states. This is the classic model of consciousness in epistemological philosophy. On the one hand, an uninterrupted flow of representations is constantly active, governed by the laws of "association of ideas." On the other, an "inner sense" enables the subject (of the verb to *represent to oneself*) to be aware of what is flowing through him and even to influence its course. Like a lockkeeper, the subject presides over the flow of his thoughts. Logic, conceived as the art of thinking, might be the regulation of this flux in the name of the great principles: the "identity principle" in formal logic, the "principle of the identity of the apperception" in so-called transcendental logic. But if the flux is not under control, if associations are freely made as in daydreams, the course of thought will follow a different pattern. It will obey, as is often said, "another logic."

The novelty of Lacan's early texts resided less in the positions taken up than in a certain tendency to invest the concept of the unconscious with an application that was independent of these psychological presuppositions. The unconscious underwent a shift; it was no longer what evades the inward focus of my attention, what presents itself only in a veiled form to my inner sense; instead it became what cannot be communicated by means of speech (*parole*) to an interlocutor. Here *parole* is not used in the Saussurean sense. Lacan's observations on the evolution of criminal law in Europe indicate that he intends a stronger sense, which is also in a way more archaic or feudal.[50] Lacan insists on the following paradox: in archaic times, it devolved upon the god to name the culprit (judgment of God, trial by ordeal); in humanist times, the culprit declared himself by confessing his misdeed, whence the need for interrogation (torture is explained by the imperative to extract an admission of guilt from the criminal); finally, in modern times, "the new man, abstracted from his social consistency, is no longer *believable*"[51] (it is no longer a matter of interrogation and punishment, but of detection and rehabilitation). This is the kind of man who will confide his problems to Freud. It is precisely in a civilization where men can no longer be believed that an art appears on the fringes of medicine, designed to cure complaints by means of the word. This is a far cry from later Lacanian constructions in which the various "complexes" and "instances" become detached from history because they are universally grounded in the relation of the subject (of the word) to language, conceived along Saussurean lines as a system of signifiers.

Lacan's conversion to the doctrine of the signifier was initially of a superficial nature. Its disastrous consequences were only gradually to emerge, alongside the proliferation of "graphs" supporting the claim to have formalized the fundamental concepts of psychoanalysis. (In reality, these diagrams are to any authentic formalization what Jarry or Duchamp's "*machines célibataires*" are to ordinary machines.)

Our theory of the signifier, says Lacan, is founded "on the fact that the unconscious is structured in the most radical way like a language, that a material operates in it according to certain laws, which are the same laws as those discovered in the study of actual languages, languages which are or were actually spoken."[52] Freud, of course, did not say this—scarcely surprising, since the discovery of the unconscious predates the semiological definition of language. According to Lacan, however, the work of Freud anticipates this progress in linguistics. For it is in fact the Saussurean notion of the signifier that succeeds in explaining the difference between medical and psychoanalytic symptoms. The medical symptom is a sign (which founds a diagnosis); the Freudian symptom is a signifier (which requires interpreting, i.e., hearing). A sign is the representative of something. A signifier signifies anything at all; it depends on the circumstances.

It is already clear that Lacan has abandoned Saussurean signifiers (whose signified is a concept) in favor of Norpois-type signifiers (whose signified is the meaning of a statement). The unconscious is structured like a language. But what kind of language? Language in the sense of discourse. All Lacanian formulas take the manifestations of the unconscious to be speech (*des paroles*). "The dream has the structure of a sentence."[53] "The symptom resolves itself entirely in an analysis of language, because the symptom is itself structured as a language, because it is a language that seeks to be delivered as speech."[54] The *structure of language* invoked in all these Lacanian edicts is thus nothing to do with the system constituted by a language. This structure is scarcely structuralist, for it is merely the grammatical construction of a sentence. One might therefore expect the theory of the signifier to be of a grammatical nature—as in certain respects it is. If a dream, for instance, could be understood as the (disguised) fulfillment of (unconscious) wishes, it must indeed be the equivalent of speech the dreamer is unaware of uttering. This speech expresses a desire of which the dreamer in his subsequent account of the dream does not wish to acknowledge himself as the subject. As Lacan rightly emphasizes, the word *Wunsch*, used by Freud to describe the dream, shows that unconscious desire is a desire expressed.

So far so good: it can be established that Freud was always in the business of interpreting signifiers. Less promising, however, is the fact that such signifiers should be speech, statements, and thus foreign to Saussurean definitions. The theory of the arbitrariness of the linguistic sign applies to words, not to sentences. The word *mare* could have been used for something other than mares; for anything at all, in fact. But it does not follow that a sentence containing the word *mare* might likewise mean anything at all. Lacan professes to use the Saussurean concept of the signifier, and thus to take it in the sense in which a word is a signifier.

"I have substituted for the word *word*, the word *signifier*. This means that it is prone to ambiguity, that is, to several possible significations."[55] So it is after all a question of the word, not of the sentence. Yes, but the word can be understood in French, as in English, in the sense of a statement: *I'd like a word with you; he had the last word; he has a good word to say for everyone; just give us the word*, and so on. And on close inspection, it is always this kind of *word* that intervenes in the examples or images Lacan gives to convey the ambiguity of language. Thus in his reply to the Congress of Rome in 1953, his example of a word without meaning is the *password*.

And so as to move from the pole of the *word* to that of *speech*, I shall define the first as the point at which the most meaningless material, in terms of the signifier, converges with the most palpable effect in terms of the symbolic. This point is occupied by the password, with its two facets: the non-sense to which it is traditionally reduced, and the truce it brings to the radical hostility of man for his fellows.[56]

This example clearly intends to oppose the sign (always the sign of this or that) and the signifier, which is linked to no fixed meaning, deriving its (symbolic) efficacy from precisely this semantic vacuum. The password, then, is the ultimate signifier. Yet the example proves exactly the opposite. The password is not a word, nor is it a Saussurean signifier; it is a message. *If he knows the password, he is one of us*. The password itself can be a word, a phrase, a sentence or anything else, for its symbolic efficacy (or "effect of the pure signifier") is inherent not in the word but in the fact that someone possesses and dispenses it. However, in Lacan's farcical variation on the Saussurean ARBOR example, the "signifiers" LADIES and GENTLEMEN are written above two drawings representing identical doors (rather than two groups: men and women).[57] The move from singular (ARBOR) to plural (LADIES, GENTLEMEN) already betrays the change of ground. The "signifiers" in Lacan's example are in the plural because grammar dictates the plural for this particular use. Thus the example does not associate Saussurean signifiers and signifieds but illustrates a context for using the notices LADIES and GENTLEMEN. They are statements (*this door is exclusively for ladies, this door is exclusively for gentlemen* would be a more appropriate expression of this "signifier").

Adherents to the Lacanian theory of the signifier may resort to the following line of defense: whereas it is perfectly true that the signifier (the "signifying material") to be interpreted is signifying in the sense that it *says* something, the crucial point is that it should state not one but several things, not simply an official truth, but something else between the lines.

The sentences have this ambiguity precisely because they are composed of Saussurean signifiers. Psychoanalysis is an analysis of language bearing upon speech, but its right to interpret is founded on the conception of language as a system of signifiers. It is because words are not signs for things that ambiguous discourse is possible.

But this defense is a piece of sophistry. Of course a word does not have the same meaning in all its uses; a word can therefore be used in several senses. This does not mean that all its various potential meanings are latent in each one of its uses. If a word does not have the same meaning in all its uses, we can say that it has different meanings in different contexts but not that it has different meanings in a single context. Otherwise I might as well say that I am on Route 6, when I am actually driving along Route 7, simply because Lyons can be reached from Paris by both routes. I can take either, but this does not exempt me from selecting one. Thus we have to say that in each of its uses, a word has the meaning it has in that particular use. Is this use the same as another use of the same word on another occasion? If so, it will already be in the dictionary. Is it different? Then it will be added to the list. What we cannot say is that a word in one context has the meaning it has in that context and simultaneously the meaning it has in other contexts different from the first. A word does not have several uses in one use. It is certainly not to this peculiar semantics that Freud turns in order to analyze phenomena of ambiguity, slips and double meanings. Instead he takes the censored text as his model. If a journalist's article must first be checked by the censor, then the writer has two interlocutors: the censor and the readership. His skill lies in getting through to his readers without alerting the censor. He must therefore write on two levels, or hold a double discourse. In each discourse, the words have precisely the meaning they have. But the two discourses are uttered simultaneously, using the same "signifying material." In order for this exercise in virtuosity to succeed, each receiver must apprehend only the discourse intended for him. The censor must hear nothing destined for the public, and vice versa. In each of the two discourses, words will have a clearly determinate use. Imagine that the censor receives a discourse in which the meaning of certain words hangs uncertainly in the context: the journalist will then have failed to overlay the text intended for the readers (or *"parole vraie"*) with a text intended for the censor.

Each time we look for several meanings in a text, we must define the various readers to whom it is simultaneously addressed. We are all too frequently informed that meaning must be "plural." Any text can give rise to an infinite number of interpretations. But in reality, it is hard enough to establish that a particular discourse is addressed, with quite different significations, to two or three groups of hearers. I believe that no demonstration has managed to surpass four. In any case, authentic hermeneutics, unlike simpler programs for a "plural reading," has always scanned the text for evidence of a plurality of intended readers. The doctrine of the four meanings of Scripture and Pascal's doctrine of figuratives are both grounded in the notion that the Old Testament must have several meanings if it already has one for the Jews. The meaning of the Book for the people whose Book it is cannot be denied by the Gentiles, who must prove instead that there is a further meaning. "A cipher has two meanings. When we come upon an important letter, whose meaning is clear, but where we are told that the meaning is veiled and obscure, that it is hidden so that seeing we shall not see and hearing we shall not hear, what else are we to think but that this is a cipher with a double meaning?"[58]

We have been told that symptoms are constructed like sentences. We are thus invited to analyze these symptoms as a signifying language (in an acceptation of *signifying* and *language* unhampered by any allusion to Saussurean linguistics). Freud defines the dream as a *Wunscherfüllung*, or wish fulfillment. It is thus the equivalent of a statement incorporating the verb *to wish* or some similar verb. Lacan asserts that desire is "produced . . . by an animal at the mercy of language."[59] The doctrine of the signifier too is a genealogy, but a genealogy of desire, and no longer one of the representative idea. It proposes to tell us of the birth of desire in an animal compelled to signify its needs in a discourse of demand. The birth of desire should be understood in the sense of mythical cosmogonies (the birth of Eros), except that the desire engendered is not mere appetite; it is desire as Freud described it. The doctrine of the signifier aims to explain why incestuous desire arises in the "animal at the mercy of language" and how an ordeal known as castration must be undergone before this desire can be transferred to other objects. It should be possible to derive the sum of Freudian theses from the relation between the human animal and the signifier. We can put this into practice by using the following instructions: "Desire is neither the appetite for satisfaction, nor the demand for love, but the difference that results from the subtraction of the first from the second."[60] Desire is the remainder obtained by subtracting need ("the appetite for satisfaction") from demand. But demand is need, signified to another person. So we must begin with need. What is the grammar of the object of need? It is more or less true that an agent has a need when the exercise or pursuit of a specific activity or set of activities (such as those that are characteristic of life) is conditional on his ability to make appropriate use—whether in consumption, absorption, expenditure, or whatever—of a portion of some element. Elements are things whose names do not allow for individuation or quantification: water, air, food, sand, coal, gold, ink, and so on. Individuation is introduced by the removal of a portion of this element: a glass of water, a breath of air, a can of food. Needs can be measured. Recipes provide a good example of the expression of needs: to make this sauce, you will need flour. How much? A spoonful; that is, the capacity of a spoon, but not necessarily the contents of the particular spoon in your hand. The grammar of the object of need requires that needs be directed at specified things, measured perhaps, but not individuated. As soon as a person claims to need not just any portion of an element, but this very one, we are already beyond need and must discover how the coveted portion became individuated. Need cannot explain a particular attachment to precisely designated individual parts, or even to certain varieties of an element if all are equally fit for their purpose. As Bergson says, the herbivore's appetite is roused by grass in general, not by any tuft in particular. When we say that nobody is irreplaceable, we are speaking from the perspective of need. Anything that will do is equivalent. Preference, choice, affinity, attraction, passion, anything that privileges differences within the element—the explanation for these must be sought elsewhere, in the object's manner of individuation. One possible reason for my alleged need for this very slice of cake might be that it was handed to my neighbor (a reason that, at the back of any rationalizations about its superior taste or size, would betray my desire to enjoy his advantages; in other words, envy). Another reason might be that the slice was assigned to me, and that it runs counter to the order of things or to a sense of fairness that anyone else should have it. In these two instances, individuation involves adding the relation of a portion of the element to a partner. This relation cannot be considered to pertain to some need on my part for that partner (one may need company or help, but not a precise companion or a specific assistant).

And so from needs to demands. The language of demand takes many forms, but these can always be paraphrased in the canonical form *I ask that p*. Thus *Water!* could be rephrased as *I ask that you give me water*. The object of demand is therefore indicated in the statement of demand by a proposition. The object of my demand is, for instance, *that I be given water*. What is requested in a demand is not a thing (like a glass of water or any other object of need), but a modification of the state of things. The grammar of the object of demand requires that it be propositional. We are asking for care, service, consideration, effort, attention, gratitude.

According to Lacan, there is a desire beyond demand because the response to demand leaves something to be desired. Whatever you demand, the response you receive can do no more than satisfy the need signified by the demand. At the same time, this response is a proof of consideration for you. To have one's demands satisfied makes one feel loved, so it may also be that a request is in reality a quest—for gifts, for evidence of love.

Here now is a signified need: *I ask you for a little water*. The Lacanian deduction tells us that satisfaction of this demand leaves a remainder, which is the object of desire. The object of need was a drink. Once water has been supplied, the need is satisfied. The water appeases the thirst. But any request is also (more or less) a demand for love. This demand is also satisfied, since it has been greeted with goodwill by the person to whom the request was made. The water as water has quenched the thirst, but the water as a thing to be asked for and given has quenched the thirst for love. Yet there is still a difference between the ways the two thirsts were appeased. The water as gift, as proof of love, does not calm thirst in the same manner as water, the liquid, satisfies the need to drink. The water as object of need is a particular reality, but the water as evidence of love is a symbol, a signifier, exchangeable against other symbols and other signifiers. The gap between the two induces the birth of desire. In his explanation of this point, Lacan adopts a Hegelian idiom that is far from clear. "Demand annuls [*aufhebt*] the particularity of everything that can be granted by transmuting it into a proof of love. . . . It is necessary, then, that the particularity thus abolished should reappear *beyond* demand."[61] By virtue of this mysterious necessity an object of desire is envisaged both in its particularity, as the object of need, and as a sign of love, the object of demand. The text goes on to show how such an object is brought about. The demand has not been altogether met; the partner has not given everything. Either something has been withheld (the object of desire is an object hidden or removed), or else it was not there to give (the object of desire is lost). Hence the initiatory formula: *Man's desire is desire for the Other*. But this absent object can only be what the Other manifests in his every action that he desires. A few episodes further on and we learn that this object is "the phallus." Unfortunately, however, we never reach this stage of the story, this key encounter between the doctrine of the signifier and the Freudian account of sexuality. For we can no longer follow the thread. We do not understand how the object of desire can be particular (in the sense that the phallus is a particular organ).

Indeed, if we duly subtract need from demand, we find that this is in no way the case. From *I ask that you give me water*, let us take away the object of need, indicated here by the direct object of the verb *to give*; we obtain *I ask that you give me something*. Suppose that the subtraction of the "appetite for satisfaction" from the "demand for love" leaves a remainder for our desire: we can formulate this remainder as *You have given me water, but I desire that you should give me something more.* The grammar of the object of desire is, as we might have expected, the same as that of the object of demand. Desires or wishes are stated by the description of a fact or situation, not by the designation of a particular thing. What psychoanalysts call "partial objects" are parts of the body. They may be the objects of "drives," whatever this may mean, but they are certainly not objects of desire.

Thus the deductive process of the theory of the signifier rests squarely upon a confusion of the Brichot-signifier (e.g., the word *water*, a signifier in the English language) and the Norpois-signifier (e.g., the fact that you give me water, a gesture whereby you signify your affection to me by means of the inference *If he gives me water when I ask him to, then he must love me*).

But this has all been confined to a general, dialectical level, which invariably leaves some available loophole. It remains to be shown by means of an example that the doctrine of the signifier cannot reach its conclusions without sleight of hand. Lacan applies his doctrine to Freud's interpretation of a certain dream, known as the dream of the Witty Butcher's Wife. Lacan begins by recounting the dream as told to Freud: "I want to give a dinner. But there's only a little smoked salmon left. I think of going out shopping, then I remember that it is Sunday afternoon and all the shops are shut. I tell myself that I'll ring round to a few tradesmen. But the telephone is out of order. So I have to give up my desire to give a dinner."[62] Freud's interpretation of this is well known: the patient has a friend who likes smoked salmon (just as she, the patient, loves caviar but does not allow her husband to give her any); the patient is jealous of her friend, but her husband thinks well of her. The friend will not be invited to dinner and will not get any smoked salmon. The patient herself desires to have an unsatisfied desire, identifying with her friend in the dream who will be deprived of salmon. How does all this translate into the doctrine of the signifier? Lacan says that the patient has a desire for caviar that she will not satisfy (by eating some). Her hysterical desire to have an unsatisfied desire is signified by a desire for caviar. As for the friend's desire, that is signified by the desire for salmon. In the dream, one signifier is exchanged for another (desire for caviar against desire for salmon). There is no mistake: the signifiers are "the desire for caviar" and "the desire for salmon,"[63] which are patently propositional (*I desire to eat caviar*). But on the next page, the signifiers as they have just been defined are nowhere to be found. In her dream, the patient has only a little salmon, not enough for a dinner. Lacan comments: "Freud, by suggesting that smoked salmon is substituted here for caviar, which, indeed, he considers to be the signifier of the patient's desire, is presenting the dream as a metaphor of desire."[64] The signifier of the patient's desire is no longer the desire for caviar (*I would like to eat some caviar*) but is now the caviar itself. And the substitution has ceased to be a matter of the friend's desire for salmon replacing the patient's desire for caviar; salmon now replaces caviar.

The formula of metaphor, according to Lacan, is "one word for another."[65] This is why the dream is a "metaphor of desire." The term *smoked salmon* is substituted for the term *caviar*. The caviar is the "signifier of the patient's desire." According to the doctrine of the signifier, the metaphorical substitution of *salmon* (which the friend will not eat as she would wish to) for *caviar* produces an effect of meaning: the patient's desire is signified in this metaphor as the desire for an unsatisfied desire. Such at any rate is the "access" provided here by Lacan to the "fundamental opposition of signifier and signified." This explanation is manifestly fanciful. For the dream to be a metaphor, it must offer "the substitution of one term for another." However, if we substitute the terms according to the preceding instructions, we find the term *salmon* being substituted for the term *caviar*. Yet it is not the butcher's wife, but her friend, who has this desire she will not be able to satisfy. In accordance with the preceding formulation, Freud's interpretation was reached by substituting one desire for another. *The patient desires to eat caviar* was the occulted signifier in the dream, for which *the friend desires to eat salmon* was substituted. By locating the signifier of the patient's hysterical desire now in the desire for caviar, now in the caviar, Lacan shows that for him caviar is both the signifier and the object of desire. This enables him to advance his second initiatory formula: "desire is the metonymy of the want-to-be [*manque à être*]."[66] By metonymy Lacan means the rhetorical figure that permits us to speak of one thing (caviar, say) while alluding to another that we do not wish to name (because it is forbidden) or cannot name (because "the word is wanting"). "Let us observe for the moment that if the desire is signified as unsatisfied, it is so through the signifier: caviar, qua signifier, symbolizes the desire as inaccessible, but as soon as it slips as desire into the caviar, the desire for caviar becomes its metonymy."[67] The signifier of the desire to have an unsatisfied desire is *caviar*—a signifier of the linguistic kind that makes it possible to speak of metonymy (or of the fact that the meaning of *caviar* is a function of the possible uses of this word in combination with other words in the language). The desire for caviar, in this case, is "the desire for something else."[68] Why then is it necessary to return from this signifier of the patient's desire—*caviar*—to the signifier of the patient's desire that had been, and is again, the desire for caviar? Lacan considers that the signifier of desire is the word (the word *caviar*) in the passages where he invokes the "laws of the signifying chain" (the so-called laws of metaphor and metonymy). But then he reverts to the idea that the signifier of unconscious desire is the desire manifest in the dream. This can no longer be a word: reference to a statement is essential. What signifies is that the butcher's wife desires to eat a caviar sandwich every afternoon, so Freud tells us, even though she has implored her indulgent husband not to let her have any. It is this situation in its entirety which justifies the view that the desire for caviar is the signifier of a hysterical desire. Now if the metonymic signifier of what Freud's patient "wants to be" ("*manque à être*") were the word *caviar*, we should be able to substitute for this word the indefinite *something else* in the statement of her desire. But this statement, as reconstituted by Freud, runs as follows: *I desire to eat a something else sandwich every afternoon.* This is hardly what we had hoped for. *I desire to be the object of the Other's desire* should in fact have been the result. To arrive at this last statement, it was necessary to substitute one completive proposition for another, not one word for another. The object of desire is necessarily described by a proposition, and this observation applies primarily to the phrase *to be the object of the Other's desire.* This phrase is literally misleading. If the friend desires to be invited to dinner, she does not desire to be an invitation to dinner, but to be the person invited. Yet the object of the Other's desire can be defined only by the grammatical object in the statement of desire, that is, *I want to give a dinner.* The doctrine of the signifier suffers from a confusion that appears irremediable.

The doctrine of the emancipated signifier would not have been so successful in Francophone anthropology had it not rendered one sterling service. Modern culture avails itself of a two-term explanatory schema for the vagaries of human activity: *this explains that.* Human deeds and gestures constitute *that* which must be explained. *This,* which explains them, is something other than what they are, something surrounding or grounding them. Thus for anthropologists there is always a temptation to fill the first half of the formula with a list of the things that are likely to influence the way people behave. Things that should act upon human agents can be drawn only from the domain of material individuals. The list of explanatory factors will thus be one of material elements or groupings; which may be why this kind of explanation is called *materialism.* There is geographical materialism (explanations in terms of soil or climate), medical materialism (heredity), economic materialism (the level of the forces of production). Such "scientific" theories have never evolved beyond the project stage, or declaration of principle. They are always caught short at the moment of application. Good anthropology is anthropology in which there is more of the (allegedly) explained than there is of the explanation. The notion of an autonomous language was therefore warmly welcomed. Emancipating the signifier meant that it need no longer be inscribed in the second list, that of the things to be explained. The state of a language need no longer be explained by the state of the world, nor the manner of the construction of statements by the way things are made, nor the existence of signifying differences by the existence of physical differences. In short, linguistics became free of anthropology (envisaged here not in terms of the case study but as a key to the sum of human activity as a whole). It would have been excessive, however, to jettison the schema itself. If language is not to feature on the second list it must be on the first, along with other factors invoked as explanations. We might describe the inclusion of the autonomous signifier on this list as a piece of anthropological accountancy, designed to balance the two columns, to equalize the factors requiring explanation, on the one hand, and the explanatory factors on the other. The excess in the first column corresponds to all the aspects of human life and behavior that seem not only environmentally ill adapted but also impervious to notions of adaptation or natural balance. (We recall that for Lévi-Strauss the "floating signifier" must account for art, poetry, magic, myth, and so on.) Thus nature explains human actions in their utilitarian aspect, and the signifier explains the rest. The signifier is explanatory and must therefore be endowed with the faculty to act upon what is to be explained: such is the "symbolic efficacy" of structural anthropology. Note that here too evident confusion surrounds the concept of language. The signifier co-opted into the list of determining elements may be a language, or it may be a statement—for instance, some utterance pronounced before a person's birth, a pronouncement concerning him that settles his fate in advance by a pure "effect of the signifier." Sometimes the determining signifier is Saussurean (one's name, for example, which is not without its "effects").[69] At others, it is a message (as in the case of the psychoanalyst's attributing a "signifying effect" to the declaration by the Rat Man's father: *This boy will be a great criminal*).

The doctrine of the emancipated signifier prides itself on having dispelled the illusion that language is composed of pointers to things. The autonomy of the signifier reveals that there is a use of language other than as *universal reportage*,* which casts the reader into relation with

---

*From Mallarmé, *Crise de vers*. [TRANS.]

things. Alongside reportage lies fiction. Human beings spend a considerable amount of time at the business of telling stories. This fact, featuring in the list of what is to be explained, clearly goes beyond any "mechanistic materialism." Semiology claims to propound a theory of fiction. Since in its view the "referent" is constituted by language operations, fictional statements present no problem. In universal reportage, reference is made to objects that are given as real. In fiction, reference is made to fictional entities. The problem of the fictional object will be the topic of my next chapter. Instead of a treatise on fiction, I have opted for an applied twist in the tale: a review of the various attempts to compile a dictionary of characters in *La comédie humaine* by Honoré de Balzac, and the efforts to identify certain fictional entities that these experiments represent.

6

Who's Who in *La comédie humaine*

The Inventory of Fictions

The idea of establishing a repertory of characters from *La comédie humaine* belongs to the realm of Balzac's fiction rather than to critical erudition. To undertake such a repertory is to play by Balzac's rules; to consult one is to fall prey to them.

I intend to show that any index purporting to be a dictionary of Balzac's characters is a fictional apparatus. We know from the author himself that *La comédie humaine* is constructed like a labyrinth. The reader may become lost and need a guide to help him find his way. In other words, *La comédie humaine* is designed to elicit a repertory or index (just as the labyrinth elicits Ariadne's thread). But if it can be established that any repertory must itself be a fiction—unable to fulfill its stated function except through fiction—it follows that the structure of *La comédie humaine* is itself fictional. By that, we should understand that although it is assuredly possible to become lost, we shall regain the thread only by means that perpetuate Balzac's fiction. Indeed, the reader would not wish it otherwise.

The text of a play normally incorporates a dramatis personae between the title and the first stage direction: *ta ton dramatos prosopa*. This list occurs before the play itself. It can operate as a notice or cast list; the actors' names are simply printed opposite the parts. This enables the audience to know *who is who* in the play, to identify major and minor characters more easily than by costume alone. Thanks to this list, the audience also knows who plays whom. Let us note in passing that the dramatis personae is not necessarily a list of names, for there may be anonymous characters (Shepherd, Old Man, Several Officers, etc.). However, names must be involved: the absence of a name indicates a gap in the cast.

The first-time reader of *La comédie humaine* soon comes up against the problem of *who was who* in the scenes he has already read. In his preface to *Une fille d'Eve*, Balzac himself acknowledged the drawbacks in his ordering of narrative. He presents this inconvenience as a "skillful device"[1] whereby his characters emerge not as novelistic creations whose history is related from birth onward, but like the people we meet in the "social world," without our always knowing their backgrounds in advance. However, on a first reading of a given episode we will lack the information necessary to appreciate the "social comedy"[2] involved. That is the real drawback to this approach. Subsequent scenes in the light of which we shall revise our earlier reaction to an episode do not follow immediately but lie much further on in *La comédie humaine*, in parts we may not read for years. In such circumstances, the tragic or comic effects bound up with the twists of the story appear doomed to failure in advance.

Une fille d'Eve contains characters such as Felix de Vandenesse and Lady Dudley, whose situation reverberates with drama and social comedy, if only their story were known; but you will be able to read it only at the very end of the work, in *Le lys dans la vallée*, which is part of *Scènes de la vie de campagne*. In short, you will encounter the middle of a life before its beginning, the beginning after the end, and the tale of the death before that of the birth.

... As the editor of this book humorously observes, sooner or later someone will draw up a biographical table of contents for the entire *Etudes de moeurs*, so that the reader negotiating this immense labyrinth may be assisted by means of entries such as:

RASTIGNAC (Eugène-Louis): eldest son of the baron and baronness de Rastignac, born in Rastignac, a province of Charente, in 1799; travels to Paris in 1819 to study law and stays at the Maison Vauquer, where he meets Jacques Collin, alias Vautrin, and becomes a friend of the famous physician Horace Bianchon.[3]

A "biographical table of contents" is necessary, then, because the order of the narration cannot and, according to Balzac, must not be chronological. "Nothing is of a piece in this world, all is mosaic. Only the story of times past can be told chronologically, a method inappropriate to the present, which is on the move."[4]

Can the idea of an index, which Balzac moots almost in jest, begin to be made concrete? Evidently some have thought so. There have been five attempts to date, all of divergent design and scope:

—Antoine Cerfberr and Jules Christophe, *Répertoire de "La comédie humaine" de H. de Balzac* (Calmann-Lévy, 1887).

—Fernand Lotte, *Dictionnaire biographique des personnages fictifs de "La comédie humaine"* (José Corti, 1952).

—In Bouteron's edition of Balzac (Pléiade), volume 11 (1959) we find two indexes by Fernand Lotte: an *Index of Real Persons and Literary References*, and an *Index of Fictional Characters in "La comédie humaine."*

—Pierre Citron's edition in the *L'intégrale* collection (Seuil, 1966) also contains two indexes: *Fictional Characters* and *Real, Biblical, and Mythological Characters.*

—Finally, in Pléiade's second Balzac edition by Pierre-Georges Castex we find four indexes: an *Index of Fictional Characters in La Comédie Humaine,* then an *Index of Real Persons and Characters from History, Mythology, Literature and the Arts Cited by Balzac in La Comédie Humaine,* followed by an *Index of Works Cited by Balzac in La Comédie Humaine* and an *Index of Works by Fictional Characters in La Comédie Humaine.* These indexes run to about eight hundred pages in volume 12 of this new Balzac edition (1981).

The first work of its kind, the 1887 *Repertory,* is a single list containing only proper names. The first entry runs as follows:

ABRAMKO: Polish Jew of Herculean strength, wholly devoted to bric-à-brac dealer Eli Magus, whose porter he was and whose daughter and riches he guarded with three fierce dogs in 1844 in an old house at Chaussée des Minimes, near the Place Royale in Paris. Abramko was involved in the Polish troubles, and Magus had saved him out of self-interest (*Cousin Pons*).

This notice is written as a succinct reply to the question, Who was Abramko in *La comédie humaine*? It is an account in the past tense of his appearance and functions in *Cousin Pons.* Yet Balzac had envisaged that the "Rastignac" entry in some biographical index would be written in the present tense. Between Balzac's suggestion and its realization in Cerfberr and Christophe's *Repertory* the following difference has therefore arisen: the *Biographical Table of Contents* as conceived by Balzac˙ was to accompany the reading in the same way as a guide leads tour groups around a monument, pointing out recondite curiosities or covert relationships between what can be seen and other factors that come into play. The *Repertory* on the other hand has a recapitulative function, using the various narratives of *La comédie humaine* as so many testimonies or sources of information, in order to gather into a single entry, like a narrative in miniature, everything we know about the character and his movements by a given date. In Balzac's (imaginary) *Table,* Rastignac comes to Paris and lives in the Maison Vauquer. But in the *Repertory,* Rastignac *came* to Paris and *lived* on the third floor of the Vauquer establishment. If the author of the *Biographical Table of Contents* is like a guide, discreetly glossing the action as it unfolds, then the authors of the *Repertory* are like historians, using the documents furnished by Balzac's narratives to compose a fresh one. The Rastignac entry is a biography of Rastignac culled from the passages in which he features, just as a modern *Life of Caesar* is a biography written with the aid of passages from the Roman historians. Taken then to its limits, this procedure would require the authors to rewrite the entire opus in a different order, grouping the information scattered throughout ninety-one novels into as many biographical entries as there are identifiable characters. *Père Goriot*, for instance, would be dismantled and its contents redistributed among the entries devoted to Rastignac, Bianchon, Nucingen, and so forth. In other words, the inconvenience of the labyrinth would have proved impossible to turn to advantage, and the labyrinth would simply have to be eliminated in favor of a kind of monadology in which the 2,472 monads (apparently) of Balzac's universe could be reciprocal expressions of one another. But since monads possess neither doors nor windows through which to act upon each other, there would be no action, and therefore no human comedy.

The *Table* envisaged by Balzac ought to be consulted as we read, whereas the *Repertory* is a kind of recapitulation that it is more appropriate to consult after the reading—the biographical narratives would otherwise interfere with the narrative proper. But in this case Balzac's *Table* is unrealizable: we would need as many tables as there are possible periods in our reading. Even if we assume that the books are to be read in a single prescribed order, as many tables as there are narratives affected by the reappearance of characters would still be required.

The *Dictionary* published in 1952 by Fernand Lotte separates fictional characters from real persons, who were not included in the *Repertory*. The *Abramko* entry is now the fourth, preceded by *Abd El Kader* ("notwithstanding his name, a beautiful English thoroughbred given by Viscountess de Grandlieu to the young du Guénic couple"), *Abel* ("the eldest of Hélène d'Aiglemont's children") and *L'Abencerrage* ("affectionate nickname given to her husband by Baronness de Macumer"). In succession, then, we have the name of an animal, a first name, a nickname, and a surname—a far more meticulous collection than we find in the *Repertory*. At the same time, the entries follow Balzac's text more closely, not only using it but quoting from it, with the result that some become incoherent. The authors of the *Repertory* took Balzac's side in their item on Julie d'Aiglemont: she was given a continuous, consistent history. This character's composite aspect is divulged, however, in the *Dictionary*. Fernand Lotte's work thus represents an intermediary stage in the execution of Balzac's idea: it is still a *biographical* dictionary, written in the past tense, but it also begins to resemble an index, with its apparatus of quotations and references making it into an appendix to this edition of *La comédie humaine* rather than a complementary volume worthy of consultation in its own right.

Lotte's later work in the first Pléiade edition explicitly constitutes an *Index*, a census recording the occurrence of names, not the appearance of characters as before. Furthermore, it encompasses real people and anonymous fictional characters. The reader is thus invited to seek useful information in either of the two *Indexes*: every single name featured in *La comédie humaine* is held to be either the name of a real person, a literary allusion (including both literary characters and book titles), or the name of a fictional character.

The next Pléiade edition of the work, with its three advertised indexes (four are actually offered), goes one stage further than its predecessors. The index of real people and literary allusions in the first edition (which in the Seuil edition Pierre Citron adapts to produce an index of "Real, Biblical, and Mythological Characters") is split into one index of real people and another of works cited by Balzac.

In principle, an index is a table of reference. It does not attempt to tell us *who was who* in *La comédie humaine* but is content with listing who is mentioned where. This shift, from characters described to names mentioned, solves the difficulty encountered earlier. Just as *La comédie humaine,* according to Balzac, vies with the real world, so *La comédie humaine* as "real world" finally undermines *La comédie humaine.* The index no longer aims to guide the reader, but simply points out the passages he should look up. Nonetheless, this ambition is renounced only to make way for another: the index purports to be complete, omniscient. It no longer attempts to tell us *who is who* in *La comédie humaine*; instead it will tell us *who is* in *La comédie humaine*— hence the inclusion of real persons and anonymous characters. But this is a perfectly exorbitant claim; the ambitions of the *Biographical Dictionary* are modest by comparison. For we can conceive of an answer to the question, Who was N in *La comédie humaine* and what was his role? But how could the question, *Who is* in *La comédie humaine* ever be answered? For those who occur in the novels may do so as named characters, or as anonymous ones, or as references to both real and fictional figures.

In Lotte's *Index,* there are seventeen descriptions of "a young man" among the anonymous characters and twenty-three of "a lady," not to mention plural designations: "ladies," or "extremely *decolleté* ladies." In the *Index* as revised by Citron, we have twenty-five individual ladies, plus collective ladies, and thirteen young men. Such inventories are clearly meaningless. Twenty-five mentions of "a lady" do not indicate that *La comédie humaine* contains twenty-five anonymous lady characters. The same lady may be counted more than once; a character may appear anonymously at first and later be identified. But the absurd side of these hypotheses simply goes to show that the question of a census of characters should not arise. The reappearance of characters is what makes *La comédie humaine* a labyrinth and necessitates a biographical table of contents. But only named characters can recur, for there is no means of knowing whether such and such an anonymous figure in this story is, or is not, the same as such and such another in a different story. The allocation of proper names to fictional characters serves precisely to permit a discontinuous narrative of this or that character's actions. For this reason the anonymous characters in *La comédie humaine* have a role but no biography. They were rightly excluded from the *Repertory* and the *Dictionary*, since nobody wonders who *a young man crossing the bridge* may be. An index of characters, on the other hand, ought to include them: they are parts that a stage or screen adaptation of the novels would have to cast. But the fact that they cannot be counted leads us to question the validity of such an index. Reading Balzac does not really demand this capacity for counting characters. In *Une ténébreuse affaire*, Napoleon shows Laurence de Cinq-Cygne his army bivouacked on the night before the battle of Jena:

"Here," said he, with that eloquence which could turn cowards into heroes, "Here are three hundred thousand men, innocent men! Why, tomorrow thirty thousand men will have died, died for their country! On the Prussian side, a great engineer, a thinker, a genius may be mown down. On our side too, we shall certainly lose unknown great men."[5]

We cannot even make a start at any identification once men are taken en masse, at least from a statistical point of view. Out of a force of three hundred thousand, losses can be expected to reach 10 percent. But such considerations affect numbers, not individuals. We do not know who is going to die, any more than we know who are the potential great men such a mass doubtless contains.

Insofar as an index of characters is actually an index of the passages in which characters are mentioned, whether by name or by means of a more or less vague description, it follows that any proper name occurring in the text of *La comédie humaine* must merit an explanatory reference in the index. This leads to the necessity for a second index, devoted to real historical people. Lotte and Citron both distinguish in their titles between fictional *characters* and real *persons*. But this distinction, where justified, is undermined (in Lotte's "Notice" prefacing his *Indexes*) by the opposition of invention (characters) and citation (real persons).[6] The authors of the indexes in the new Pléiade edition have indeed dropped this distinction, opposing fictional characters to real characters. In reality, the separation of the two indexes is a consequence of using two criteria whose simultaneous application is obviously inconsistent. We are asked first to distinguish the fictional from the real, and then to distinguish Balzac's invention from his borrowing. We are thus confronted with such surprising classifications as "literary characters and references" (Lotte) or "real, biblical, and mythological characters" (Citron in *L'intégrale*), or again, "real persons and characters from history, mythology, literature and the arts" (second Pléiade edition). All these headings betray the same malaise, as if the separation of the fictional and the real, so obvious at first, had led to difficulties in classifying all the names in one or the other list. Names of mythological *characters* are thus set alongside names of real *persons,* blurring the distinction between characters and persons as a result. A new difference now emerges: on the one hand we have "literary references," persons (or characters) whose names are merely quoted; on the other, literary uses of certain names, in order to situate the characters in the story. Notice that all these indexes count Melmoth and Don Juan as fictional characters in *La comédie humaine*, although they were not Balzac's creations. Yet figures from *The Iliad* or *The Arabian Nights* appear among the real persons, as references. If we were to pool these distinctions, we should expect to arrive at four lists of names:

1. Names of characters invented and used by Balzac.
2. Names of characters borrowed (whether from literature or life) and used by Balzac.
3. Names of characters borrowed and cited by Balzac (but not used).
4. Names of characters invented by Balzac and cited as if they were part of public consciousness and could be mentioned exactly like legendary or biblical figures.

Now this little point of order expresses the fatal flaw of *indices nominorum*: they do not and cannot distinguish between references to real persons and their incorporation in a narrative. Balzac does not mention only Don Juan; he includes Napoleon, Talleyrand, Louis XVIII, and more among the personnel featured in *La comédie humaine*. In the cases of Don Juan and Melmoth, the *Indexes* choose to consider that Balzac has wholly appropriated the traditional figure. They do not differentiate between a character that has been invented for use and one that has been borrowed for use. Why is this solution not adopted in the parallel case of authentic persons, borrowed from life, who appear in the novels? In fact, we shall find all the names of real persons in the index that is not the index of Balzac's fictional creations. But each rubric will give space to these persons insofar as they are held to play a part in the narrative. Under *Napoleon*, for instance, two kinds of information are therefore included: allusions to Napoleon and views about him voiced by characters (and the author), but also a section headed "Napoleon as agent in *La comédie humaine*."

In one sense the division of fictional and real figures is unavoidable. But this does not mean it is easy to justify it or to state clearly who belongs in which category. What justifies it is the very function of a biographical dictionary: if such a biographical table of contents is to enlighten us as to who is who in *La comédie humaine*, it cannot also be telling us who is who beyond it. Napoleon's biographical entry cannot be of the same kind as Rastignac's; at least not if the reader is required to take the name *Napoleon* in its usual sense as referring to the emperor. It is assumed that readers already know who Napoleon is; not who he is in *La comédie humaine* but who he was in the acceptation of that name current in the French language at that stage of history. To know the meaning of the words *Napoleon*, *Fouché*, *Talleyrand*, and so on, is to share in the linguistic knowledge required for the reading of the narratives. But as the reader's ability to understand words taken in their so-called common acceptation naturally fluctuates with the times, it falls to the experts to compile an index of Balzac's *references*, in case readers no longer know who such and such an actress or minister was, or what were the political leanings of such and such a contemporary broadsheet. This kind of learned index is in no way similar to a *Repertory of "La comédie humaine"*; it is rather more an *Encyclopedia of the Nineteenth Century*. Balzac's fiction would then appear to demand a single biographical notice for names like Napoleon or Talleyrand; for if we read in the *Index of Real Persons* that Napoleon is such and such a person outside *La comédie humaine* but such and such a character inside it, we shall have to recognize that Napoleon the real person and "Napoleon" the fictional character invented by Balzac have fused—and in this way Balzac's narrative accedes to its rightful place in the history of the period. This effect of fusion is inevitable. If the authors of the *Index* had repositioned the entry under "Napoleon as agent in *La comédie humaine*" in the other *Index* devoted to fictional characters, the meaning of the word *Napoleon* would have become ambiguous. When the emperor is only cited in the story, he is Napoleon in the usual sense: the emperor Napoleon whose remains lie at the Invalides. But when he features in the story as an active participant, he becomes a character, a kind of imaginary double. Nothing in the text, however, alerts us that some names are to be taken in one of two senses.

Nothing warrants the doubling up of an index of names, except perhaps that we are already familiar with certain names while others are new to us—although our own ignorance of a name does not prove that Balzac has invented it, any more than a familiar ring to a name should enhance its effect of reality. We are left with the awkward result that all proper names appearing in *La comédie humaine* are used in exactly the same way, according to exactly the same rules. There are no indexes of fiction or reality, as if the word "Napoleon" were imprinted with a reference to one or the other index: "Napoleon$_1$" or "Napoleon$_2$." So Napoleon must be the same in every case: as real in *La comédie humaine* as in the *Mémorial de Sainte-Hélène*, yet as fictional in *La comédie humaine* as Nucingen or Goriot, Z. Marcus or Birotteau. All this shows how urgently the notion of the "fictional character" requires clarification. The difference between the fictional and the real must be extremely tenuous if it cannot be used as the basis of a coherent index.

Fictional Names

The weakness of these theories of fictionality, when applied to the various repertories, doubtless lies in their uncritical equation of fiction and invention. Any character invented by Balzac is a fictional character. But Balzac did not invent Napoleon, and Napoleon is therefore a real person. This kind of genetic approach is inadequate. What if we discover that an invented character is unmistakably modeled upon a real person whose existence at the time is well documented? Now that the character can no longer be seen as an invention, can it still be called fictional? Everything depends, we might think, upon whether Balzac actually knew the person. What matters is not therefore the existence of a person endowed with a given place in the real world, but the meaning of the use of a certain name by the author. If Balzac uses a name in a sense commonly accepted by those around him, then it is the name of a real person. On the other hand, any name for which Balzac invents a use that has not hitherto existed in French is the name of a fictional character. And this applies in every case, including that of proper names that may happen to belong (unknown to Balzac, perhaps) to real people.

But how are we to approach the idea that Balzac invents uses for certain words, in which these words name fictional people? How can a fictional person be named? There seem to be four possible answers to this question:

1. To name a fictional person is to name someone who does not exist

in this world, the real world, and yet still subsists after a fashion in an imaginary or fictional world.

2. To name a fictional person is to name a person held to be real in a work of fiction.
3. To name a fictional person is to name someone who does not exist, but who might have existed and so exists in a "possible world."
4. To name a fictional person is to name nothing at all, since the fictional person is precisely someone whom nobody is.

Of all these answers, only the last—the denial of any kind of reality to characters in fiction—is consistent. I believe this answer would be more readily accepted if it did not appear to beg the entire question of reading. We feel that this Parmenidean way of denying a name to nothing is an attempt to deprive us. It looks to us like a bid to cheat us of the pleasure of reading. If fictional characters have no kind of reality, we do not know whose imaginary adventures we are reading, and storytelling has merely a semblance of meaning, which we could only imagine that we under-stood. The first three answers have the advantage of "salvaging fiction," clarifying what it is we understand when we allow ourselves to listen to "stories." But before long it emerges that the answers conceding some reality to fiction have nothing more to give us than the Parmenidean response; what they propose is moreover unintelligible, and thus unable to shed light on anything.

Answer 1, if it means anything, must mean the same as answer 2. Fictional persons are those who, unlike real people in the real world, are real in an unreal world. Napoleon is real in the real world, Goriot is real in the unreal world. But to be real in an unreal world is tantamount to being unreal. If the first answer is not to be reduced to the Parmenidean version, it must be shaped into a theory of the construction of the world. This would hold that what we call "a world" is not given wholesale, but constructed out of more immediate data. Apply this idealist doctrine of the "world as representation" and the way out is clear: in the course of his reading, the reader encounters clues that enable him to construct a world—the *Comédie humaine* world. The characters defined as "fic-tional" are those posited as real in the *comédie humaine* world, whereas they would have to be posited as unreal had we adopted the perspective of life, from which the world of life is constructed. As we have just seen, the first answer is saved from identicality with the fourth only by merging with the second.

This second answer, meanwhile, is purely verbal. It requires assertions of existence to submit to operators that render them relative to a "universe of discourse." We shall not say that Napoleon is a real person and Rastignac a character in fiction. We shall instead profess that in reality Napoleon is real and Rastignac is not, but that both are real in *La comédie humaine*.[7] Answer 2, then, suggests that we adopt a certain manner of speaking that differentiates between what is real in the real and what is real in this fiction (not in fiction or fable in general, as before). To say that Rastignac is a fictional character, that is, nonexistent yet endowed with a quasi-existence which precludes outright dismissal, is to say that there is a narrative in which Rastignac is considered real. This answer is manifestly no more than verbal: to say that a character is fictional because only in a fictional tale is he considered real is simply another way of saying that he is fictional, and it ignores the question of why the fictional should be anything other than the unreal, pure and simple.

The third answer is not verbal. It is, on the other hand, false. Here the world of fiction is viewed as a possible world: the idea is not to relativize existence but to modalize it. We are asked to reason as follows: It would be absurd to think that the individuals actually in existence at a given period are the only ones who could ever have existed at that time. According to circumstances, some of them might not have existed, whereas others might have done so. A fictional character is a possible individual, provided we refer to a kind of literature governed by the conventions of "realism." Of course Rastignac never existed. Nonetheless, his description (to be found in the *Repertory* or the *Dictionary*) is logically possible, presenting no inconsistencies or contradictions. If the description of a young man (and subsequently of an older one) called *Rastignac* is logically possible in itself, it must be the description of a possible individual. There never was a young man with the same curriculum vitae as Rastignac's, but there might have been. Rastignac did not exist, but he *might have*. The writer of fiction is thus one who exploits the contingency of human affairs or the fact that the possible is always richer than the real. This answer is obviously derived from the notoriously equivocal notion of the "possible individual." When we say that the individuals who existed at a given date were not the only ones possible, we are simply acknowledging the consequence of contingency in human affairs. Napoleon, for instance, might not have been born had his parents not been who they were. By the same token, other individuals who were not born at that time might well have existed but for some quirk, itself arbitrary, in the lives of persons one generation before. But to speak of other *individuals* encourages confusion, for we should be hard put to say who these individuals are (or were, or might have been). At any event, the individuals who did not exist in 1819, but who might well have existed, and who might well have met in a Latin Quarter guest house, would not have been Rastignac, or Bianchon, or Goriot, or Vautrin, or any of the characters from *La comédie humaine*. All these names from Balzac's story are supposed to present us with well-defined individuals, wholly credible from all points of view, whereas "possible individuals" suffer from not being *individuated*. They are "people" without being "these very people." We cannot therefore confuse the following statements, the first entirely legitimate:

It would have been possible in 1819 for other individuals to exist than those who did exist in 1819,

and the second absurd:

There are individuals (Rastignac, Bianchon, etc.) who, albeit nonexistent in 1819, might have existed in 1819.

Let us take the character of Rastignac. What have we just admitted in saying "take the character of Rastignac"? Answer 1 is impossible, for there is no imaginary character called Rastignac, and to say that an imaginary person is Rastignac is to say that no one is Rastignac. The second answer, which might be termed "constructivist," turns out to be equally disappointing, for to say that in the world which *La comédie humaine* invites us to construct there is a real person called Rastignac is to say that in reading Balzac, we recognize that there is someone called Rastignac but fail to examine what exactly is being recognized in this. Last, the answer invoking possible worlds also founders: there is no possible world that is Balzac's very *world*, even if among "possible worlds" there are some that resemble it (the one most closely resembling it is no doubt the real world).

  Perhaps the considerations above will impress none but the already converted. If there is anyone who thinks that purely logical reasoning is irrelevant to that other world, the world of literature (as it is to the world of dream or fantasy), he can always object that any effort to apply the patterns of thought belonging to this world to that other world is misguided. Although the preceding arguments are entirely conclusive in my opinion, I shall nonetheless reinforce them with a more straightforward description.

  The difference between characters in fiction and real people justifies itself by the necessity of distinguishing two universes, that of *La comédie humaine* and that of everyday reality. If this is so, then opting for one system or the other ought to resolve our difficulties. If I consult, from the standpoint of reality, the index of persons mentioned by Balzac I shall encounter only names attested to in the outside world, whereas if I bury myself in Balzac's world I shall only find the names of characters whom I

earlier deemed fictional (unreal) and whom I now call persons who are
real in fiction—or again, to go by the other version, possible individuals
described in their possible world, a world that might have existed and
must be described as if it had. But these alternatives do not work, and the
division proves useless. Even if we immerse ourselves in fiction, pretend-
ing that real in fiction persons are simply persons, we shall still come up
against other fictional or imaginary persons who are fictional in fiction.
The divide between fictional and real reappears in the fictional world.
Characters in *La comédie humaine* sometimes resort to pseudonyms, for
instance, names of people who do not exist—but who are taken for real
so long as their incognito remains undetected.

  Thus Vautrin is presented at the beginning of *Père Goriot* as a man
named *Vautrin*. It makes no odds whether one registers this from the
perspective of reality or of fiction—either Balzac has introduced a fictional character by the name of Vautrin, or a person named Vautrin is
staying at the Pension Vauquer where Rastignac lodges. For anyone
accustomed to the French language, the word *Vautrin* automatically
implies a surname, the name of a member of the Vautrin family. But there
is no Vautrin family in *La comédie humaine*, and so there is no individual
called *Vautrin*. Vautrin is a genuine fictional character from *La comédie
humaine*; he is a character who does not exist in *La comédie humaine*,
even though his only hope for a stake in existence resides there. Unlike
Rastignac or even Jacques Collin, who have fictional substance, Vautrin
is nothing—nothing in life, naturally, but nothing in fiction either. He is a
fiction within a fiction. This returns us to our earlier problems: is Vautrin
endowed in Balzac's fictional reality with a fiction of fictional reality? Or
is he an unreal entity taken for real by other unreal entities? Or is he a
possible character—not actualized, admittedly, in the description of that
possible world, the world of Balzac—but who belongs to another possible world, the world that might have been Balzac's fictional world?

  If *Vautrin* is a pseudonym, *Vautrin* cannot be the name of a (real in
fiction) Balzac character, and there is no character by the name of
Vautrin in the world of *La comédie humaine*—a world that is, fictionally
speaking, taken for real. And this was Balzac's intention. Bibi-Lupin, the
policeman (who is himself introduced as falsely identical to the nonexistent Gondureau, a Parisian stockholder), holds forth as follows to
Mademoiselle Michonneau, the "Venus of Père Lachaise": "Well, His
Excellency [the minister of police] is now quite confident that *the alleged
Vautrin*, lodging at the Maison Vauquer, is a runaway convict from the
penal colony at Toulon, where he goes by the name of *Trompe-la-Mort*
[the Death Dodger]."[8] *The alleged Vautrin* is none other than the man
who calls himself Vautrin and professes to be him but is nothing of

the kind. From now on the man hitherto designated as *Vautrin* becomes the man who hides behind that pseudonym, *the false Vautrin*, as the fake Gondureau (alias Bibi-Lupin) suggests: "Coming here, Trompe-la-Mort adopted the guise of a respectable gentleman, and masquerading as an honest citizen, he took rooms in a decent establishment. . . . This *Monsieur Vautrin*, then, is a man of substance, who conducts important business. . . . The minister fears that if by mistake we arrest *a real Vautrin*, he will find commercial circles in Paris and public opinion turning against him."[9] The false Vautrin is an escaped convict. The real one is a respectable Parisian gentleman. But only the false Vautrin exists in fiction, only the man who pretends to be Vautrin and acts out the role of an upright citizen. The real Vautrin does not exist. Therefore no character exists who might be what Vautrin must be in order to be.

But we may object that names are not an essential feature of character. Vautrin is perhaps a false Vautrin according to Balzac, but it is nonetheless by means of this pseudonym that we ourselves, in the wake of the author, prefer to designate Jacques Collin. The final part of *Splendeurs et misères des courtisanes* contains this passage: "Jacques Collin, known as Trompe-la-Mort in the penal world, and who will no longer be called by any name but his own, was . . . [etc.]."[10] Until now, the demands of narrative have necessitated a series of designations for Jacques Collin. He was Father Carlos Herrera for some, Trompe-la-Mort or Collin for others acquainted with his real identity, and for the uncertain he could be either. This oscillation gives rise to some remarkable turns of phrase, one of which occurs earlier in the same story: "Nevertheless, Jacques Collin or Carlos Herrera (for we must call him by one or other of these names, according to the exigencies of the situation) had a long-standing acquaintance with the ways of policemen, courts and prisons."[11] Collin or Herrera, because for some he is the first and for others the second. But Collin and Herrera are not like Jekyll and Hyde, alternately one or the other. In fact, he sometimes admits to being one, sometimes pretends to be the other. The *Collin or Herrera* disjunction disjoins nothing, being equivalent to the conjunction *Collin and Herrera*; for whatever the real Collin does, the false Herrera also does (so long as a false Herrera persists), and vice versa. Nor for that matter is anything conjoined, for only one character, affecting to be another, is involved here.

All well and good, but it is nevertheless remarkable that the decision to give Collin no other name but his own should occur toward the beginning of a section headed "The Last Incarnation of Vautrin." Yet *Splendeurs et misères des courtisanes* contains no mention of Vautrin, either real or false, and only barely recapitulates the episode in which the false Vautrin was unmasked several years before the opening of the present story. In the title of the fourth part of *Splendeurs et misères*, the Vautrin whose last incarnation we read of is the false Vautrin, according to the world of *La comédie humaine*, while for us he is the only, the true Vautrin. Are we to conclude that the real Vautrin is the false one and that the false one is the real one (since in any case there is no other)? In reality, we reserve for the man who claims to be Vautrin the name by which he was originally introduced. This does not mean that we take him for an authentic Vautrin, but simply means that we refer to whoever it was we first encountered under that name. If the real Vautri is the man whom the alleged Vautrin claims to be, then there is no real Vautrin: the pseudonym is taken *de dicto*. However, if we understand the pseudonym *de re* to signify whatever person entered the narrative with that name, then Collin is Vautrin.[12]

There is genuine ambiguity in a pseudonym, but it can be resolved by an unequivocal statement on whether we take *Vautrin* to be the name of the pretender to that name or, conversely, to be the name of a Vautrin born and bred. There is no avoiding this distinction, as we can see if we compare two of Collin's aliases, *Vautrin* and *Herrera*. Vautrin does not exist; therefore Collin is not Vautrin, for no one can be someone who does not exist. Nor is Collin Herrera, this time because Herrera exists (at least until he succumbs to Collin). Collin is not Vautrin because there is no Vautrin, and he is not Herrera because there was a Herrera. These contrary reasons may be formulated as follows:

1. In order that Collin might pass for Vautrin, Collin must disappear. since it is to hide Collin that Trompe-la-Mort creates the false Vautrin (but as soon as Collin becomes visible once more, the false Vautrin is discarded).

2. In order that Collin might pass for Herrera, Herrera must disappear, for Trompe-la-Mort aspires to produce a new Herrera (but as soon as we learn that the priest Herrera with whom we were familiar is a false Herrera, we realize that the real one has been liquidated).

Thus there are pseudonyms and pseudonyms. The name *Herrera* is a pseudonym for Collin, but this false name is the real name of another character. Collin and Herrera constitute two characters, and the first passes himself off as the second. The name *Vautrin* is also a pseudonym for Collin, but it belongs to nobody; Collin and Vautrin together constitute a single "real within fiction" character, even though each has a distinct identity. Of these two pseudonyms, *Vautrin* is the one that produces the problem of the status of fictional entities. The relationship of the fictional to the real is not that of the false name *Herrera* to the real name *Collin*. It would be better understood on the model of the relation between the false name *Vautrin* and the real name *Collin* (real in fiction, of course). When Collin claims to be Herrera, he is appropriating someone else's name; but when he calls himself Vautrin, he is doing no such thing. The name *Vautrin* signifies a member of the Vautrin family; no one actually bears that name, and Collin adopts it. Similarly, we might say that *Rastignac* is a name indicating a member of the Rastignac line, and a name no one actually bears. In this instance, however, the name *Rastignac* has not been fraudulently assumed by a person of flesh and blood (real in reality), unless perhaps by some undercover agent as a pseudonym. But it is irrelevant to us whether the name has served as a pseudonym; this knowledge is superfluous with respect to our ability to understand it in a sentence. Any name, whether real or invented (by Collin or by Balzac) can serve as a pseudonym provided it sounds plausible.

A look at the way pseudonyms are treated in the dictionaries of *La comédie humaine* will be useful here. The *Repertory* and the *Dictionary* set out to catalog fictional characters. Both, predictably, have a policy of including one entry for each real fictional character. False fictional characters (fictional within fiction) are ignored. The *Repertory* mentions the escaped convict Trompe-la-Mort under *Collin*. The nickname *Trompe-la-Mort* appears as one of Collin's aliases rather than as a separate character. The *Vautrin* entry reads: "Vautrin, most notorious of Jacques Collin's assumed names." Under *Herrera*, we find a biography of the real Herrera, which notes at the end that Collin "killed him, stole his belongings, and eventually adopted his name and persona, down to the last detail, until about 1830"—facts that pertain to the real Herrera's history. In Lotte's *Dictionary*, mention of Herrera is only to be found under *Vautrin*, in an entry that begins: "False identity assumed by Jacques Collin, and his most famous incarnation." The remainder of the entry refers to Collin by whichever of his names is appropriate to the episode described. The *Collin* entry in the same *Dictionary* refers us back to *Vautrin*. Again, only one entry appears for *Herrera*, and naturally deals with the Spanish priest himself. In both works, then, we encounter either characters who are "real within fiction" or names that are actually used by these "fictionally real" characters. No ontological distinction is ever suggested that would make it possible to supplement such characters with other, "fictional within fiction" creations. Everything changes, however, as soon as we turn to the "Indexes" at the back of the first Pléiade edition. These are analytical in form, referring us to the appropriate pages instead of summarizing the lives. Each name therefore requires an entirely separate entry. Thus *Collin, Herrera, Trompe-la-Mort* and *Vautrin*, not to mention *Barker*, the false Herrera's pseudonym, all warrant separate entries as characters in their own right; each entry refers us to pages where we shall effectively find a Balzac character by that name. For instance, the *Vautrin* entry begins as follows:

VAUTRIN (M.). His origins are revealed to Poiret and la Michonneau by Gondureau, alias Bibi-Lupin. He is the convict, Jacques Collin, who has broken out of the Toulon penal colony [etc.].

Likewise, under the name "Herrera" we have two entries, one headed HERRERA (*Father Carlos*) and the other HERRERA (The False Father Carlos). This provides us with two fictional characters, that of the real Herrera and that of the false one: two full-fledged characters where previously there were only two names. In its passage from biography to the index of names, the pseudonym becomes a character. The biographical approach told us that a certain character was variously known under four different names (a surname, a nickname, and two pseudonyms, one invented and the other usurped). But the index details four characters as different as their respective entries, yet linked by the sign of identity. Four identical characters, and not the same character four times—the suggestion is plainly absurd. The last Pléiade edition of Balzac reverts to the policy of single entries; but these remain analytical, so that we are no longer sure, as we read, which persona the character is adopting in this or that episode. Such a solution lacks coherence, falling between the two stools of biography and index.

Of all the various tabulations we have reviewed, those adopting the biographical approach are undoubtedly most in keeping with Balzac's suggestions (except for their use of the past tense rather than the present, which embodies the limitations of the enterprise). We can now see why: such biographical repertories belong to the realm of Balzac's fiction, and to read them we must enter into the dance or the masquerade, prepared to treat fictional characters as though they were real. There is no question therefore of two lists, as if there were two kinds of character according to origin. All the characters in *La comédie humaine* exist on the same level. To transpose a Balzac story to the screen would require living actors for every part, and no one would contemplate filming the invented characters in black and white while the real ones appeared in color. It is because we have settled into the tale as though it were real life that the lifelike difference between real and false can emerge: the difference between appearance and reality, or pseudonym and name. In the biographical repertories, we only find characters and names; there are no fictional characters regarded as entities distinct from the pseudonyms adopted by the characters themselves, and this leads to a preponderance of names over characters.

In the indexes appended to the scholarly editions of Balzac, a line is drawn between fictional characters and real persons with a part to play in the story. In other words, there are two kinds of character. As a result, all the fictional characters are fictional to the same degree, producing, remarkably, as many characters as there are names in that group. But on the side of real persons, names outnumber persons, not that we find this in the least perplexing. Under *Otrante (duc d')*, for instance, we read not: Name of a real person identical to Fouché, but "See Fouché." Fouché and the duc d'Otrante are not two identical persons; they are the same person. The "Indexes" present us with a distinction alien to the story, whereby the characters invented by Balzac and the figures borrowed from real life belong to separate orders. At the same time we are denied a distinction—which the story does make—between persons presented as real in the story and those presented in the story as fictional. The notice preceding the "Index" in the new Pléiade edition contains a startling declaration to the effect that the reader will find in it "characters imagined by other characters . . ., or who appear in their dreams . . ., and figures from imaginary novels. These are products of the author's imagination, comparable to characters presented more directly, and as such deserve a mention in any index of fictional characters."[13]

The concept of "fictional character" as it is invoked in these indexes and in literary criticism generally suffers from an excess both of breadth and of narrowness. It is too broad inasmuch as it does not allow for a distinction between a character who is dreaming and a character who is dreamed about. This insensitivity afflicts the kind of reader for whom Don Quixote's Dulcinea exists on a par with the peasant woman whom Sancho Panza courts on his master's behalf. It is necessary to differentiate in the story between Vautrin and Collin. At the same time, the concept is too narrow, forcing us to regard Napoleon as he appears in *La comédie humaine* as a different kind of character from Rastignac. If we felt as we read Balzac that some figures were real and others invented, this would preclude all understanding. Let us take the conversation between Laurence de Cinq-Cygne and Napoleon in *Une ténébreuse affaire*. Here Laurence speaks to Napoleon, and Napoleon speaks to her. They address one another, and their exchange is what constitutes the action. But if we really were to distinguish the historical figure (Napoleon) from the fictional character (Laurence), we could say that Laurence speaks to Napoleon or that he speaks to her, but never that they speak to each other; there would be no action. This may easily be shown with the aid of the logical distinction drawn, in the tradition of Frege and Quine, between contexts that are transparent to the reference and contexts that are opaque to it. It appears that certain so-called intentional verbs constitute a context which may be "transparent" and "opaque" by turns—for example, the verb *to write* (*a letter*) *to*. One might think that this verb is always transparent to the reference. If I write a letter to someone, there is someone to whom I write a letter. But in fact I may well have been deceived; I can write a letter to Santa Claus, but there is no Santa Claus to write to. In this case, the verb *to write to* has induced a context that is opaque to the reference, inasmuch as the referent of the designation *Santa Claus* is a purely intentional object; it is possible to construe it only as the complement of the verb *to write to*. These observations have a bearing on the example from *Une ténébreuse affaire*. To say that Napoleon, in the book, is for us the name of a real person implies that we are using a particular interpretation of the verb *to write* (*the story*) *of*. In the statement *Balzac writes the story of Napoleon*, the verb constitutes a transparent context. When Balzac tells us that Napoleon grants an audience to a young lady on the eve of Jena, we take it that there is a man, Napoleon, about whom Balzac writes that he grants an audience to a young lady on the eve of Jena. But the "Index" would have us treat *Laurence de Cinq-Cygne* as the name of a fictional character. In other words, *to write about* must be understood as opaque to the reference in the sentence *Balzac writes that Laurence meets Napoleon on the eve of Jena*. In this scene, then, Balzac must be telling two stories at once: an imaginary episode in the life of Napoleon, and an episode in the imaginary life of Laurence. The two episodes can never coincide so as to generate action, because the verb *to write about* means something different in each of the two contexts.

Any explanation of the concept of "character in fiction" must thus satisfy two conditions:

1. Napoleon must really be Napoleon and be able to be named in *La comédie humaine*.
2. Napoleon must be able to meet Laurence de Cinq-Cygne; otherwise there can be no story.

Any theory of fiction reluctant to concede these conditions must necessarily conclude that we are incapable of understanding what we read when we are reading Balzac. Otherwise it would be impossible to read him. Yet it is of course possible, and any theory that did not acknowledge this at the outset would be erroneous and absurd.

We understand what we read because we know who's who in *La comédie humaine*, even in the case of recurring characters. This knowledge is not gleaned from some *Dictionary* in the absolute, be it a dictionary of Balzac's language or a dictionary of nineteenth-century French; for names have no reference in the dictionary, but only in the context of the sentences in which they occur. This is why the *Who's Who* must always be relative to a particular use, the use that is commonly understood. If this is so, we should start from the fact that certain proper names used by Balzac, already in use before him, retain their acceptation in his work: Napoleon is Napoleon. The proper name *Napoleon* names the emperor Napoleon. Other proper names used by Balzac, however, are his own inventions, and these are sometimes referred to as fictional names. But what is meant by the term? Is an invented name a fiction of a name or a name that designates a fiction? In other words, are fictional names fakes posing as names, or are they a special kind of name? They are neither. They are not fictions of names, at least not to the same degree as *Oytis* (*Nobody*), for example—the name Ulysses adopted for the benefit of Polyphemus. A fiction of a name is a sign that cannot really serve to name: witness, in this case, the immediate equivocity of *Nobody*. Balzac's proper names are authentic names in that they are potential or virtual names in the French language, proper names virtually contained in French (or in another language, when the invented name is foreign). But although fictional names are names, they name only fictional or potential persons. The fictional name *Rastignac* is to the actual name *Napoleon* what *Vautrin* is to *Collin* in Balzac's work, except that *Rastignac* is nobody's pseudonym. It is a genuine proper name, because it would name a member of the Rastignac line, if such a family existed; this is what we understand upon reading the name. Now FICTION, in the sense of the discourse of fiction, consists precisely in a particular use of proper names. Virtual proper names are used as though they enjoyed actual currency in the language. This is naturally quite a different procedure from using potential proper names in order to invest them with a concrete function in the language. When some of Bonaparte's adversaries began deliberately to call him *Buonaparte*, they were conferring an actual use upon a possible name. In order to show that a fictional name names someone, it has been argued that the novelist selects a potential proper name and confers upon it a specific actual use, which is to name a particular kind of person: the fictional kind. But a fictional character is neither real in imagination nor possible. Such a character is an impossible person, being the person whom the fictional proper name chosen by the novelist would name, if this name could at once remain a possible proper name and be invested with an actual use while in this virtual state. A fictional name must remain a possible name for us to be in the realm of fiction, otherwise it would be the pseudonym of someone (we do not need to say, someone real). And it is in this virtual state that it is *actually* used in the story. Thus the inability to designate anyone is an intrinsic part of the very notion of the fictional name.

We have seen how precarious the difference is between "person" and "character." In reality there are only persons (no need to say real persons) and names. Any name affords a meaning inasmuch as it presents the object in a particular way, as Frege has shown. A "character" is exactly that: a way of being given or presented.[14] It would be clearer still to speak of *masks* rather than of *characters*. We are in no danger of confusing persons and masks. In *La comédie humaine*, Collin is supposed to be a person and Vautrin a mask—Collin's mask. Similarly, Herrera uses the pseudonym *Barker*. Barker is Herrera's mask. But Herrera is Collin's mask, so that Barker is the mask of a mask. In this way we can avoid the elision of characters that are presented as real and their borrowed personalities under the common designation of "fictional characters." In *La comédie humaine*, there are more names than there are characters presented as real. This means that there are masks of masks, over and above the masks known as Collin, Rastignac, Nucingen, and so forth. And it allows us to see that although there is a difference between Collin and Vautrin (they are separate masks), a confusion of the two persists (one is a mask, the other a mask of that mask). Finally we return to the possibility that Napoleon might meet Laurence de Cinq-Cygne and that she might meet him. Both Laurence and Napoleon are masks in *La comédie humaine*. Balzac's work contains a Napoleon mask inasmuch as the name *Napoleon* serves to present someone in the guise of a French emperor. The two masks meet in *Une ténébreuse affaire*. The sole difference between them is that the emperor mask is also the mask of the emperor, whereas the mask of a girl from the Cinq-Cygne family is not the mask assumed by any particular girl. As in carnival, some wear the masks of legendary figures while others are disguised, often in caricatures, as this or that well-known "personality." A dragon mask is not the mask of any one dragon.[15] We can recognize a dragon mask and identify it, but we cannot identify anything of which this dragon mask might be called the mask. Conversely, a president mask is likely to be the mask of one particular president. We can identify both this particular president mask (this mask or that one) and the president whose mask it is. That is the difference between the mask of some-thing and the mask of no-thing. It does not disqualify them from parading side by side in the procession of masks.

Notes

Chapter 1 The Escape of Meaning

1. Ian Hacking, *Why Does Language Matter to Philosophy?* p. 51.
2. Or more precisely, cannot explain them without reiterating in their explanation the very formulations of the propositions in question that had originally required elucidating.
3. See Edmond Ortigues, "Destiny and Oracles," in *Religions du livre, religions de la coutume.*
4. Clément Rosset, *Le réel et son double*, pp. 38–39.
5. Martin Heidegger, *Unterwegs zur Sprache*, pp. 97, 121–22.
6. The obsession with the model of interpretive understanding provided by translation leads to excesses that have been well documented by Jacques Bouveresse in his article "Herméneutique et linguistique."
7. Martin Heidegger, *Treatise on Categories and Meaning in Duns Scotus.*
8. Antoine de Rivarol, *De l'universalité de la langue française* (1783). See Wittgenstein's comment in *Philosophical Investigations*, 336.
9. Denis Zaslawsky, *Analyse de l'être*, p. 24.
10. Ludwig Wittgenstein, *Philosophical Investigations*, 664.
11. Jacques Bouveresse, *Le mythe de l'intériorité: Expérience, signification et langage privé chez Wittgenstein.*
12. Michael Dummett, *Frege: Philosophy of Language*, p. 472.

Chapter 2 The Linguistic Turnout of Contemporary Philosophy

1. John Searle, *Speech Acts*, p. 17; Dummett, *Frege: Philosophy of Language*, p. 681.
2. John Searle, *The Philosophy of Language*, p. 1.
3. Alasdair MacIntyre, "Essence and Existence," p. 59.
4. Richard Rorty, *The Linguistic Turn: Recent Essays in Philosophical Method*, p. 3. This definition contrives to reconcile the view that philosophy

ultimately "solves" its problems by adopting the "linguistic" method, with the opposing view that these problems are superseded ("dissolved") by such an approach. Rorty himself takes a third view, for he believes the "linguistic turn" is already a thing of the past.

5. Who was Franz Mauthner? The author of *Contributions to a Critique of Language*, 3 vols. (1901–2) is not well known in France. Mauthner (1849–1923) was a contemporary of Frege (1848–1925) and Nietzsche (1844–1900), as well as William James (1842–1910). He was ten years younger than Brentano (1838–1917) and ten years older than Husserl (1859–1938) and Bergson (1859–1941). Wittgenstein, who quotes Mauthner here, was himself a contemporary of Heidegger (both were born in 1889). I have just named most of the thinkers we will be dealing with, explicitly or otherwise, in this chapter.

6. In the French class of philosophy, the word *empiricism* is normally used pejoratively. It implies the lack of a guiding idea (and therefore of an overall plan, but also of principles of conduct or morality); it suggests shoddy work with neither method, direction, nor merit. Like any defect, the empiricist flaw can be presented as a superior agenda—has anything great ever been achieved without chance or good fortune? Throughout this exposition, I shall use the concept of empiricism in a sense devoid of reproach, to designate the philosophical school that offers an unadorned version of the modern claim that experience lies at the basis of any instructive declaration.

7. Rorty, *Linguistic Turn*, p. 39.

8. See Norman Kretzmann's well-documented article "History of Semantics," p. 393.

9. As Jean Cavaillès notes in *Sur la logique et la théorie de la science*, p. 11.

10. William Kneale and Martha Kneale, *The Development of Logic*, p. 320.

11. "As we can have no knowledge of what is without us, but by the help of the ideas which are within us; the reflections that may be made upon our ideas are perhaps the most important part of logic, because it is the foundation of all the rest" (Antoine Arnauld and Pierre Nicole, *Logic, or The Art of Thinking*, 1662; trans. John Ozell [William Taylor Printers, 1723], p. 32. A more recent translation is available: *The Art of Thinking: Port-Royal Logic*, trans. James Dickoff and Patricia James [Indianapolis: Bobbs-Merrill, 1964]). Louis Marin has shown that the Port-Royal *Logic* was in fact a description of language (*La critique du discours*). "We must emphasize that the Port-Royal *Logic* has to do purely with language" (p. 39). Yes, but it requires an interpretive reading to assert this. As Marin also notes, "The Port-Royal *Logic* speaks of nothing but language, but rarely speaks of it by name" (p. 37). This oversight on its part impedes the analysis.

12. Arnauld and Nicole, *Logic*, p. 89.

13. Namely the paradox of *Through the Looking Glass* (the name of the song is called "*Haddocks' Eyes*," but the name is "*The Aged, Aged Man*," while the *song* is called "*Ways and Means*," when in fact it is "*A-sitting on a Gate*"). This paradox has been formulated by the Czech logician K. Reach ("The name relation and the logical antinomies"), quoted by Elizabeth Anscombe

(*An Introduction to Wittgenstein's Tractatus*, pp. 83–85) and Peter Geach (*Logic Matters*, pp. 208–9). The relation between the doctrine of *suppositio* and modern theory of quantification is studied by Geach in *Reference and Generality*.

14. In this example the words *king of Rome* are considered an appellative term (a logically simple sign) and not a definite description (a logically analyzable sign). Otherwise the proposition would be predicative. Similarly, *Waterloo Station* is a simple sign if it refers to Waterloo Station in London, but a complex descriptive sign if it refers to the station in Waterloo, assuming there is only one station there).

15. Herbert Spiegelberg, *The Phenomenological Movement*, 1:92, 93, 2:649.

16. Edmund Husserl, *Ideas: General Introduction to Pure Phenomenology*, vol. 1, para. 55. On this broadening, see Dagfinn Føllesdal, "Husserl's Notion of *Noema*" and "Brentano and Husserl on Intentional Objects and Perception," and Michael Dummett's critique from the perspective of Frege, *The Interpretation of Frege's Philosophy*, pp. 56–61.

17. On *material object, formal object,* and *intentional object,* see Elizabeth Anscombe, "The Intentionality of Sensation: A Grammatical Feature," in *Collected Philosophical Papers*, 2:3–20.

18. Husserl, *Ideas*, vol. 1, para. 89.

19. Donald Davidson, *Actions and Events*, pp. 162, 182.

20. Husserl, *Second Logical Investigation*, para. 8.

21. Husserl, *Ideas*, vol. 1, para. 131. See Ernst Tugendhat's commentary, which I follow here, in his *Vorlesungen zur Einführung in die sprachanalytische Philosophie*, p. 362.

22. Husserl, *Ideas*, vol. 1, para 131.

23. Richard Rorty, *Philosophy and the Mirror of Nature*, pp. 134–35.

24. Maurice Merleau-Ponty, *The Structure of Behaviour*, p. 186.

25. Maurice Merleau-Ponty, *Phenomenology of Perception*, p. 204.

26. Jacques Derrida, *Speech and Phenomena*, p. 104.

27. In Derrida, *Speech and Phenomena*, see the whole of chapter 7, entitled "The Supplement of Origin."

28. Ibid., p. 93.

29. Ibid., pp. 96–97.

30. Ibid., p. 96.

31. Michel Foucault, *The Order of Things*, p. 306.

32. Merleau-Ponty, *Phenomenology of Perception*, p. xv.

33. Edmund Husserl, *Cartesian Meditations*, para. 16.

34. Martin Heidegger, *Nietzsche*, 1:169: "die Grundworte sind geschichtlich."

35. Eugen Fink, "L'analyse intentionelle et le problème de la pensée spéculative."

36. Ibid., p. 67.

37. Ibid.

38. Ibid., pp. 67–69.

39. Merleau-Ponty, *Phenomenology of Perception*, p. ix.

40. Jean Beaufret, *Dialogue avec Heidegger*, 3:161.

41. Ibid., p. 162.
42. Ibid., p. 221.
43. All the italicized words appear in Beaufret; for example, 3:11–12, 221.
44. Ibid., p. 185.
45. Ibid., Beaufret's italics.
46. Ibid., p. 82.
47. Aristotle, *On Interpretation*, 16ᵇ23–24.
48. Beaufret, *Dialogue avec Heidegger*, 1:32; see also 3:80, 83.
49. G. W. F. Hegel, *Encyclopaedia of Philosophy*, §166.
50. Arnauld and Nicole, *Logic*, bk. 2, chap. 3, 128.
51. Merleau-Ponty, *Phenomenology of Perception*, p. 289.
52. Ibid., p. 294.
53. See Maurice Blanchot's commentaries and references to Mallarmé in *La part du feu*, *L'espace littéraire*, *Le livre à venir*, *L'entretien infini*, and *L'amitié*. In what follows, the allusions to Mallarmé are intended to evoke the Mallarmé of Blanchot and his followers. This is not the place to discuss the partial nature of their interpretation.
54. Gustave Flaubert, *Le second volume de Bouvard et Pécuchet*, compiled and introduced by Geneviève Bollème (Paris: Denoël, 1966), p. 57.
55. Jacques Bouveresse, *Wittgenstein: La rime et la raison*, p. 64, n. 32.
56. See Jonathan Ree's interesting article on certain "analytical" versions of Marxism in the August/September 1980 issue of *Critique*: "Les philosophes anglo-saxons par eux-mêmes."
57. *The Language of Morals* is the title of a celebrated work by R. Hare. In *After Virtue*, Alasdair MacIntyre tells the amusing parable of an analytical philosopher's landing in Polynesia with Captain Cook and accounting, unperturbed, for the concept of taboo by means of a would-be logic of the prescriptive statement.
58. Anscombe, *Introduction to Wittgenstein's Tractatus*, p. 13 and passim. Michael Dummett's work has developed the idea that Frege is the most decisive modern philosopher for us because he does away with the primacy of epistemology. See especially "Can Analytical Philosophy Be Systematic, and Ought It to Be?" (1975), reprinted in *Truth and Other Enigmas*.
59. Great Books of the Western World, no. 31 (Chicago: Encyclopaedia Britannica, 1952), p. 22.
60. Ludwig Wittgenstein, *Zettel*, 420, p. 73.
61. Ernst Tugendhat, *Selbtsbewusstein und Selbstbestimmung*, p. 119.
62. Aristotle, *Prior Analytics*, 1.38.
63. See Peter Geach, *Mental Acts*, no. 28, pp. 124–29, and Elizabeth Anscombe, "The Intentionality of Sensation," in *Collected Philosophical Papers*, 2:14.

Chapter 3 The Present Interest of Transcendental Philosophy

1. There are in fact two philosophies of the transcendental argument. J. L. Austin, for example, writes "This is a *transcendental* argument: if, there were not in existence something other than sensa, we should not be able to

do what we *are* able to do (viz. name things)." ("Are There *a Priori* Concepts?" in *Philosophical Papers*, p. 3.) The transcendental argument, then, begins with ourselves, with what we do and are capable of doing, and draws conclusions about what there is. The same doctrine is propounded in Peter Strawson's *Individuals*, p. 40, and also *The Bounds of Sense*, p. 18. But according to other authors, the transcendental argument begins with an experience, held to be incontestable, and draws conclusions relative to the subject of this experience, his capacities and status. See Charles Taylor, "The Validity of Transcendental Arguments."

2. The positivist, for his part, maintains that only he can attain an authentically critical attitude, for speculative philosophy has failed to free itself entirely from the ancient subjection of the mind.

3. The third alternative reduces the critique of what is, inasmuch as it is, to futility. For although we must accept that *anyway, every thing is a certain way*, we may not infer from this that *there is a certain way in which, anyway, every thing is* (there are no properties necessary to all objects). Still less may we infer that *every thing is in a certain way anyway* (there is no way that any thing may remain indeterminate). See Clément Rosset, *Le réel, traité de l'idiotie*, p. 9.

4. *Ontology* is understood here in the Anglo-Saxon sense, as the answer to the question *An est? What is there?* For Willard V. O. Quine, for example, the "ontological problem" is not *What is being?* but *What is there?* (Cf. "On What There Is.")

5. If we are to believe certain articles by Jacques Poulain, this transcendental pragmatics of language is soon to suffer the same fate as the first transcendental philosophy of action, associated with Fichte and the post-Kantians. It will be condemned to hover in a vacuum, founding exigencies on other exigencies (*it must be that it should have to be that . . .*), or it will turn into anthropology, by admitting that the pragmatic conditions for linguistic communication are themselves conditioned by facts of a physiological nature. The fact of communication is subject to the observance of certain pragmatic rules, but this observance is subject in its turn to the factual satisfaction of other, biological conditions. See "Les paris de Saul Kripke," "Richard Rorty ou la boîte blanche de la communication," and "Le filtre de vérité."

6. Garbis Kortian has suggested that the eternal recurrence in post-Kantian philosophy of the question *Quid juris?*—or the question of validity—is proof of this philosophy's inability to return to the origin of the division between "facts" and "values." Having instituted *pure reason* as the supreme court that would justify it, subjectivity rapidly concedes that everything is unjustified. Henceforth nothing separates the critical enterprise of legitimation from an illegitimacy suit brought against human activities as a whole. See Kortian's "De quel droit?" and his more recent *Métacritique*.

7. Immanuel Kant, *Critique of Pure Reason*, "Introduction," A12, B25. *Prolegomena*, 13 and "Appendix," n. (ed. Vorländer, Meiner, p. 144; trans. P. G. Lucas [Manchester, 1953], p. 146).

8. Spiegelberg, *Phenomenological Movement*, 1:126.
9. Heidegger, *Kant and the Problem of Metaphysics*, 3. *Die Frage nach dem Ding*, p. 138. But see also *Der Satz vom Grund*, pp. 133–35.
10. See *Violence and the Sacred* by René Girard.
11. On this question, see Odo Marquard's perceptive article "L'homme accusé et l'homme disculpé dans la philosophie du XVIIIe siècle" ("Der angeklagte und der entlastete Mensch in der Philosophie des 18. Jahrhunderts," in *Abschied von Prinzipiellen*).
12. "The modern form of ontology is transcendental philosophy, which itself becomes a theory of knowledge" ("Ueberwindung der Metaphysik," 5 in *Vorträge und Aufsätze*, 1:66).
13. Jean Beaufret, *Introduction aux philosophies de l'existence*, p. 168.
14. If we insist on this sense of the term *ontology*, we will not be able to say that there is an ontology of Aristotle. On the history of the word, see Etienne Gilson's remarks in *L'être et l'essence*, p. 168n.
15. For example, Thomas Aquinas explains that the error of Avicenna is to treat the transcendental adjective *one* as though it signified in the same way as the predicamental adjective *white*: "E contrario Avicenna … credidit quod unum quod convertitur cum ente addat rem aliquam supra substantiam entis sicut album supra hominem. Sed hoc manifeste falsum est: quia quaelibet res est una per suam substantiam" (*Summa theologica*, Ia q.11, a1–1um). To my knowledge, Aquinas does not yet use the adjective *transcendentalis*, confining himself to the remark that a term is among those that transcend. (For example: "Ad tertium dicendum est quod hoc nomen *res* est de transcendentibus" [Ia q.39, a3–3um]. In other words, it is the name that is transcendental, it is *hoc nomen res* that signifies a substance, a relation, etc., according to context. There is no question of any mysterious *transcendental thing*.)
16. Aristotle, *Metaphysics*, 1003^b27–30.
17. For myself, I have no idea what *beingity* is, except that here it should be to *being* what falsity is to false or solidity is to solid. Perhaps it would be preferable for this hypothetical property, *ens/esse*, to speak of *entity* (on the model of *entitas*, or *Seiendheit*). Unfortunately, entity is already used nowadays in the literally incorrect sense of an ill-identified object.
18. From notes taken during his lectures in 1935 (cf. *Wittgenstein's Lectures, Cambridge 1932–1935: From the Notes of Alice Ambrose and Margaret Macdonald*, pp. 124–25).
19. "We say, 'There is an x such that x is a dog and x is white and x barks'; now the different status of 'dog' among these predicates can be brought out by considering that 'There is an x such that x is first white and then not white' ('first barks and then does not bark') raises no problems; but 'There is an x such that x is first a dog and then not a dog' should prompt us to ask 'What, then, is the x that is first a dog and then not a dog?'" (Elizabeth Anscombe, "Aristotle," in *Three Philosophers*, p. 74). Such, from the contemporary viewpoint, is the raison d'être of the Aristotelian difference between a predicate belonging to the category of substance and predicates belonging to other categories. In "There is an x such that x barks and then does not bark,"

we understand that the same x is meant. But how are we to interpret the letter "x"? If the predicates successively attributed are like *to be white* and *not to be white, to bark* and *not to bark*, we can find the general term that enables us to identify the subject of attribution twice over ("first a certain surface is white and then it is not white," "first a dog barks, then the same dog does not bark"). When the predicate has meaning in the category of substance, we no longer have any general term to interpret. The "pseudo-concept of object," as Wittgenstein was to call it, cannot act as a general term, because we cannot say *the same object* in the same way as we say *the same dog.*

20. "The word *thing* is not a generic name" (*Wittgenstein's Lectures*, p. 125).

Chapter 4 The Grammatical Reduction of Ontological Propositions

1. "Nominalists make the mistake of interpreting all words as names" (Wittgenstein, *Philosophical Investigations*, 383).
2. Husserl, *Ideas*, vol. 1, para. 24.
3. Aristotle, *Posterior Analytics*, 2.7.92^{b}14.
4. Ludwig Wittgenstein, *Philosophical Grammar*, p. 332.
5. Willard V. O. Quine, *Set Theory and Its Logic*, p. 1.
6. Kant, *Critique of Pure Reason: The Ground for the Distinction of All Objects in General into Phenomena and Noumena*, A250.
7. John Locke, *Essay concerning Human Understanding*, 1, 4, No. 18.
8. Ibid., 2, 23, No. 2.
9. Kant, *Prolegomena* No. 46, See David Wiggins's commentary, *Sameness and Substance*, p. 5 and passim.
10. Geach, *Mental Acts*, pp. 19–20.
11. Husserl, *Fifth Logical Investigation*, para. 10. See Tugendhat's commentary (*Einführung*, p. 97), which I am following here.
12. Husserl, *Ideas*, vol. 1, para. 84.
13. *Der Korrelatgegenstand* (ibid.).
14. Husserl, *Cartesian Meditations*, vol. 2, 17.
15. Ibid., 14.
16. Gilbert Ryle, "Phenomenology," in *Collected Papers*, 1:171.
17. Martin Heidegger, "The Origin of the Work of Art," in *Basic Writings*.
18. Verbs (predicates) or propositions may be denied, but not names (Aristotle, *On Interpretation* 2.16–30). It is certainly possible to speak of the Antipope or the Antichrist (a sign that here the words *Pope* and *Christ* have a descriptive, not a nominative, function); but it is not possible to speak of the Anti-Hector.
19. See Ernst Tugendhat's work on consciousness and self-determination (*Selbstbewusstsein und Selbstbestimmung*).
20. *Critique of Pure Reason*, "The Idea of a Transcendental Logic," A58, B82.
21. Wittgenstein is no doubt referring to the celebrated passage in Kant on the definition of truth and the impossibility of a standard for *adaequatio* (con-

sidered as a relation, whose existence must be verified, between two partners: the proposition and its object). He says: "The limits of language are met in the impossibility of describing the fact that corresponds to a proposition (to this fact that is the translation of it) except by repeating this proposition. (Here we are dealing with the Kantian solution to the problem of philosophy.)" (Note, 1931, in *Vermischte Bemerkungen*, p. 27.)

22. Kant, *Critique of Pure Reason*, A158, B197.
23. Ibid., Introduction, B2.
24. Ibid., B6.
25. In this way, several writers have maintained that two concepts of the object, albeit in different contexts, are to be found in Kant: one that holds for sensible individuals (house, sun, stone), the other signifying the objective validity of what is represented in a true representation (the object, for instance, might be the fact that the stone is hot because the sun has warmed it). See Heidegger, *Die Frage nach dem Ding*, pp. 107–9, and also Tugendhat, *Einführung*, pp. 359–61.
26. Kant, *Critique of Pure Reason*, "Preface to the Second Edition," B17.
27. Ibid., "Second Analogy of Experience," A190–91, B235–36.

Chapter 5 The Inn of the Emancipated Signifier

1. Emile Benveniste, *Problèmes de linguistique générale*, 2:51.
2. See Ian Hacking's remarks in *Why Does Language Matter to Philosophy?* p. 164.
3. This episode is, of course, related by Freud in *Beyond the Pleasure Principle*.
4. Alan Gardiner, *The Theory of Speech and Language*, p. 88.
5. Ibid., 26.
6. Gilbert Ryle, "Use, Usage and Meaning," 2:223.
7. J. L. Austin, *How to Do Things with Words*, p. 98.
8. There is no other species of duchess—that is, fictional duchesses—besides those who exist in flesh and blood (see chap. 6).
9. Benveniste, "La forme et le sens dans le langage" (a paper presented at the Congress of Francophone Philosophy Societies in 1966), in *Problèmes de linguistique générale*, 2:215–38.
10. See Jacques Lacan, *Le séminaire*, 1:272, 2:322.
11. Benveniste, *Problèmes de linguistique générale*, 2:63.
12. Ibid., p. 51.
13. Ibid., p. 225.
14. Ibid., p. 47.
15. Ibid., p. 224.
16. Ibid.
17. Ibid., p. 222 (Etienne Gilson glosses this text in *Linguistique et philosophie*, pp. 263–83).
18. Wittgenstein, *Philosophical Investigations*, 99.
19. Benveniste, *Problèmes de linguistique générale*, 2:64.

20. Ibid., p. 224 (my italics).
21. Ibid., p. 226.
22. Ibid.
23. Ibid., pp. 226–27.
24. Certain writers distinguish the reference of the name *(Smith* refers to Smith) and the reference of the speaker (in saying *Smith,* I refer to a certain person I believe to have that name). Of course, an analysis of language need not deal with what occurs simultaneously in the minds of two partners in a conversation, so long as their thoughts do not affect the form of the proposition. See Geach, *Reference and Generality,* p. 8, and Saul Kripke, *Naming and Necessity,* p. 25n.
25. Paul Ricoeur, *La métaphore vive,* p. 132n.
26. Ibid., p. 97.
27. Ibid., p. 275; see also p. 166.
28. Ibid., p. 278.
29. Benveniste, "Nature du signe linguistique" (1939), in *Problèmes de linguistique générale,* 1:52.
30. Ibid., p. 51.
31. Oswald Ducrot and Tzvetan Todorov, *Encyclopedic Dictionary of the Sciences of Language.* (The entry "Arbitrariness" pp. 130–37, is credited to Ducrot.)
32. See Elizabeth Anscombe's article "The Question of Linguistic Idealism" (1976) in her *Collected Philosophical Papers,* 1:112–33.
33. Benveniste, *Problèmes de linguistique générale,* 1:173.
34. The *Laches* is quoted earlier in the book, ibid., p. 124.
35. I am following Peter Geach's analysis in "Good and Evil."
36. This is what Alan Gardiner failed to see in his reply to Benveniste, "De Saussure's Analysis of the *Signe Linguistique.*"
37. "One may mock at the pedantic silliness with which diplomats of the Norpois type go into ecstasies over some piece of official wording which is, for all practical purposes, meaningless. . . . Childishness has this compensation. . . . Chargé d'Affaires in countries with which we had been within an ace of going to war, M. de Norpois, in his anxiety as to the turn which events were to take, knew very well that *it was not by the word 'Peace,' nor by the word 'War' that it would be revealed to him,* but by some other, apparently commonplace word, a word of terror or blessing, which the diplomat, by the aid of his cipher, would immediately read and to which, to safeguard the honor of France, he would respond *in another word, quite as commonplace, but one beneath which the Minister of the enemy nation would at once see written: 'War.'*" (Marcel Proust, *The Guermantes Way,* translated by C. K. Scott Moncrieff [New York: Modern Library, 1933], pp. 355–56; my italics). The word *war,* for which the Saussurean signified would be "war," is not a word by which the threat of war would be signified to us in diplomacy.
38. Roland Barthes, *Mythologies,* p. 109.
39. Ibid., p. 116.

40. Ibid., p. 113.
41. Roland Barthes, *Elements of Semiology*, 1.22, p. 27.
42. Claude Lévi-Strauss, "Introduction à l'oeuvre de Marcel Mauss," p. xlix.
43. Ibid.
44. Ibid., p. xlviii.
45. Ibid., p. xlix. Jacques Derrida too likens the totality of the signifier to a book:
    "The idea of the book is that of the totality, finite or infinite, of the signifier"
    (*Of Grammatology*, p. 30).
46. *Ecrits*, p. 233.
47. See, in *Speech and Language*, materials under the heading "De nos anté-
    cédents" and also "Le complexe, facteur concret de la psychologie familiale"
    (not included in *Ecrits*).
48. Jacques Lacan, "Aggressivity in Psychoanalysis," in *Ecrits*, p. 28.
49. "Theoretical Introduction to the Functions of Psychoanalysis in Crimin-
    ology," *Ecrits*, French edition, p. 130 (not included in Tavistock edition).
50. See the article quoted in note 49.
51. Ibid., p. 138.
52. Lacan, *Ecrits*, p. 234.
53. Ibid., p. 57.
54. Ibid., p. 59.
55. Jacques Lacan, "Yale Declaration," p. 34.
56. Jacques Lacan, "Actes du Congrès de Rome," p. 245. This text annotated by
    Lacan does not appear in the French edition of *Ecrits*.
57. *Ecrits*, p. 151.
58. Blaise Pascal, *Pensées*, 678 (Penguin Classics edition, p. 108).
59. Lacan, *Ecrits*, p. 264.
60. Ibid., p. 287.
61. Ibid., p. 286.
62. Ibid., p. 280, n. 22 (a reference to Freud, *Gesammelte Werke*, 2–3:52).
63. Lacan, *Ecrits*, p. 257.
64. Ibid., p. 258.
65. Ibid., p. 157.
66. Ibid., p. 259.
67. Ibid.
68. Ibid., p. 167.
69. According to the French daily *Libération* (21 April 1983), a decree published
    in the *Journal Officiel* of December 1982 authorizes the bearers of certain
    embarrassing names to change them: Baizé to Balze, Bordel to Bardel,
    Labitte to Lafitte, Verge to Verger. (The original names give more or less
    phonetic renderings of terms whose English equivalents would be Fuck,
    Brothel, Prick, and Dick.) These changes of signifier are quite commensurate
    with what the doctrine of the signifier refers to as metaphor. For no sooner
    has the erstwhile Mr. Prick amended his signature, in all legality, to *Mr.
    Frick* than his previous name becomes more conspicuous still.

Chapter 6 Who's Who in *La comédie humaine*

1. Honoré de Balzac, *Une fille d'Eve*, in *Oeuvres complètes*, 2:266, Edition Castex, Bibliothèque de la Pléiade (Paris: Gallimard).
2. Ibid., p. 265.
3. Ibid., pp. 264–65.
4. Ibid.
5. *Une ténébreuse affaire*, in *Oeuvres complètes*, 8:681–82.
6. Fernand Lotte, in the preceding edition of the Bibliothèque de la Pléiade (*Contes drolatiques*, p. 1127). Apparently Balzac himself was indifferent to this distinction, as attested by his preface to *Une ténébreuse affaire*.
7. This solution is outlined, for example, by Leonard Linsky in *Referring*. The theory of imaginary individuals is subjected to what is, in my view, a decisive critique in Peter Geach's article "The Perils of Pauline" (which appears in *Logic Matters*). On this point, Geach defends Russell's classic position (though he does not espouse Russell's doctrine of the proper name).
8. *Le père Goriot*, in *Oeuvres complètes*, 3:189 (*Trompe-la-Mort* is italicized in the original; my italics: *the alleged Vautrin*).
9. Ibid., pp. 191–92.
10. *Splendeurs et misères des courtisanes*, in *Oeuvres complètes*, 6:812.
11. Ibid., p. 703.
12. The distinction between the meaning of *de dicto* and the meaning of *de re* applied originally to propositions. Take the proposition *The author of "La comédie humaine" might not have written "La comédie humaine"*. Understood *de dicto* this is nonsense, for it speaks of the person, if that person exists and whoever he may be, about whom it is true to say that he wrote *La comédie humaine*. Understood *de re*, it refers to Balzac and, by the same token, will be considered false unless we maintain an inexorable fatalism. Once a doubt has been sown as to the real identity of the person we know as Vautrin, the surname *Vautrin* begins to hover between two significations. On the one hand, *Vautrin* refers to a person thereby presented as someone called Vautrin (i.e., *Monsieur Vautrin, a man of substance who conducts important business*). On the other, *Vautrin* refers to someone who introduces himself as the man presented by the name *Vautrin* (i.e., *the alleged Vautrin*).
13. In Balzac, *Oeuvres complètes*, 12:1137.
14. This idea derives from Peter Geach's article "Two Kinds of Intentionality?"
15. There is of course neither this dragon nor that dragon nor any kind of dragon (for reasons that are evidently physical rather than logical). But there is always this particular mask, which is perfectly identifiable and can moreover be reproduced many times so as to appear at several points in the masquerade (just as the name *Vautrin*, like any name, can be used several times).

Recent Works Cited

Anscombe, Elizabeth. *An Introduction to Wittgenstein's "Tractatus"*. London: Hutchinson, 1959.
————. *Collected Philosophical Papers*. 3 vols. Minneapolis: University of Minnesota Press, 1983.
————, with Peter Geach. *Three Philosophers*. Ithaca: Cornell University Press, 1963.
Austin, J. L. *How to Do Things with Words*. 2d ed. Oxford: Oxford University Press, 1975.
————. *Philosophical Papers*. 3d ed. Oxford: Oxford University Press, 1979.
Barthes, Roland. *Mythologies*. Paris: Seuil, 1957; Points, 1970. (*Mythologies*. London: Jonathan Cape, 1972; trans. Annette Lavers, Saint Albans: Paladin, 1973.)
————. "Eléments de sémiologie." In *Le degré zero de l'écriture*. Paris: Gonthier, 1971. (*Elements of Semiology*. Trans. Annette Lavers and Colin Smith. London: Jonathan Cape, 1976.)
————. *S/Z*. Trans. Richard Miller. London: Jonathan Cape, 1975.
Beaufret, Jean. *Introduction aux philosophies de l'existence*. Paris: Denoël-Gonthier, 1971.
————. *Dialogue avec Heidegger*. Paris: Minuit, vols. 1 and 2, 1973; vol. 3, 1974.
Benveniste, Emile. *Problèmes de linguistique générale*. Paris: Gallimard, vol. 1, 1966; vol. 2, 1974.
Blanchot, Maurice. *La part du feu*. Paris: Gallimard, 1949.
————. *L'espace littéraire*. Paris: Gallimard, 1955.
————. *Le livre à venir*. Paris: Gallimard, 1959.
————. *L'entretien infini*. Paris: Gallimard, 1969.
————. *L'amitié*. Paris: Gallimard, 1971.
Bouveresse, Jacques. *Wittgenstein: La rime et la raison*. Paris: Minuit, 1973.
————. *Le mythe de l'intériorité: Expérience, signification et langage privé chez Wittgenstein*. Paris: Minuit, 1976.

————. "Herméneutique et linguistique." In *Meaning and Understanding*, ed. J. Bouveresse and H. Parret, pp. 112–53. Berlin: Walter de Gruyter, 1981.

Cavaillès, Jean. *Sur la logique et la théorie de la science*. 2d ed. Paris: Presses Universitaires de France, 1960.

Davidson, Donald. *Actions and Events*. Oxford: Oxford University Press, 1980.

Derrida, Jacques. *De la grammatologie*. Paris: Minuit, 1967. (*Of Grammatology*. Baltimore: Johns Hopkins University Press, 1976.)

————. *La voix et le phénomène: Introduction au problème du signe dans la phénoménologie de Husserl*. Paris: Presses Universitaires de France, 1967. (*Speech and Phenomena, and Other Essays on Husserl's Theory of Signs*. Evanston, Ill.: Northwestern University Press, 1973.)

Ducrot, Oswald, and Tzvetan Todorov. Translated by Catherine Porter. *Encyclopedic Dictionary of the Sciences of Language*. Baltimore: Johns Hopkins University Press, 1979.

Dummett, Michael. *Truth and Other Enigmas*. London: Duckworth, 1978.

————. *Frege: Philosophy of Language*. 2d ed. London: Duckworth, 1981.

————. *The Interpretation of Frege's Philosophy*. London: Duckworth, 1981.

Fink, Eugen. "L'analyse intentionnelle et le problème de la pensée spéculative." In *Problèmes actuels de la phénoménologies*. Paris: Desclée de Brouwer, 1952.

Føllesdal, Dagfinn. "Husserl's Notion of *Noema*." *Journal of Philosophy* 66 (1969): 680–87.

————. "Brentano and Husserl on Intentional Objects and Perceptions." *Grazer Philosophische Studien* 5 (1978): 83–94.

Foucault, Michel. *Les mots et les choses*. Paris: Gallimard, 1966. (*The Order of Things: An Archaeology of the Human Sciences*. New York: Pantheon, 1972.)

Gardiner, Alan. "De Saussure's Analysis of the *Signe Linguistique*." *Acta Linguistica* 4 (1944): 107–10.

————. *The Theory of Speech and Language*. 2d ed. Oxford: Oxford University Press, 1951.

Geach, Peter. "Good and Evil." *Analysis* 17 (1956): 33–42.

————. *Mental Acts*. London: Routledge and Kegan Paul, 1957.

————. *Reference and Generality: An Examination of Some Medieval Theories*. 2d ed. Ithaca: Cornell University Press, 1968.

————. *Logic Matters*. Oxford: Basil Blackwell, 1972.

————. "Two Kinds of Intentionality?" *Monist* 59 (1976): 306–20.

Gilson, Etienne. *L'être et l'essence*. Paris: Vrin, 1948.

————. *Linguistique et philosophie*. Paris: Vrin, 1969.

Girard, René. *La violence et le sacré*. Paris: Grasset, 1972. (*Violence and the Sacred*. Baltimore: Johns Hopkins University Press, 1977.)

Hacking, Ian. *Why Does Language Matter to Philosophy?* Cambridge: Cambridge University Press, 1975.

Hare, R. *The Language of Morals*. Oxford: Oxford University Press, 1952.

Heidegger, Martin. *Basic Writings*. London: Routledge and Kegan Paul, 1978.

————. *Kant und das Problem der Metaphysik*. Frankfurt am Main: Klostermann, 1951. (*Kant and the Problem of Metaphysics*. Bloomington: Indiana University Press, 1962.)

————. *Die Frage nach dem Ding.* Tübingen: Niemeyer, 1962.

————. *Der Satz vom Grund.* Pfulligen: Neske, 1957.

————. *Nietzsche.* Pfulligen: Neske, 1961.

————. *Vorträge und Aufsätze.* Pfulligen: Neske, 1967.

————. *Unterwegs zur Sprache.* Pfulligen: Neske, 1965.

Husserl, Edmund. *Logische Untersuchungen.* 2d ed. Halle: Niemeyer, 1913. (*Logical Investigations.* London: Routledge & Kegan Paul, 1970.)

————. *Ideen zu einer reinen Phänomenologie und phänomenologischen Philosophie.* Vol. 1. Husserliana, vol. 3. Halle: Nijhoff, 1950. (*Ideas: General Introduction to Pure Phenomenology.* London and New York: Macmillan, 1931.)

————. *Cartesianische Meditationen und Pariser Vorträge.* Husserliana, vol. 1. Halle: Nijhoff, 1963. (*Cartesian Meditations.* Halle: Nijhoff, 1960.)

Kneale, William, and Martha Kneale. *The Development of Logic.* Oxford: Oxford University Press, 1962.

Kortian, Garbis. *Métacritique.* Paris: Minuit, 1979.

————. "De quel droit?" *Critique* 37 (1981): 1131–44.

Kretzmann, Norman. "Semantics, History of." In *The Encyclopedia of Philosophy,* ed. Paul Edwards, 7: 358–406. New York: Free Press, 1973.

Kripke, Saul. *Naming and Necessity.* Oxford: Basil Blackwell, 1980.

Lacan, Jacques. "Le complexe, facteur concret de psychologie familiale." In *Encyclopédie française,* 8:8.40.5–16. 1938.

————. "Actes du Congrès de Rome." *Psychanalyse* 1 (1956): 242–55.

————. *Ecrits.* Paris: Seuil, 1966. (*Speech and Language in Psychoanalysis.* Baltimore: Johns Hopkins University Press, 1968.)

————. "Conférences et entretiens dans des universités nord-américaines." In *Scilicet,* nos. 6–7. Paris: Seuil, 1976.

————. *Le séminaire.* Paris: Seuil, vol. 1, 1975; vol. 2, 1978.

————. "Yale Declaration." In *Scilicet,* nos. 6–7. Paris: Seuil, 1976.

Lévi-Strauss, Claude. "Introduction à l'oeuvre de Marcel Mauss." In *Sociologie et anthropologie,* by Marcel Mauss, ix–lii. Paris: Presses Universitaires de France, 1950.

Linsky, Leonard. *Referring.* London: Routledge & Kegan Paul, 1967.

MacIntyre, Alasdair. "Essence and Existence." In *The Encyclopedia of Philosophy,* ed. Paul Edwards, 3:59–61. New York: Free Press, 1973.

————. *After Virtue.* Notre Dame, Ind.: University of Notre Dame Press, 1981.

Marin, Louis. *La critique du discours: Sur la "Logique de Port-Royal" et les "Pensées" de Pascal.* Paris: Minuit, 1975.

Marquard, Odo. *Abschied von Prinzipiellen.* Stuttgart: Reclam, 1981.

————. "L'homme accusé et l'homme disculpé dans la philosophie du XVIIIe siècle." *Critique* 38 (1981): 1015–37.

Merleau-Ponty, Maurice. *La structure du comportement.* Paris: Presses Universitaires de France, 1942. (*The Structure of Behaviour.* Trans. A. L. Fisher. London: Methuen, 1965.)

———. *Phénoménologie de la perception*. Paris: Gallimard, 1945. (*Phenomenology of Perception*. Trans. Colin Smith. London: Routledge and Kegan Paul, 1962.)

Ortigues, Edmond. *Religions du livre, religions de la coutume*. Paris: Sycamore, 1981.

Poulain, Jacques. "Les paris de Saul Kripke." *Critique* 36 (1980): 901–19.

———. "Richard Rorty ou la boîte blanche de la communication." *Critique*. 37 (1982): 130–51.

———. "Le filtre de vérité." *Critique* 39 (1983): 215–31.

Quine, Willard V. O. "On What There Is." In *From a Logical Point of View*. 2d ed. Cambridge: Harvard University Press, 1961.

———. *Set Theory and Its Logic*. Cambridge: Harvard University Press, 1969.

Reach, K. "The Name Relation and the Logical Antinomies." *Journal of Symbolic Logic* 3 (1938): 97–111.

Ree, Jonathan. "Le marxisme et la philosophie analytique." *Critique* 36 (1980): 802–17.

Ricoeur, Paul. *La métaphore vive*. Paris: Seuil, 1975.

Rorty, Richard. *The Linguistic Turn*. Chicago: University of Chicago Press, 1967.

———. *Philosophy and the Mirror of Nature*. Princeton: Princeton University Press, 1979.

Rosset, Clément. *Le réel et son double*. Paris: Gallimard, 1976.

———. *Le réel, traité de l'idiotie*. Paris: Minuit, 1977.

Ryle, Gilbert. *Collected Papers*. Vols. 1 and 2. London: Hutchinson, 1971.

Saussure, Ferdinand de. *Cours de linguistique générale*. Paris: Payot, 1915. (*Course in General Linguistics*. Trans. Wade Baskin. New York: Philosophical Library, 1959.)

Searle, John. *Speech Acts: An Essay in the Philosophy of Language*. Cambridge: Cambridge University Press, 1969.

———, ed. *The Philosophy of Language*. Oxford: Oxford University Press, 1971.

Spiegelberg, Herbert. *The Phenomenological Movement*. Vols. 1 and 2. Halle: Nijhoff, 1965.

Strawson, Peter. *Individuals*. London: Methuen, 1959.

———. *The Bounds of Sense*. London: Methuen, 1966.

Taylor, Charles. "The Validity of Transcendental Arguments." *Proceedings of the Aristotelian Society* 79 (1979): 151–65.

Tugendhat, Ernst. *Vorlesungen zur Einführung in die sprachanalytische Philosophie*. Frankfurt: Suhrkamp, 1976.

———. *Selbstbewusstsein und Selbstbestimmung*. Frankfurt: Suhrkamp, 1979.

Wiggins, David. *Sameness and Substance*. Oxford: Basil Blackwell, 1980.

Wittgenstein, Ludwig. *Philosophische Untersuchungen*. Oxford: Basil Blackwell, 1958. (*Philosophical Investigations*. Trans. Elizabeth Anscombe. Oxford: Basil Blackwell, 1953.)

—————. *Tractatus logico-philosophicus.* London: Routledge and Kegan Paul, 1961.

—————. *Zettel.* Oxford: Basil Blackwell, 1967.

—————. *Philosophische Grammatik.* Oxford: Basil Blackwell, 1969. (*Philosophical Grammar.* Trans. Antony Kenny. Oxford: Basil Blackwell, 1974.)

—————. *Vermischte Bemerkungen.* Frankfurt: Suhrkamp, 1977.

—————. *Wittgenstein's Lectures, Cambridge 1932–1935: From the Notes of Alice Ambrose and Margaret Macdonald.* Ed. Alice Ambrose. Chicago: University of Chicago Press, 1979.

Zaslawsky, Denis. *Analyse de l'être: Essai de philosophie analytique.* Paris: Minuit, 1982.

Index